Dear Brother Gene,

You have been a loyal friend and constant source of support. Thanks brother!

For the Service

Semper Fi!

William R. Uhlar

1-20-87.

Gene —

Welcome Home!

God bless and keep up his work!

Phil Dunn
"River Rat"
68-69

— VIETNAM —

THE OTHER SIDE OF GLORY

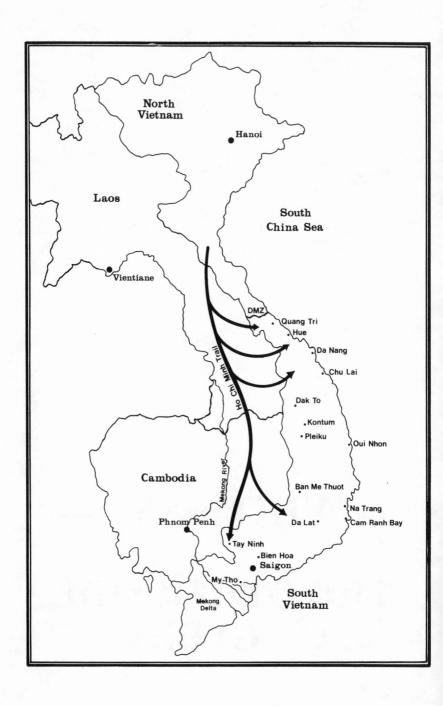

— VIETNAM —

THE OTHER SIDE
OF GLORY

by
William R. Kimball

Daring Books
Canton • Ohio

Published by Daring Books,
Box 526, Canton, Ohio 44701

Library of Congress Cataloging-in-Publication Data

Kimball, William R.
  The other side of glory--Vietnam.

  Vietnamese Conflict, 1961-1975--Personal narratives,
American. 2. Vietnamese Conflict, 1961-1975--
Religious aspects. I. Title.
DS559.5.K56 1987   959.704 '38   86-19948
ISBN 0-938936-57-3

Printed in the United States of America.

Dedicated to the brave Americans
who lived and died and have yet to return

Our small convoy of jeeps and deuce-and-a-halfs crept cautiously along the muddy track, occasionally grinding gears as we negotiated the slippery ruts. Under the whine of jeep transmissions and the throaty cough of diesel engines, we were suddenly jolted to our senses by the popping of small arms fire from the jungle fringe. I glanced sideways and caught the unmistakable look of a green medic, fresh from the States. The sporadic shots had elicited a grimace of wide-eyed apprehension. It was a familiar look among the uninitiated. I was about to say something reassuring when all hell broke loose. A swarm of olive drab men tumbled out of the vehicles, sprawling face first in the reddish mud before scrambling for the nearest cover. Against the acoustic backdrop of rifle cracks, the shrill scream of incoming mortar rounds, and the stuttering of machine guns, the confused cacophony of men grunting, splashing through mud, the bark of orders, and the personal sounds of pounding hearts, cursing, and private prayers punctuated the chaos. The deadly blossoms of gray-black were bursting their way towards our column, threatening to send red-hot splinters of shrapnel tearing through the gas tanks and supplies in a matter of seconds. Unloading the trucks under the barrage of incoming was essential but highly risky. At least the medic had enough sense to grab some of the critical medical supplies in our mad dash from the truck. We were desperately trying to form a protective perimeter when the firing abruptly stopped. Charlie had melted back into the densely packed jungle surrounding us. One minute the firefight had enveloped us with the sounds of machine guns and mortar fire, then we were left with an uneasy stillness and the melancholy cries of wounded men. I turned to survey the carnage, when I noticed the young medic sprawled in a pool of his own blood, with his jugular vein ripped open from shrapnel. He didn't have much to leave behind for his one day legacy in Vietnam. In a lethal split second, he had become a sudden statistic in what seemed a senseless war. I was long since acclimated to death and dying, but such a wholesale waste was still hard for me to stomach.....

Ray P. Lockman
Rifleman, 173rd Airborne
Sept. '67 - Sept. '69

Table of Contents

Preface

The polished black panels of the Vietnam Memorial stand in Washington D.C. in solemn reminder of those who died in Vietnam.

Its very dedication touched a sensitive chord in the hearts of millions. I remember, to my surprise, the tide of emotion which swept over me with warm waves of tears as I watched the cameras panning the names carved in white.

It speaks as an oracle to America — a reverent reminder to a wounded nation. It is not silent, nor does it lay to rest the confused impressions of Vietnam. If anything, it calls us to remember and reflect once again.

To some, its Spartan simplicity, even its mournful profile, is just another in a long series of subtle insults to those who gave their all. To others, its black backdrop gives the appearance of a painful scar etched in the earth and stands as a fitting commentary to the senseless loss and tarnished glory of one of the darkest pages in American history.

But for most, it is more than a melancholy monument. It says something far more profound than the black and white. Its stark contrast in shades symbolizes an unspoken understanding in the hearts of many which transcends the darkness. The engraved names of 58,000 men and women tell us more. They tell us that they didn't die for nothing. They tell us that the lives of the living and the dead who passed through the long shadows of 'Nam were not in vain. It doesn't just speak for the dead, but for the living.

Some pass and pause before those somber panels and think, "What a waste — what a tragedy!" Some only see the black, while others stand and consider.

But there remains another message of hope and inspiration between the lines — another untold story, another side of glory.

William R. Kimball

Acknowledgments

I want to especially thank Spanky and Mary Allio, who planted the seed thought for this book and provided an untiring base of support and encouragement. I also want to extend my appreciation to Linda Murley, secretary extraordinaire, who possesses the uncanny ability to translate my handwritten hieroglyphics into legible type.

A special note of recognition is also due to John Piette, and Ron Mason, fellow Vets, who stood faithfully beside me through the emotional roller coaster of this undertaking.

Though it may go without saying, I want to also express my indebtedness to the fourteen men and one woman who contributed their personal stories to this book. Without their sacrifice, this work would not have been possible.

And finally, I want to express my gratitude to my wife, Rose, and my daughters, Angela and Rachel, for providing the loving support to fulfill this burden.

August 22, 1945 - October 12, 1986

William L. Landreth
1st Lieutenant, U.S. Army
Infantry Officer
4/21st Inf. 11th Brigade
Americal Division
Oct. '68 - Jan. '69

1

Short Tour

I was three weeks in country, a raw lieutenant fresh from the States, and leading an afternoon patrol west of Duc Pho in the central Highlands.

Our "Kit Carson" scout had brought news to the company commander of a V.C. location in our area of operation. Shortly after, my radio man informed me, "Eight-one, you got a call from eight-one papa." The lot fell on my platoon to recon a ridge line where the suspected V.C. position was dug in. Our orders were to find it, make contact with any Charlies, and destroy them. It took us most of a day of back-breaking effort to hump our way up the ridge, chow down, and set up our night defensive position.

Early the next morning, Sergeant "Ski" took a patrol out along the eastern flank of the ridge. A short time later, we heard sporadic shots and received word that Ski's point had surprised three enemy soldiers and nailed two of them. After stripping their bodies of weapons and papers, the customary calling card — the ace of spades — was left in their mouths.

I led out the afternoon patrol in a sweep along the west flank of the ridge. I was eager to earn the respect and confidence of my men. That could be a formidable task for a green lieutenant. Leading men who already had more jungle savvy than you usually generated an undercurrent of suspicion and distrust. The line grunts generally operated with the premise that most new infantry officers were inept glory-boys, a little reckless, or both. But I didn't arrive with any of that duty-honor-country nonsense in my head. There were no misconceptions about the righteousness of that filthy little war. I could care less about scoreboards and kill ratios. My primary concern was not with body counts; what mattered to me was getting each of my men home in one piece. I was determined to allay their fears and prove to them that I wasn't going to ask them to do something I wasn't prepared to do myself. That afternoon, I walked point for the first time.

The air was hot and heavy moving through the thick jungle undergrowth, so thick that the trail was only wide enough for one man. Except for an occasional splinter of sunlight which penetrated the dense canopy, we were enveloped in a dappled maze of green twilight. The jungle gave the impression of being swallowed up in a shadowy underworld of living matter. As we moved through this shielded green labyrinth of plant life, I could smell the scent of wet earth and damp mold, rotting vegetation and sour sweat. I threaded my way down the narrow corridor between solid walls of lush vegetation, pausing every few paces to listen. Trickles of sweat burned my eyes as I strained to see any trip wires, punji pits, or ambushes up ahead.

I was acutely aware of the lethal seriousness of what I was doing. I was filling the vacancy left by the previous platoon leader who had tripped a booby trap earlier walking point, sending a jagged shard of shrapnel tearing through his throat. As I moved nervously down the path, I couldn't shake the uncomfortable feeling that my neck was naked and exposed. At that moment, there were no illusions of Hollywood heroics coursing through my brain — only the rush of adrenaline. With each step, my heart was pounding so hard that I was convinced everyone in the column could hear it. Every new sound or curvature in the trail sent another surge of adrenaline pulsing through my system as I moved stealthily through the steamy, shadowy tangle.

In places, there was double and triple jungle canopy overhead. The trees, foliage, and tangled vines were damp and dripping from the perpetual humidity. Everything seemed to be sweating with nervous anticipation. An oppressive stillness hung in the moist air like an ominous refrain. Even the jungle seemed devoid of life — no birds or monkeys. The only life, if you could call it that, was white, inchworm-like ground leeches. They littered the jungle floor in a state of dormancy until the noise of a gentle footfall, or the sound of a heartbeat pumping blood through veins awakened them to the approaching meal. Then, like a scene from a bizarre horror movie, they would raise their heads in unison, homing in on their potential victims, and start inching their way methodically towards us by the thousands. Our army-issue repellent was the only thing that kept them at bay. It didn't seem to discourage the mosquitos much, but it was death on those blood-sucking slugs. That very morning, I had awakened with a leech feeding on my upper lip. The sight of them closing in made our skin crawl but encouraged us to keep moving forward.

The jungle was so impenetrable that we were forced to stick to the trail. If we tried hacking our way through the undergrowth, our thrashing would warn Charlie of our approach. It was a perfect set-up for a V.C. ambush, so we snaked along the trail as cautiously as possible. The only comfort of the trail was the knowledge that it went both ways. Charlie took his chances on the trail just like

us. Often, our point man and the enemy's point man
would surprise each other, empty a magazine, and it
would be over in a few seconds — just that fast. I know
a lot of guys came over thinking that fighting in 'Nam
involved slugging it out with the enemy for days on end.
This happened only rarely. The jungles of Vietnam didn't
accomodate the tactics or rules of conventional warfare.
"Firefights" were called such because we expended a lot
of firepower in lightning time. Like the speed of a brush
fire, the killing flared up, then quickly died down. It happened so fast that some guys didn't have time to react
before the shooting stopped. Time sped up for a few frantic moments, then it was all over. The only thing that took
time to return to normal was your system which was over-
amped with adrenaline.

That afternoon patrol included about fourteen men,
two squads of six each, myself and the radio operator.
We must have been out about two hours and hadn't gone
too many klicks. I had been moving slowly because it was
the first time I had pulled point and I didn't want to make
any stupid mistakes. Suddenly, I felt a tug on the ba' ';
of my web gear. The man behind me pulled me back and
motioned with hand signals for me to look to our right
about thirty feet on the uphill side of the trail. There was
a crude concrete bunker, overgrown with jungle growth,
with a sinister dark slit staring right at me.

The next minute, everything came to a dead standstill.
In that heart-stopping moment, I knew I was dead meat
and clearly in the "kill zone". Tense seconds ticked by,
but no muzzle flashes were seen or rifle cracks heard. I
began to hope there wasn't anyone in the bunker. "Maybe
it is abandoned," I thought. I couldn't get any lower or

move; my buttons were in the way and my legs seemed a little limp. Three or four men checked out the bunker and found it was empty.

A few meters down the trail, we spotted a tin-sided, one room building. I motioned the men on line to do a "reconnaissance" by fire. In other words, shots were fired into the shed to see if anyone would fire back. None did. We checked it out and found it empty. A little farther on, we ran into a company-sized complex of about fifteen hooches, scattered about fifteen yards apart along the slope of the ridge. Some were barracks, others were aid stations, and one was a regular chow hall! Pigs from the mess hall pen were running everywhere and squealing in terror as we lobbed in fragmentation grenades to clear the tunnels adjoining the barracks. However, there were no V.C. By all the evidence, they had fled in a hurry when they heard our recon fire a few minutes earlier.

The barracks were dug back about four feet into the damp earth with a huge mat suspended lazily about eighteen inches above the earthen floor. The woven mat was large enough for 10-12 men to sleep on. Some of the hooches were open on one side with a thatched roof and three sides; others were fully enclosed with just an open door. They all had an attached tunnel which sank into the hillside about six feet deep, then made a 90-degree turn for four feet, and made a final 90-degree turn with a tunnel exit. These zig-zag tunnels served as makeshift bomb shelters.

By the time we had thoroughly cleared the V.C. encampment, it was nearly dark. I radioed permission from the C.O. to pull back to our previous R.O.N. site for the night because the size of the V.C. camp suggested that we would be outnumbered if the enemy returned, but permission was denied. The C.O. suspected that we had a good chance of uncovering some weapons or ammo caches in the vicinity and wanted us to hold the position overnight.

I broke the men into three groups of 4-5 men each and stationed them in the hooches which seemed the most suitable for a perimeter. Then, under the cover of my poncho liner and with the aid of my flashlight, I plotted our registration sites in case we had to call for "artie." While calculating the artillery coordinates, it dawned on me that we were on the reverse downslope of the steep ridge in relationship to the direction of fire from our artillery fire support base. At that angle, it made it extremely difficult to accurately adjust artillery fire around our positon. With little margin for error, a change in wind velocity or a couple of graduations on the elevation sights of a howitzer could suddenly transform friendly fire into deadly incoming.

After the darkness settled in, four of us slipped into one of the bamboo barracks near the trailhead at the edge of the camp. I was tucking the grid map away in my rucksack when one of my men whispered, "Sir, there is someone coming down the trail with a flashlight." We peered through the thatched siding and caught glimpses of a silhouette behind the dancing beam of a flashlight making its way towards us. He stepped over the trip wire vine I had strung about 30 yards down trail without even noticing the grenade tied to the back of the tree. We were dripping with hot sweat as he headed towards our barracks. The suspense was so thick you could almost cut it with a knife. He was either going to pass by, or turn down the side path leading up to our hooch. He decided to enter our barracks.

I was standing just inside the entrance, concealed in the darkness. The tiny spotlight was pacing across the ground like the probing nose of a bloodhound tracking its prey. I rolled a half turn out of the doorway, with my back on the ground facing up towards the approaching soldier. In the shaft of light, I could only see his Ho Chi Minh sandals on the dirt trail. I had to react. In a second, he would have raised his hand and caught sight of the intruders. I fired three rounds point-blank into the figure before he crumpled in front of me with his back to my face.

I could hear him in the darkness speaking to me with a plaintive voice. I couldn't understand what he was saying in Vietnamese, but it didn't take an interpreter to know he was pleading for his life. He was just laying there in his own crimson pool, a young man not so different from me, begging us in very human terms to have mercy. I was scared and a bit sick to my stomach at the same time. My muzzle flashes and his groaning were giving his friends a good fix on our position. I had little choice. He would die in a few agonizing moments anyway. To put him out of his misery, I fired a final, carefully placed bullet into his spine, right between the shoulder blades. I grabbed a grenade, pulled the pin, let the spoon fly, then tossed it down trail to discourage any V.C. who were coming up the path and to cover our retreat to one of the other barracks.

When we reached the other hooch, I radioed in to the C.O., reported our situation, and requested immediate fire support. Within a few moments, a parachute flare popped overhead with its flickering orange ball, followed by four high explosive rounds with delayed fuses. I had purposely lied about the proximity of my men in order to get the incoming right on top of us. Normally, this would have been suicide, but unless we received a direct hit, Charlie's earthen bomb shelters provided us protection, coupled with the fact that the pattern of the shell bursts would be spread out due to the reverse angle of impact.

After the initial salvo ripped through the jungle, my radio operator informed me that the battery pack on the radio was going dead. Without that lifeline, our chances for surviving the night were slim. The C.O. told us to conserve energy by breaking squelch twice for a fire mission, once to end it. The juice was so low that we couldn't afford to transmit any longer by voice.

Surrounded by a company of V.C. in the pitch black jungle, holed up in a dirt cave with only the sound of two static hisses a heartbeat between life and death, was enough to make you panic. I remembered the childhood fears of sleeping in a darkened bedroom, but our predic·· ment gave a new meaning to the word terror. I was gripped by a cold, cramping fear. I was just glad we were huddled in the blackness so my men couldn't see the expression of icy terror on my face.

We waited and listened for movement. After the dust cleared, we could hear a faint rustling in the jungle around us. They were very close — so close that we could smell their spicy sweat. The Vietnamese poured a rotten fish sauce over their food called "nouc-maum", and once you caught wind of it, you never forgot its distinctive odor. It was one of those pungent Oriental smells that Occidentals seldom get accustomed to. As we sat there drenched in our own sweat, I wondered what we smelled like to them with our C-rat sweat.

After a few tense moments of waiting for them to filter in from the jungle, I depressed the transmission button on the handset, sending the double "break squelch — break squelch!" Miles away, the gun crews of an artillery battery were feverishly loading huge brass shells into their big guns, rechecking their firing trajectory, and, with the tug of the lanyards, the "boom, boom, boom, boom!" of H.E. rounds were answering our urgent summons, sending their deadly delivery right down Charlie's throat.

Overhead, a lone spotting flare flickered to life, filtering a pale yellow light through the jungle canopy. We braced ourselves and covered our ears as the gutteral sound of incoming passed in a steep descent overhead. Suddenly, the bright orange flashes, followed by the deafening "crump! crump! crump! crump-crump!" accented the darkness. The jungle seemed as if it had been seized in a violent convulsion of fire and steel. The ground was quivering with each impact as the jungle was being ripped apart by the hail of flying shrapnel. Pieces as big as my fist tore through the flimsy barracks overhead. Slivers of serrated steel were scything their way through broad leaves, branches, and lush vegetation.

Then, that which I feared came upon me. It was like someone had ripped open a huge canvas overhead, sending a torrential downpour upon us. It was raining steady and hard. I couldn't hear or smell Charlie. I was blind and deaf and had lost my sense of smell. I started to pray steady and hard — what we referred to as "P & P's": prayers and promises. I bartered with God; if He would turn off the rain and just let me live through the night, I would go to a church and support it when I got back home. Almost immediately, the downpour stopped and I could hear Charlie groping around again.

A second time, my fingers transmitted the "break squelch — break squelch," and again, gun crews raced to remove spent shell casings and reload their breeches. There were two more fire missions called down on top of us before the sky began to wash with grays. It was 0500. Charlie had given up and slipped back into the jungle.

With the advancing light of dawn, the rest of the company arrived. We blew a hole in the jungle canopy with det cord and C-4 to provide an LZ for choppers to get in. Some of the rear area brass flew in to survey the tunnel complexes and the rain of destruction we had unleashed on the V.C. encampment. It was the customary P.R. picture-taking for the desk jockey lifers to get a feather in their cap and extol their imaginary contribution to the war effort.

I was left with only the haunting memories of the darkness, the terror, the pleading voice of the wounded soldier, and the snapshots of his wife and kids that I had taken from his body. I tried to console myself with the fact that he would have done the same thing to me if the tables were turned. He had an AK-47, the safety was off, it was loaded with a full magazine, a round was chambered, and the selector switch was on full "rock and roll". But it didn't ease the guilt. His dying somehow conferred on the V.C. a humanity that I hadn't been willing to bestow before. I sensed that I had done something I didn't have the authority to do: I had taken another man's life. Oh, I knew it was either "him or me, kill or be killed," but I didn't feel comfortable playing God. He, alone, was the author and designer of life itself — who was I to take it away?

As I replayed the nightmare in my mind, I also remembered that God had answered my prayers. I didn't know why yet, but I sensed that He had covered us with His hand. Still, the images of the dying soldier sobered me with a profound consciousness of my own mortality and a painful awareness of the value of human life.

Back home, life unwinds at its monotonous pace, but in a war zone the mechanics of dying accelerate it. Life can end so abruptly, like the North Vietnamese soldier who tried to forage something to eat from one of our throw-away C-rations we had buried at one of our night positions. He fell for the stay behind ambush set-up for V.C. scavengers. His simple attempt to find food was terminated with a single bullet through his head.

His body was still warm when our platoon passed his corpse. I found out why they call the brain "grey matter." He was lying there face up, staring skyward, with the glassy eyes of a dead fish. Trickles of caked blood had drained from his ears and what remained of the right side of his head. I remember the gruesome sight of bees crawling in his skull and ears — wherever there was blood; they were searching for food, also.

The sight of his wretched remains made me question the sanctity of human life. That body, which once housed the sacred breath of life, seemed so desecrated. It was just lying there like a delicate porcelain bowl which had been shattered, spilling its contents. The near mythical illusions of invincibility so coveted by youth were forever erased from my mind. I understood at that moment of manhood that life, even my life, was so very temporal. As I passed by, I couldn't help wondering what really happens after the fragile shell we call our body finally dissolves. What happens when we depart for our long home? Death could be so decisive — so final. It so accentuates our mortality. But what was the ultimate end? War produces a lot of questions like that to consider.

As a reward, our unit was pulled back to the relative safety of a fire base. During Thanksgiving, some Chinooks flew in a hot turkey dinner in large chow cans which, unbeknownst to us, had previously been used to transport gasoline. The cooks had not scoured the cans sufficiently before using them as food containers. Within twenty-four hours, the entire base was plagued with a bad case of the trots. I'll never forget the half comical sight of two long lines of troopers shifting nervously from one foot to the next behind the sanctuary of the waiting latrines. Every so often, four or five men could no longer maintain control and peeled off for some desperate place to dump. At that moment, we were so vulnerable that a handful of V.C. could have overrun the entire base.

For the next murky month, we endured the endless misery of rain and drizzle. The relentless drumming pelted poncho liners, sandbags, and tin cans strung along the perimeter wire until it reached a level as insufferable as a Vietnamese version of the Chinese water torture. We spent most of our time soaked to the skin in flooded foxholes, damp bunkers, or sloshing through dripping jungles, up one unforgiving mountain ridge and down another. It was a sodden month under dirty grey skies, awash in a sea of brownish red mud, mildew and monsoon rains.

In January, the rains subsided and brought a welcome respite from the grey monotony. On January 19, we received word that we would be airlifted the following morning to a village in the rice paddy lands west of Chu Lai. S-2 had information that about ten V.C. were conscripting forced labor from the local villagers, forcing them to dig cache holes and carry rice. Our orders were to go in and clear out the enemy. The job was assigned to A Company. One platoon would be set down as a blocking force north of the village while my platoon and the other platoon would sweep in from the south, forcing the V.C. into the blocking force ambush. It was the classic hammer and anvil tactic, straight from the pages of a military textbook. It seemed simple in the classroom, but it didn't always come off so flawlessly in the field.

At 0530 hours, we loaded the bulbous green Hueys in groups of eight amidst the usual prayers and nagging question of whether or not it would be a hot LZ. The choppers assembled overhead, then veered off in the direction of the objective. The assault force gave the appearance of a swarm of dragonflies bobbing up and down in a gentle sea of invisible currents. Against the noise of buffeting winds and the whine of the chopper motors, we were each secretly reassuring ourselves that there would only be ten Viet Cong. Our muscles tensed as we gradually descended over the patchwork of palm groves and emerald rice paddies. The golden sunrise gilded the surrounding landscape with an almost enchanting beauty. All seemed so serene in the early morning stillness. I could see the saffron colored roofs on the hooches as we approached the village. Before we jumped clear, the customary order to "lock and load" was issued. None of us could hear the metallic sounds of bolts chambering their rounds under the relentless hammering of the chopper blades. The Hueys set us down in the flooded rice paddies just south of the village as a copper colored sun was just clearing the eastern horizon. It would nearly be the last sunrise I would see.

The Huey I was riding in had accidentally veered off course and dropped us off with the wrong platoon. We lunged out of the hatch into muddy, knee-deep water and headed across the field to link up with the other position. My radio operator, a couple of other men, and I just reached one of the low dike footpaths bordering the rice paddy when we heard the rattle of rifle fire coming from the direction of the village. The radio crackled to life with word that the point man in the other platoon had been killed. The cluster of men following me were in a crouched position, slogging through the shallow water, when I noticed that the thatched roofs we had observed from the air were deceptively camouflaging thick concrete bunkers. When my fire team reached the second platoon, a number of the men were huddled together crying. They were overcome with grief at the death of the point man who was a close friend. Some were in a state of semi-shock, not from traumatic wounds, but from the pain of losing a buddy.

The early morning mist was burning off, bringing the details of the village into clear focus. I could see V.C. soldiers maneuvering towards a tree line bordering the village. They were jumping like black fleas from bunker to bunker, dodging and running to rifle pits and trenches to take up position. We'd obviously landed in the midst of a large force of Viet Cong and were in imminent danger of being outflanked.

I ordered my men to link up with the other platoon who were digging in about 300 yards away on a flat, sandy island ringed by palm trees. It was lying out in the middle of the expanse of rice paddies. We popped a smoke cannister to cover our movement while one of the men started firing his 40mm grenade launcher towards the enemy to keep their heads down. Under the clatter of helmets and web gear, sloshing water, and grunting men, we re-deployed. Our dash to the island left us breathless with hearts pounding. I told my radio man to stay behind while I skirted the perimeter to find the other platoon leader. The men were feverishly digging shallow depressions around the sandy island in a circular perimeter.

The occasional snap of rounds, followed by the report of AK's, punctuated the air around us. The sporadic stutter of a machine gun could be heard in the distance. Our situation was rapidly deteriorating. I knew we had to do something. We had to regain the initiative, but our options were limited. I got behind one of the M-60's and started working over the windbreak two hundred yards to our front where the enemy had taken up positions. I was pumping staggering bursts of six shots a few feet above the rice paddies towards the tree line where Charlie was dug in. The intermittent tracer rounds streaked in quick succession, probing the tree line like a deadly finger.

Somewhere off in the distance, a V.C. mortar crew was releasing an 82mm round down the mouth of a tube, followed by the hollow cough. About 75 yards to our front, a huge geyser of mud, water, and dirt clods erupted, showering the surrounding paddy with a thousand tiny splashes and sending shock waves rippling across the muddy water.

My men were accustomed to fighting in the highlands, trudging up and down rugged jungle ridges. Nobody wanted to hump heavy mortar tubes and base plates, along with a couple rounds per man, up those back breaking slopes. Because of the density of the jungle canopy, we couldn't fire mortars even if we wanted to. Most of my platoon had never been exposed to the terrifying "KaRUMph!" of incoming mortar rounds.

With the first burst, I figured Charlie was firing bracketing rounds to find our range: one long, one short. When they found our distance, they would open up for effect. I assumed the first explosion had been the short round, to be followed by another. I thought we had a few precious moments to prepare. Little did I realize that the mortar crew had already overstepped us with a spotting round and were loading their tubes to walk rounds across our island.

I moved out to warn my men, who were dug in along the natural berm which ringed the island, to get down. As I passed from position to position, I noticed an old bomb crater gouged into the fringe of the island. I remember having the strongest inclination to dive into the hole, but I ignored the thought and passed by. I was in mid-stride when an enormous blast of hot air picked me up and slammed me to the ground. There was no sound — just that awful rush of dragon breath. The next instant, I was sitting upright in the dirt with my right leg cocked underneath me and my chin resting on my chest. I remember wondering who had poured hot tomato soup down the front of me. In my stunned stupor, it felt like someone had spilled scalding liquid on my chest. Then

I realized that it wasn't tomato soup at all, but my own hot blood. I was hemorrhaging from the neck. My throat had been ripped open, jugular vein severed, vocal cords paralyzed, and my right leg lacerated by shrapnel. With each heartbeat, my life blood was spurting out of my neck.

I knew I was bleeding to death, yet I had a matter-of-fact indifference to it all. I thought to myself, "So this is what it's like to die. Dying is not so bad after all." Everything was winding down. I couldn't hear anything and was only vaguely conscious of my surroundings. It was a glassy daze in that silent, slow motion world. The grey-black bursts were sounding their final exclamations across the paddies as I faded from this life. I just sat there in a state of detached consciousness while the firefight sputtered out. It was all so strange, yet so very real.

As my life drained out of my wounds, I was overwhelmed by a bright light. It was faint at first, but gradually intensified to such a blinding brilliance that it was like trying to look straight at the sun. The illumination bathed me in a peace which transcended the battlefield. There was no apprehension — just an awesome glory and a deep sense of knowing, as though every question I could ever have asked was already answered.

I felt incredibly light, like I was suspended in mid-air. My clinical assumption was that it was due to a rapid loss of blood, but what began to unfold convinced me otherwise. It seemed like two bands were severed at my shoulders, and I began to rise a few feet above my body. I looked down and saw the top of my head. My navel had ascended to the height of my head. I lowered my chin a little more and could see through my new body. I had a shape and form, but I could see the ground through my chest. It was all so mysterious, yet not menacing. There was no longer any real attachment to my body. I suppose it was kind of like a snake shedding its old skin. The real me was floating upwards. It was such an exhilarating and euphoric sensation. Such an intense joy overwhelmed me that it seemed like the sheer rapture of all the accompanying joys of humanity were compressed into one intense moment.

Then, a soothing, almost fatherly voice asked me if there was any reason why I wanted to stay. I remembered that I had only been married for five days before I shipped out for 'Nam. I felt a sense of obligation to my wife not to leave her alone so soon. Suddenly, there was a commanding voice which said "NO!" and my soul and spirit shot back into my body like a taut rubberband which had snapped. The "here and now" quickly colored in around me, and the sights and sounds returned. The light faded, but that awesome peace remained.

Just then, I heard the voice of a soldier asking, "Anybody hit?" I reached up with my right hand and pinched the surface skin to stop the flow of blood, but it was hard holding a firm grip with slippery blood all over my neck and trickling between my fingers. I couldn't speak so I lifted my left hand over my head and waved for Taylor, my radio operator, to help. Along with Hernandez, the medic, they started an I.V. of albumin to help aid the coagulation of blood. Taylor then radioed in for a med-evac. However, none of the med-evacs in the vicinity wanted to abort their dust-off's to risk landing in a hot LZ and jeopardizing the lives of the wounded they already had on board. Taylor responded, "If you don't come down now, eight-one will die!'' I could overhear the ''... eight-one will die!'' but I had such a confidence I would live that it didn't bother me.

The battalion commander was circling overhead and happened to pick up Taylor's transmission over his radio. He ordered his personal chopper down to pick me up. Hernandez was also peppered in the back with shrapnel, so they flew both of us to an intermediate aid station to stabilize our condition. I remember the stone-cold calmness of the door gunner as the chopper tilted its nose forward and climbed across the paddy. I was slumped in the chopper bay with my throat laid open when he casually turned, flicked his cigarette, and offered me a smoke. It wasn't because I didn't smoke that it seemed so strange. Maybe it was just out of habit — a standard dust-off courtesy. It was all so melodramatic, like offering a last cigarette to a dying man or supplying a macho prop for a wounded soldier.

When we landed at the aid station, I remember   the riveted stares of the onlookers as the medics lifted me off the Huey. I remember the deep concern etched into the haggard lines on the doctor's face. I knew those looks. It was the stare that strains to see the Death Angel as he completes his gruesome last work. It is the look of morbid curiosity and icy fear which tries to steal a glimpse of the ultimate unknown.

Because of the massive loss of blood, my veins had collapsed. The doctors had difficulty registering another I.V. needle. But, through it all, I still maintained a confidence that I was going to pull through. They loaded our stretchers onto another chopper and rushed us to the 312th Medevac Hospital at Chu Lai.

When we arrived, the E.R. was a scene of borderline chaos. The hut was filling up with a flood of incoming wounded. In a room designed to accomodate about seven patients, over twenty were crammed into that space. Some of the men were lying on gurneys, while others were lying on the floor on stretchers. Doctors were sorting the wounded through triage, with the more critical patients receiving immediate care. I remember a V.C. in black pajamas lying on a gurney next to me writhing in agony. The doctors had alotted him a last priority.

The doctors were working feverishly on some other grunts while I lay there waiting for my number to come up. Then dear old Hernandez started demanding that someone look at his platoon leader. In moments, a covey of medics were cutting away my fatigues and jungle boots. That's when the guilt settled over me like a leaden sky. Just a few air miles away, my men were in a tug-a-war with death while I was in the safety of a hospital emergency room. I know it wasn't rational, but I felt like I had deserted them in their time of need. It wasn't that I felt so indispensible to them — it's just that I cared so much for their welfare, much like a protective father feels for his children. That oppressive cloud of guilt stayed with me for the next twelve years.

In a few days, I was transported to Cam Ranh Bay, then to the 249th General Hospital in Tokyo. Two weeks later, I was flown stateside to Fort Belvoir, Virginia, outside of Washington D.C. The shrapnel had so damaged my vocal cords that I could barely whisper for a year. In time, the healing process returned my left vocal cord to near normal. I was medically retired from the Army in 1972.

I'd only served in 'Nam for three months, but that short tour was destined to alter the rest of my life. In that space of time, I had acquired an addiction to adrenaline. The intensity of combat always keeps your system on the ragged edge. Every sensation is electrified. Your mind functions smoother, your thoughts are more lucid, your reflexes more adroit. No artificially-induced high could equal it. I found myself taking up skydiving and scuba diving just for the sheer thrill of the rush. I was driven by an insatiable craving to live on the cutting edge of life. It wasn't worth living, to me, if you didn't beat the odds — if you didn't put your life on the line.

So, I rode the fast lane. I slept lightly, always keeping a full rucksack by my bed, 200 rounds of ammo, a high-powered rifle, a .45 cal. pistol, and an assortment of knives. I controlled it better than most, or maybe concealed it better than most, but the residual madness was as intimate a part of my private life as alcohol is to a closet alcoholic.

After five years, my wife could stand no more and ended up divorcing me. In turn, I was sinking deeper and deeper into a black hole of cynical despondency. I tried EST and Transendental Meditation in a last ditch effort to get my head together, but I was out of control and hopelessly unraveling.

Through it all, I never remembered the prayer and promises I had uttered to God. But He hadn't forgotten. Maybe that's why He hadn't forsaken me when that mortar round nearly stole my life. As a young boy of ten, I had gone forward in a church service and asked Jesus to be my Savior, but the troubled complexities of adolescence and early adulthood had long since erased that former innocence.

I finally reached a point in my life where I longed for an end to my misery. I went to the local Vet center in Seattle, WA. They tried their best to help with the typical rap group and psychological approach, but all we accomplished was a rehashing of painful memories and a cosmetic catharsis. It was like putting a band-aid on a bullet hole. They could diagnose the presence of delayed stress, but they couldn't heal it.

During that time, I married a beautiful lady named Jan. She was an answer to prayer. She was a sympathetic sounding board, yet didn't let me wallow in self-pity. Instead, she encouraged me to read the Bible. She stuck with me and loved me even though I dragged her through a nightmarish world of mental and emotional torture. I couldn't keep a job for more than two years and was running out of excuses. Finally, the paranoia reached a place where Jan was even afraid to go to the bathroom at night for fear I'd shoot her with the .45 I had under my pillow.

It wasn't until I reached rock bottom that I decided to open the pages of the Bible and read. I'd tried everything else the world and secular psychology had to offer, with dismal results. That Book was the only thing left.

Within a few minutes, the awesome power of God's Word had brought me to tears. I found myself begging God for forgiveness and He not only forgave me, but He did in an instant what the rap groups and therapy could never have accomplished. I got up from my tear-soaked carpet a healed and restored Christian, transformed by the grace of God and delivered from the oppressive years of guilt, anger, and fear.

Since that turning point, I've often reflected on the words of a song which Richie Havens sang at Woodstock·

A soldier came down from Dien Ben Phu with
tears in his eyes.
He told of many a night when fire was in the
sky.
He told of many a morning when the bravest
of men would cry,
Knowing that through Satan's earthbound
magic, many more would have to die.

Those haunting lyrics were written for me. I was the soldier with tears in his eyes — tormented by Satan's earthbound magic. But I found that the oppression was not isolated to the hellish nightmare of 'Nam. That was only the tip of a much larger iceberg — a much larger war. Oh, I had struggled silently along with thousands of other vets to put Vietnam behind me, but it took years for me to realize that there was another far more insidious conflict which I was warring against. That battle was not restricted to the rice paddies or jungles of 'Nam. The combatants were not green-clad soldiers or peasant farmers. They were the sum total of humanity. That war is not for flesh and blood, but a spiritual conflict over soul and spirit.

I had survived the short tour which nearly cost me my life but returned to fight an unforseen foe on an unforseen battlefield which would rage for twelve long years before that special peace was declared.

Bill Landreth and his wife Jan currently live in Seattle, Washington. They have two children. Bill works full time for the Seattle Division of Safeway Stores and is the President of Point Man Ministries which offers a comprehensive outreach service to Vietnam vets and their families. Bill and his wife Jan are extensively involved with Vietnam-era vets and their wives around the country.

Postscript

Bill Landreth was taken home to be with the Lord October 12, 1986, leaving this testimony:

I have fought the good fight, I have finished my course, I have kept the faith:
Henceforth there is laid up for me a crown of righteousness, which the Lord, the righteous judge, shall give me at that day: and not to me only, but unto all them also that love his appearing. **(II Timothy 4:7,8)**

David C. Shaffer
Captain, U.S. Army
Green Beret
Special Operations Group
Dec. '67 - Nov. '69

2

Night Flight

The night was sticky and hot — one of those anxious nights when all the men in my A-Team were tight and ready. The night was alive with exotic sounds of insects, frogs, rock apes, and jungle birds which reminded each of us that we were far from home. As we waited for our upcoming mission, our minds drifted wistfully to the things we would do when we got back, but our eyes and ears never left the present tense of 'Nam. We all knew that the intensive training we had received as members of the Special Forces would soon be put to the test. That's what we all wanted. Sitting around got old real quick. We were ready to fight that unconventional war that the Special Operations Group was trained to fight.

As elite members of the Special Operations Group (S.O.G.), we carried out covert counterinsurgency operations deep in enemy territory for months at a time. We were waging a top secret war which you didn't read about in the papers back home. Only a select handful even knew that we existed. Our standing orders were not to be seen. Our true identity was a closely guarded secret. If we made contact with the enemy, we were to take no prisoners, leave no survivors. If caught, our government would disavow any knowledge of our existence. If captured, we faced excruciating torture and inevitable death. We, therefore, were prepared to die as a preventative. It was somewhat like "Mission Impossible" — except it was for real.

Dawn came early the next morning. It was one of those daybreaks you both love and hate. You love it because

the sun is bright and the world is alive with color; you
hate it because it is already hot and getting hotter. Most
of that day was spent getting our gear ready. It was hard
to prepare for something when you didn't know what you
were going to be doing or even where you were going to
do it. Sometimes, I think back to those days and wonder
how I made it through it all. After all, we were executing
some of the most hazardous missions of the entire war.
We spent more time in Indian country surrounded by
Charlie than we did with the friendlies. But a still, small
voice inside my head invariably reminded me that He was
with me, even then.

Before I entered the briefing tent, I was given a security check by the M.P.'s. Several senior officers were seated
in the stuffy tent with a lone individual in a suit. I was
shown to a chair and told that two other men were due
to arrive soon.

Not more than three minutes passed before a high rank-
ing General entered the tent. He started to address us
when his aide whispered something to him. He was
noticeably perturbed, but sat down. About ten minutes
later, two M.P.'s escorted in another guy wearing a suit
and silver-tinted sunglasses. The man was carrying a brief-
case handcuffed to his wrist. He walked up to the General
and asked him for the key. The General took some papers
out of the case, glanced over them, and looked straight
at me. I was the lowest rank in the room and felt uncom-
fortably out of place.

The General looked at the bird colonel and asked if
I was the man who was going to lead the mission. He
told him I was.

"Captain, are you and your men ready?"

I stood to attention and said "YES SIR!, we are sir."

"Captain, do you know where you and your men are going?"

"No sir, I don't sir."

"Captain, I will give you an envelope. You are not to open it till you are 25 minutes from your jump-off point. Do you understand?"

"YES SIR!"

"You and your men are to go over to the security shed and turn in anything in your possession that is U.S. made: no identification, and, most of all, you must be absolutely positive that no one has any personal items with them. Do you understand?"

"Yes sir."

"I've given orders that you and your men are not to be fed any food made by our people. You will only eat food cooked by local people so you will smell like the Vietnamese. You will be given weapons taken from the V.C. The exact time of departure from camp will be given to you only one hour before takeoff. Do you have any questions? If you do, Mr. Jones will be in camp to offer assistance. Good luck, Captain Shaffer, and good hunting." He then gave me a brisk salute and left the room.

The full colonel came up to me and said we were to be on the flight line at 1900 hours. No one was to discuss what was said inside the tent. I was not to tell my men anything until we were airborne and on our way to the drop zone. "Yes sir," was my answer, but in the back of my head that small voice was reminding me that here we go again. This was not the first time I had been in that kind of a briefing. My mind raced back about nine months to the last mission like this. It was just before we went out for a "little walk in the woods," as the General put it. It took us five and a half months to walk back out, and then only by the grace of God.

One week later, we were told to saddle up. We had not received any mail or had any contact with the outside world in all that time. None of us knew where we were going. My team was given Russian AK's and ammunition. The uniforms and web gear were foreign issue as well. The food and smokes came from the locals. Oh, how I wanted an American cigarette — even some C-rats looked good. Before we boarded our C-130 for our mysterious destination, we were given one last search to make sure we weren't carrying anything which could incriminate the U.S. With all the precautions, you might think we were on a secret mission to infiltrate the Soviet Union.

The General and his two aides in suits came into the cargo hold and told us to have a good trip. Looking at those rear area personnel, I wondered whether they knew what life in that part of the world was like without their bennies, air conditioning, officers' clubs, and all the frivolous conveniences they brought over from the States.

When the pilot and crew boarded, we took off and headed north. Our destination was somewhere above the boundary marked on the maps as the DMZ. Looking at the landscape below, all you could see was an endless carpet of green vegetation interrupted occasionally by a stream, river, or village clearing. Gazing at the picturesque countryside, you couldn't even tell there was a war going on. The steady drone of the props continued and several monotonous hours passed before a voice screeched over the loudspeaker, alerting us that we had 25 minutes till the jump-off point. I was suddenly very much awake. I tried to keep my mind busy as the jump time neared, but the nervous anticipation heightened with each passing minute.

Those were the hardest times for me. Once I was out of the door, my mind would click into high gear. My all-consuming thought would then be the mission and my men. They had been with me all through AIT; we were a team in every sense of the word. We had been together for fifteen tight months, and our sense of esprit was unrivaled. To this day, I can't explain how a group of men can get so totally in tune with one another as we were. We did not have to talk to know what each other was going to do — we just knew it. Our reflexes were perfectly synchronized.

It was time to open that ominous brown envelope containing our secret orders. I always dreaded tearing into those sealed envelopes because it meant that we were going to be placed between the hammer and the anvil. Our mission was to take and secure an NVR camp. The camp was a suspected transfer point for all heavy troop movement flowing southward through that sector. A Montagnard ground unit would provide our local ground support. I always liked working with the "Yards." They were gutsy fighters. My team had spent much of our first year living with this group. Because I only had 25 of them to assault the camp, I felt like we were being put out on the line to dry, but this was nothing unusual for a Special Operations Group. You get accustomed to being reminded that your government will not acknowledge your existence if captured — whether dead or alive.

I took one last look at my orders, tucked the map in

my rucksack, and burned the rest of the papers in the special container we carried on board. This was to be our last covert mission before R & R. As the final minutes ticked by, I uttered a silent prayer: "If there is a God up there, and You are hearing me, please keep my men safe."

We spent the last 20 minutes talking about what we were going to do when we got back home. I kept thinking about all we had gone through as a team, and what was to come. Back in camp, I had overheard Mr. Jones mentioning to a friend that they were going to throw a big party for us before we took off. When he was asked why, Jones stated matter-of-factly, "We don't expect any of them to come back." As we approached red light, I wished I could get that statement out of my head. The light flicked on and the buzzer scared half the team, who were deep into their own dreams, back to reality. We stood up, hooked up, and got ready to file out the door. Standing in the door, I took one last look at the map. The seriousness of the moment suddenly hit me like a ton of bricks. There was no turning around once out of the door.

Looking out of the door, all that could be seen was a small fire on the ground. I hoped that it was the signal fire the Yards had set for us. The only light I could see was from that fire. I knew the tribal chief and was confident that he would not light a fire if the V.C. were in the vicinity. As we made our first pass over the drop area, a blue light flashed on and off giving us the "all clear" to come in.

No sooner had we hit the ground and gathered our chutes when our contact met us. I was happy to see Twan.

He was the chief of the group which would be working with us. He grabbed my arm and pulled me to cover. Once out of the clearing, he told me that one of his runners had just made contact with a V.C. patrol closing in about 5 klicks out to the north. They had obviously picked up our approach. I directed Mike to form a protective perimeter to our north, but the Viet Cong were on us just like flies on a hog. Suddenly, the head of one of the younger Yards just exploded like a pumpkin hit with a baseball bat. Automatic fire erupted all around us. Grenades were exploding and people were screaming in pain all around the clearing.

Twan tapped me on the shoulder and pointed down. I couldn't believe my eyes. The black mouth of a tunnel opening disappeared into the ground right in front of me. Twan had purposely set up our landing site a few feet away from the abandoned tunnel complex for a quick escape route in case we got hit. I told my men to follow as I descended into the hole. It was an eerie feeling crawling through the darkness of one of those tunnels. It was pitch black, damp, and reeked with the nauseating stench of human excrement. Twan was leading us through the underground maze with a small flashlight. We had to walk hunched over because the ceiling was only about four feet high. Some of my men slipped a couple of times because the floor of the tunnel was like polished mud. None of us wanted to know what the tunnel was filled with. We must have traveled about a half a mile through the labyrinth before we started up a steep incline. The slimy ascent was even harder going, but we pressed on.

We emerged into the sweet smell of fresh air. I was relieved to see the top of the trees instead of their roots.

Twan told us to stay put until he found out how the V.C. had known we were coming. I asked if he had anyone new in his village. He told us that about two weeks ago, a family in his village had had relatives come to visit. My men and I took cover and gave Twan two days to return with the answer. If trouble started, we were to withdraw back into the tunnel and fork to the left of the "Y," opposite the way we had come in. I did not want to go back down into that hole for all the tea in China.

We set up our NDP and camped in for the night. We all sensed it would be a long one. Just after everyone was settled in, the bush to our right started to rustle. It sounded like something was slowly circling us in the dark. This kept up for several hours. Then, just before dawn, the stalking sound drew closer. No one dared to move or make any noise which might give our position away. I sent Dou and another Yard forward to check the source of the rustling, when the sound shifted to our rear. It continued in a gradual circle until it reached our front, where Dou was supposed to be. I tried to see what was happening, but the undergrowth was too dense.

All grew quiet for what seemed like a lifetime. No one drew a breath for fear of what might happen. I looked over at Mike with a look of puzzlement; but before he could respond, a loud noise, unlike anything I had ever heard or wanted to hear again, roared out of the jungle. I don't know how to describe it — it was like being inside a lion's den at feeding time. Suddenly, Dou broke through the brush with an expression of stark, raving terror on his face. What was right behind him is what scared me. It was about ten feet long and the biggest cat I had ever seen. What do you do? I wasn't trained to fight a

600-pound tiger. You have a hungry cat coming at you, but you can't shoot for fear you would alert Charlie. Looking back, my response was pretty stupid. I pulled out my knife, as if that would do any good! About three feet in front of our line, the tiger lunged at Dou and took one huge bite which tore half of his side out. The tiger then looked straight at me with menacing eyes. I grabbed a grenade and was ready to pitch it when a shaft went by my left ear. It hit that tiger right between the eyes and dropped him in his tracks. I looked over my shoulder into the business end of a crossbow, then turned around to see what happened to the cat, only to notice that if I had extended me arm, I could have touched him on the nose. It was experiences like that which convinced me that God was standing only a hairbreadth between myself and death.

When the two days were up, Twan returned with his grisly trophies. He was carrying the heads of two people hanging from a bamboo pole. One was a man about 20 years old; the other was a woman about the same age. Their eyes were open. The woman's face had a look of fear, frozen just a moment before the blade came down. The lips of the man were curled in a snarl, and the eyes had a final look of defiance for his executioners.

It was that particular brand of frontier justice which this war bred. Twan told me that the V.C. knew that we were in the area and advised us to call off the mission. I said "NO!" I had never scrubbed any mission, and I wasn't planning on starting now. He informed me the V.C. had doubled the number of troops at the outpost, and it would be suicide trying to take it now. By his look of concern, I knew he was questioning whether I would go ahead. I told him I was, and nothing was going to stop us. Mike had overheard Twan's caution and asked me what my problem was. It was unlike me to unnecessarily risk the lives of my men. I said that I saw no reason not to proceed with the mission, but told him that if it would make him feel better, I would send a message back with a runner. We had a predetermined contact point where we had buried a short-wave radio for a message transfer in case we ran into problems. That temporarily calmed Mike's fears. I coded a message and had Twan send a runner back to the emergency contact point with it. Just to be on the safe side, I sent a second runner an hour later carrying the same message. I knew what the answer would be; but to keep Mike and the other men happy, I sent the message anyway.

During the next two days, we fought a running skirmish with the V.C. They would find us and hit us with all they had. We would fight back to cover our retreat as we melted back into the jungle. We would then lay an ambush and kick the dog out of them as they pursued us. This continued for two days and three nights until the designated time to link up with our runners to get word on what to do next. The plan was to use the Yards in a diversionary move to draw off the V.C. while we moved to rendezvous with our runners.

The Yards opened up on the V.C. just after midnight on the third night of our running battle. There were tracers all over the place, but none from the V.C. camp. Something was wrong. I sent two of my men back to see what was going on. They returned and informed me that the V.C. had left only a small contingent of men in camp, while the main body had pulled out to the southwest. I sent Doc with five Yards ahead to the contact point, while the rest of us pursued the V.C.

It took about an hour and a half for us to come up on the rear elements of the V.C. They were taking no precautions at all, so we almost walked into them. The plan was to see if we could take one of them alive to find out what was going on and why they had pulled out of the area so hastily. Mike, Phil, and Veto flanked their left to distract the last two or three of them, while John and I went up the right side with six of the Yards. At a given point in the trail, Mike and his group opened up. The V.C. did just the opposite of what they normally did. The front of the group took off running, while the back five dug in to cover their retreat. It was unlike any maneuver I had ever seen the V.C. take. They were fighting as though they had to hold that section of ground at all costs.

We hit them from three sides at once with everything we had, even though we still wanted prisoners. The battle raged on for almost an hour, with the loss of several of the Yards. Twan was on one side of me and this little Yard was on the other. At one point in the firefight, a grenade rolled into our position and the little guy to my right smothered it with his body. Luckily, it did not go off. He just looked at it and started laughing hysterically. He picked up the grenade and showed it to us. The V.C. who had thrown it was so freaked he forgot to pull the pin. As he stood there showing us his prize, a bullet hit him on the right side of his neck and exploded out the left side, showering us with blood and tissue.

The battle seesawed back and forth without either side gaining the upper hand. Then, all of a sudden, the V.C. firing stopped. The only sound was from our weapons.

I called a cease-fire and an uneasy silence fell over the jungle. Not even the usual noises could be heard. The peace was a welcome respite. We all stopped to catch our breath and burn off the adrenaline.

What happened next I thought you only read about in comic books. Just in front of us were four V.C. with their hands in the air, begging us to take them prisoner. That was almost unheard of from the V.C., but four of them were coming towards me with a white flag. Not only did they surrender, but they were only too willing to talk. However, at the moment, I didn't feel like talking. My anger had reached the boiling point. I wanted to kill them with my bare hands. I started to take a step towards them when that small voice stopped me. Even then, that small voice was trying to keep me straight. I didn't always obey, but He was still there directing my steps toward that day when I would fully respond to Him.

The first V.C. started to chatter so fast that I had to stop him and call our interpreter over to see what he was saying. He was scared, but not of us. I asked why they were left behind to die. The one in command explained they were ordered to stay back and hold us in that place till the main body could get out. When I asked him why, he told me that they had three Chinese advisors with them who didn't want to be captured. When I asked them why they surrendered, I was startled by their answer. It seemed that the Chinese had made their lives miserable through constant drilling, indoctrination, and back-breaking labor. Doung, the oldest of them, said that the Chinese had stripped them of all their personal belongings, burned their village, forceably conscripted them, and lied to them about the reasons they were fighting the

South. He had a brother living in the South who had told him a completely different story than what the Chinese were saying. Doung also said that he and about ten of his comrades had spent the last month looking for a way to escape. When I asked him why they kept fighting after the others pulled out, he said they were just scared. They were told to keep fighting until reinforcements came back for them. They gave up because they had exhausted their ammunition and had nothing to fight with and nothing to lose. They knew if they didn't show a white flag, we would kill every one of them.

When Twan asked about the base camp we were to take, Doung said that it not only contained two companies of Viet Cong but had been reinforced with four NVR companies and one company of Chinese Regulars. I was relieved to hear that. If we had tried to take our objective, we would have walked into a death trap. Our only recourse was to head back the way we came, in hopes of linking up with Doc. We trussed up our prisoners and headed out. My mind was fielding a host of questions but not getting any satisfactory answers. I couldn't figure out how we got lucky enough not to stumble into such a suicidal situation, still I knew instinctively that it was more than coincidence.

After 9 klicks, we finally linked up with Doc. He was white as a sheet and out of breath from a hard hump through the bush. All I could get from him was that about four klicks out from our original contact point, he had run across three companies of North Vietnamese Regulars with about ten Chinese officers headed in our direction. That news spared us again from walking into a no-win situation. A strange sense of providence swept over me.

We doubled back to the contact point for message transfer, hoping we could send an emergency message to get picked up.

When we arrived, we could see signs that a battle had taken place. Doc searched the area and found the bodies of the two runners we had sent ahead a few days before. They were both staked spread-eagle to trees, mutilated almost beyond recognition. The V.C. had tortured them to extract what information they had. Trem, the youngest of the two, had both his eyes carved out and the skin peeled off his back in strips. He was stripped naked and castrated. The other Montagnard runner was even more brutally butchered. It looked as if they had forcibly pulled his left arm off. It appeared that every bone in his body had been broken. His tongue was ripped out of his mouth and his teeth kicked in.

After finding that grisly scene, my immediate concern was whether they had uncovered the emergency transmitter. I said a small prayer asking for it to still be buried where we left it. It was our only link to the outside. I don't know what I would have done if it wasn't there. Thank God it was. I dug it out of the hole, unwrapped it, and sent the coded message for help. No response, so I sent it again. Still nothing, so I started to check the unit. Just as I turned it over, it crackled and came to life. Mike sent a short coded message which prompted a resonse to call back in three hours.

We saddled up and moved out in the opposite direction from our last contact with Charlie. We wanted to put as much real estate between us and the V.C. as possible before the choppers came in to lift us out. However, it was slow going because the rain forest was so congested with vines, bamboo stands, and tangled undergrowth.

After grueling hours pushing through the jungle, we ran into one of the worst possible obstacles that we could have confronted. A river is not one of the things you like to see at a time like that, but we found ourselves with our back to one which was about 100 meters across and swift moving. The lush vegetation grew to the very edge of the water making it nearly impossible to tell if anyone was dug in on the other side waiting. It would be extremely dangerous crossing it in the open, but we had no choice. Charlie was closing in. Twan and one of his men stepped into the water and immediately went under like lead weights. When they didn't come up, I thought, "What a lousy way to go after making it through so much." Just then, about twenty meters downstream, Twan bobbed up. He tried to swim to the other side, but the current was too strong.

I called him back to our side of the river and sent five Yards and Veto upstream, and Doc with five Yards downstream, with instructions to go two hours out, or until they found a suitable crossing, then return. An ambush was then set up in case Charlie came to cross the river before our teams returned. Those two hours seemed like they took two days. We were all extremely jittery listening to the sounds of the jungle as we waited for our teams to return.

The shadows were lengthening when Veto's group returned. He had bad news. They couldn't find a shallow crossing upstream and had sighted a company of Regulars heading towards us about four klicks back.

We moved downstream in a hurry, trying to reach Doc's group. About 30 minutes later, we met Doc and his people. They were wet and excited. They had found a way across and hadn't made any contact with the enemy. Twan suggested we leave a diversionary trail to give the impression we were a small recon team so we could buy time to set up an ambush at the crossing site. Doc described the opposite bank of the river as a sandy rising about 25 meters by 100 meters wide with little ground cover. At the top of the incline was a thick tree line. He had already positioned two of his men there to cover our crossing.

Mike called in another coded message requesting a lift out and giving the map location of a hill about two klicks to the rear of the river crossing where the choppers could land. We were instructed to be at the pick-up point in twelve hours. We would be cutting it very close! In less than an hour, the enemy would overtake us and we didn't know if we could hold them off for that long.

While Twan sent about ten of his Yards on a diversionary maneuver away from the river, the rest of us headed for the crossing in a roundabout way, trying to cover our trail as we went by replacing the trampled undergrowth and arranging the thick foliage to cover our tracks. We spent about three miserable hours slashing our way through the almost impenetrable jungle. The insects and suffocating humidity were miserable. The going was slow, wet, and sloppy through the dripping undergrowth. Our only consolation was that it would be slow going for Charlie, also.

When we finally reached the river crossing, all was still — almost too still to be safe. On the opposite side was a small boat, the kind that the locals used to cross the river. Twan led us to another dugout a short distance away which we used to cross over with. Paddling out in the middle of that river, completely exposed to possible gunfire, was a harrowing experience. Once on the other bank, we worked our way around to the far side of the open slope at the river crossing. The two men Doc had left behind to cover the crossing were dug in at the top of the clearing. When we reached them, they told Twan that no one had been there, and they were starting to think we had abandoned them.

We climbed down to the river and crossed back in the same boat we had borrowed from the other side. With one lethal exception, we beached it the way we found it. We booby trapped it by placing a grenade with its pin pulled underneath in such a way that if the boat was disturbed, it would blow up. Veto and I planned where to set up our booby traps and discussed what we were going to do about the ten men Twan still had out. The plan was set: we planted four claymores on both sides of the trail just at the bend before the river, then put some plastique at the base of two large trees just before the river's edge so they would fall back onto the trail when they exploded. We would detonate them by remote control. The next step was a little more tricky. We mined the river bottom at the point they would begin to cross and the bed where they would come out on our side. To stop any that made it past this lethal gauntlet, we hid claymores in the scrub brush on the sandy slope they would have to climb to get to us. To make sure we funneled them in the direction we wanted, we set up a field of crossfire with the two M-60's that Twan's men had positioned at the top of the clearing. Another advantage we had was the fact that if they didn't show up for two hours, the blinding glare of the setting sun would be directly in their eyes.

I told Twan to leave two of his men behind to make contact with the other ten men who would be coming back. While we waited, John and Yep got on the radio to see if there was any traffic from the other side. There was only the usual chatter. We dug in and waited for the action to start. In the back of my mind, I hoped that we would get out without making contact and having to fight our way out of there.

The sun was sinking behind the tree line when Veto signaled that Twan's men were coming in with Charlie hot on their trail. As they crossed the river, the jungle behind them exploded. Veto detonated the first set of claymores, then blew the second set. Firing started on the other side, but not in our direction. It sounded like dozens of jackhammers were pounding away in the jungle. The NVR were shooting as if we were still on the other side. One of Twan's men came up to him laughing like mad. The company of Regulars had followed Twan's men into the ambush, while about twenty Viet Cong that had picked up our trail converged on the Regulars at the same time. They were across the river shooting each other to pieces. When Veto set off the first set of claymores, the Regulars opened up on the Cong thinking that it was us. When Veto set off the second set, the V.C. thought it was us again and started lobbing rounds into the NVR position. We sat back and watched the fireworks for about ten minutes. One of the V.C. must have gone for the boat because, all at once, there was a loud "Vavoom!" which hurled him into the air amidst the splintered remains of the boat.

The explosion ignited the firefight for another five minutes before everything died down. They must have discovered who they were shooting at because we could see them coming around the bend in the trail towards the crossing point. Veto blew the charges which amputated the trees at stump level. One of the trees crushed about five of them, and the other fell just missing about ten more. When the trees started falling, some of the gooks fled into the jungle, while the rest dived into the river. Veto pulled back up the hill as more jumped into the river. With more than half of them wading downstream, the riverbed mines suddenly went off sending arms, legs, blood, mud, and water everywhere. The last vestiges of sunlight were fading as the remaining Regulars opened fire out of the cotton wool mist of smoke floating over the river.

If we could keep them on the other side for a half hour, we could leave one man behind to set off the remaining charges and make the pick-up point just in time to be pulled out. I no sooner had that plan go through my head when they all started across the river again. About fifteen made our shore when the bed mines went off sending more bodies, blood, and junk into the air. Some of the survivors were cut down by the M-60's; the rest fell back to the other side and started to send us incoming mail. We opened up on their muzzle flashes with everything we had for ten mintues then quit, hoping they would think we had pulled back. It worked. They started across for the third time. We stayed very quiet and low while they waded across. We could see the Regulars with green uniforms and web gear, clutching AK's, and looking noticeably nervous coming at us. Veto let most of them reach our side before he detonated the first of five pairs of claymores, ripping through their ranks with thousands of searing steel pellets. The Yards then cut loose with their machine guns. So far, we hadn't lost a man. The enemy was not that lucky. The beach was drenched with blood. Some of their dead were piled on top of one another at the water's edge; others were lying motionless on the slope. Severed limbs were strewn across the sand. The river was dyed with their blood, sending a crimson current drifting lazily downstream.

It was time for us to clear out. I decided to leave Twan and Veto behind to cover our rear as we moved west to our pick-up point. As soon as the enemy saw that we had left, they started across again. The Yards waited until they reached mid-river, then cut them to bits with their M-60's. Just as Twan and Veto were ready to pull back, they started across again. Veto put timers on the claymores that were left, setting the explosives to go off at the top of the slope first, then walking them down the hill as the V.C. fell back.

We had nearly reached the top of the hill when we heard the muffled whacking sound of approaching choppers coming in from the south. The olive drab Hueys without markings hovered in under the relentless clamor of slapping blades as we broke into the clearing. When I reached the first chopper, I told the pilot to hold for five — we had two men coming. He started to say he could give us only three when the concussion from the first of the claymores ripped through the jungle, followed by the second, third, and fourth. He looked at me and then at the jungle with a panicked expression which said, "Let's get the hell out of here!" Mike told him we still had a couple of men out there and needed two more minutes for them to reach us.

The jungle was washing with greys as we loaded into the choppers. The door gunner swiveled his M-60 in the direction of the tree line, flipped off the safety, and anxiously scanned the jungle fringe from where my team had emerged. We could hear a running gun battle in the jungle which was drawing closer by the second. Suddenly, Veto broke into the clearing on a dead run with Twan right on his heels. Both were firing short bursts back over their shoulders at pursuing Regulars who were only 30 meters behind them. The rotor blades were spinning faster as the pilots throttled down. The skids of our half-hovering chopper were nervously shifting from side to side in eager anticipation of lift-off when Veto dove into the bay. With a final surge of power, our Huey tilted its nose forward and lunged upwards. Rounds slammed into the hull as the pilot fought for altitude.

In those final, slow-motion seconds waiting for Twan to make the second ship, I was again reacquainted with prayer: "Oh God, get us out of here — please get us out alive!" The prop wash from the second chopper was churning up a swirl of dust and leaves just as Twan grabbed one of the skids. As it lifted off, the door gunner opened up on the swarm of Regulars who were pouring into the open. In the twilight, we could see some of Twan's men struggling to pull him into the chopper, but not before a parting round slammed into his back. As we climbed over the tree line, we could clearly see the orange muzzle flashes from the enemy gunners in the clearning below. Miraculously, we all made it out of that hell hole that time. I said "that time", for I knew we would be going back, but I also knew that He would get us out alive.

Coming back to the world was the easy part; adjusting was not. The window dressing was still the same, but I was a different person. The passage back to the lifestyle I'd left behind was fraught with post-traumatic pitfalls and uncertainties. I'd spent two incredibly tense years coiled tighter than a steel spring, and unwinding wouldn't be easy. My physical senses had grown so acute that they couldn't adjust to the normal sights and sounds of home. The backfire of a passing car, a simple walk across a lawn, a casual tap on the shoulder, walking in a crowd, or being suddenly awakened from sleep triggered instant responses conditioned by the sustained stresses of combat. Even the simple comforts and conveniences of clean beds and dry sheets, hot showers, ice water, washed clothes, and cooked meals seemed strangely alien to me.

Back in 'Nam, I was a professional with a license to kill. I was a seasoned master in the deadly art of stealth and sabotage. I'd learned to live an earshot from death, to hunt humans, to survive off the land by the cunning and resourcefulness of my fine-tuned skills. Stepping out of that role into the monotonous mainstream was a psychological impossibility. I'd thrived in a pressure vacuum for too long to acclimate to normalcy overnight.

The Army could teach you how to waste people with proficiency, but they couldn't teach you how to return home the same way you left. I wasn't the same. I was an adenaline junkie, hooked on my own self-induced high. I was addicted to the lethal rush of warfare. Coming cold turkey off that two year run was as impossible to me as doing the backstroke across the Pacific. Besides, I had secretly learned to love the habit and wasn't ready to kick it just yet.

Still, I came back to the world — like a million others — to pick up where I left off, to resume the traditional quest for the American dream. However, stepping back on the well-worn treadmill was an exercise in futility. I tried to interface with the old routine at first, but it didn't work. I tried playing by society's rules, but the role was as uncomfortable as a pair of shoes two sizes too small. I got a regular job teaching at a junior college, but that lasted all of six months. I tried to act normal, but I had lived in the fast lane too long to suddenly slam on the brakes. I was hopelessly out of place and couldn't conform to an environment which was as alien to me as the planet Mars.

I started chumming around with some old friends who had taken up with an outlaw motorcycle gang. I soon found myself dropping out on weekends and riding the roads with my misfit fraternity of bikers. It wasn't just the defiance or the freedom of the wind blowing through your hair on a wide open stretch of road — it was the tightness of the gang. We watched out for each other. We stuck together. We were a team. It was like being in 'Nam all over again.

In short order, I chucked the rat race and took up with my adopted family. For eleven years, I lived the rootless existence of a nomadic rebel, drifting along the asphalt arteries of America. However, it wasn't a carefree existence — I was slowly dying. They were unhappy years of running hard and raising hell. During that time, I exploded through my second marriage. It was a tumbleweed existence of violence, drugs, and sex. It was a life that accommodated the smoldering rage and sub-surface stress which I had entombed deep within my soul.

But the low life grew old. Those years of knocking around led me nowhere except to the end of my rope. I'd finally reached a place of desperation one day in a sleazy bar, high on drugs, where I cried out in brokenness for Jesus to set me free. That was the turning point which changed me from a cold, calloused, uncaring drifter into a man who wanted to love and live again.

Dave Shaffer is now happily married and raising his two boys from his second marriage and the youngest of three from his first. Dave is actively involved in ministering to the large Vietnamese community in the Minneapolis, Minnesota area and has established a 24-hour hotline called "Viet-Help Line" to reach out to the Vietnamese.

Note

The accounts depicted in this story are factual. However, isolated details, locations, and names have been altered to protect the anonymity of the persons involved and safeguard the sensitive nature of certain incidents.

David C. Shaffer

David E. Knight
Captain, U.S. Army
Chaplain
4th of 47th Inf. Battalion
9th Inf. Division
Nov. '67 - Nov. '68

3

Supreme Six

I'd just melted into my rack after an exhausting Sunday schedule, in hopes of stealing a couple of hours of sleep before our early morning mission, when I was awakened by a sheepish, somewhat apologetic squad leader named John. "What do you mean, Chaplain, you must be born again? I just can't seem to get those words out of my head." I was physically spent, but I could tell by the plaintive tone of his voice and the troubled look in his eyes that he really needed to talk.

There were some chaplains who would have rolled over with a "We'll talk about it in the morning," but I hadn't volunteered for chaplaincy duty in 'Nam to keep my own hours. With two years behind me as an infantry officer during the Korean conflict, I was already acclimated to the fact that your life was not your own in the military; it belonged to the officers over you. After years of serving as an Episcopalian priest and re-enlisting for active duty at the age of 37 to attend to the spiritual well-being of the soldiers in 'Nam, I arrived with the knowledge that my life also belonged to a higher authority — to Supreme Six, the Army's slang for God. It was with that conviction that I received my orders assigning me to the Mobile Riverine Force operating along the yellow-brown waterways and patchwork rice lands of the Mekong Delta.

With John's words, I bolted awake. It was as if God had suddenly awakened me from my stupor. I hadn't actually preached those words that morning — only read that familiar verse in passing. Yet that passage had pierced his heart deeper than any piece of shrapnel could have ever penetrated. We talked about the meaning of those words from the lips of Christ until the early morning call to "saddle up" was issued.

I remember the joy which overwhelmed the both of us while anchored on that barracks barge on the muddy Mekong as he recited the sinner's prayer and asked Christ to come into his heart. John disappeared into the pre-dawn darkness a different man.

A month later, a P.F.C. confided to me, "You will never believe what happened to John, Chaplain. That guy used to be a pain in the rear. Every time we'd get into a firefight, that coward would hide. He was supposed to be our squad leader, but he'd cringe behind some tree and let us fend for ourselves. He even faked being bit by a rabid rat by pinching his stomach with a pair of hand pliers so he'd be pulled off the line and sent to a hospital in Saigon for rabies shots. But he's really changed. Now he's like some old mother hen. He never leaves us, and whenever we get into a firefight, he risks his life to save us. He's not the same guy. If that's what coming to Christ will do, I'm all for it!"

I must admit, when I first arrived in country, I was just as skeptical about the sincerity of "foxhole conversions" as some in the States were of deathbed confessions. But testimonies like John's began to show me that God was very much alive in the affairs of men, even amidst the carnage and corruption of Vietnam. I also saw that God was able to make sense out of the confusion.

I can empathize with the many men who never saw beyond the desperation and dying. Everything seemed so utterly hopeless in that war-torn country. After years of uninterrupted conflict, Vietnam gave every impression of being a terminally ill patient. I think we all knew the South Vietnamese had long since lost the will to resist. Even their army was too weary or just too indifferent to bleed anymore. The only thing that kept Vietnam from its inevitable collapse was the massive infusion of U.S. dollars and adolescent blood.

Everything associated with our involvement in 'Nam seemed like a black-and-white negative of futility. It was a war without fronts against an elusive enemy. By day, he could be a harmless peasant farmer plowing his paddy in time-honored fashion behind a water buffalo; while at night, he'd stalk the jungle in black pajamas, planting homemade explosives which would blow our men away in the morning. Often, it seemed like we were not fighting men at all, but booby traps which indiscriminately maimed and killed. We were hopelessly entangled in a conflict without clear objectives. Except for the "kill ratios" chalked on some battalion scoreboard, we had no way of knowing whether we had won or lost. Rules of engagement which designated "free-fire-zones" versus a "don't shoot unless shot at" policy posed an insane dilemma for the common grunt who risked his life each day in an endless field of fire. In a war where we would take a hill, let Charlie reclaim it, only to sacrifice more men to re-take it again, a chronic sense of wholesale waste was fueled. It was a war whose moral mission, its very heart and soul, had been ripped out by student riots and political dissent back home. So, for many, Vietnam was a worthless war as denuded of ethics and reason as the Vietnamese jungles which had been stripped bare by our defoliants and bombings.

Yet, in some sovereign way, the Lord cut through the

insanity of it all to show me that He was still in command, even if America had lost her way through that dark nightmare. Even through the sin and suffering, He made me realize that "all things" do "work together for good to them that love God, to them who are called according to his purpose." I had come with that scripture a firm part of my world view but, once there, God would cause the glory of that truth to shine as relentlessly upon me as the midday brilliance of a Vietnamese sun.

I had reenlisted in the Army with the belief that it was simply God's will. But as our chartered jet made its final descent from 30,000 feet over the South China Sea, I was suddenly seized by a sickening fear that I had made a terrible mistake. There had been an almost festive spirit on the plane until we left the runway of Clark Field in the Philippines. I remember the jubilation of one young officer who told me, "It's as if I've been looking forward to this moment all my life. I am a professional soldier, and now I have an opportunity to try my wings." I must admit, I was caught up with the same naive idealism. I longed to experience that sacrament of war — my baptism by fire. Yes, I also came with lofty notions of the justness of our cause — a soldier pitted against the godless forces of Communism. I was an officer and minister in the Army of God, with a mandate to carry that "terrible swift sword," but God would temper us all during those months in Indochina. I would come home with no illusions of the righteousness of war, but a poignant reminder of God's ability to redeem something eternal out of the blood, sweat, and tears.

I'll never forget the sober change of mood that filled the cabin as the stewardess announced, "Gentlemen, our next stop is the Republic of South Vietnam." The childlike days of playing soldier abruptly ended. This was the moment of truth. There was no turning back. The atmosphere was charged with the troubled questions of men lost in the private inventory of their manhood. "How will I react in this test? Will I prove a coward? Will I run the first time I'm shot at? Will I make it home?" I also wondered, "How many would make the return flight a year from now? How many would go home early without arms and legs? How many would make the passage home in a box? How many would die in spirit? And how many would meet their Maker in one way or the other?" I wondered, too, if I would make any difference in the lives of those whom I would serve.

I sat back in my seat facing forward in quiet resignation to my fate when His Word overshadowed my moment of weakness: *"My grace is sufficient for you, for My strength is made perfect in weakness."* It was as if He had casually brushed aside the self doubts and fears. I was there because I was supposed to be. My orders had not come down through Army channels but from God above. His Word was encouraging me that His grace would sustain — that I was sent with a purpose. It was not to kill, but to offer life to those who craved it the most. Maybe that is one of the sublime ironies of war — that some men only seek God in the midst of death and dying. There were countless times during my tour that I would tell new arrivals, "Men, most of you probably never thought about the Lord before, but I guarantee you'll think a lot about Him over here." They did, and some followed in the footsteps of John. Many found grace in their living and in their dying.

There was Sully, an infantryman with a family back in the "real world," who had calloused his heart and turned his back on God. He made no attempt to conceal the fact that he was living in open sin. His life was a proverbial case of the "pig that returns to wallow in the mire." I hadn't approached him as yet — maybe because he was avoiding me like the plague. I guess I represented a physical reminder of the conviction which was already troubling his soul.

Our battalion had been engaged in a series of waterborne search and destroy sweeps to rout out V.C. sanctuaries along the gridwork of canals and rice paddies in the Mekong Delta. Because of my prior experience as an infantry officer, I spent the majority of my duty in the field slogging through the wet world of the rice lands alongside of the men in the line companies. I didn't have to be out in the field, but that's where the harvest lay. I wanted to show the men that God was not cloistered in the safety of some rear area chapel.

However, on one particular operation, I was prevented from taking part in the assault because I was preaching at a fire base at Tan An. I arrived after our battalion had pulled out. I headed over to the Tactical Operation Center to monitor the battalion's progress. The radio frequencies were cluttered with garbled chaos. They were taking heavy casualties. Med-evac choppers were only a few minutes out, inbound to our M.A.S.H. hospital. I hated the sickening feeling of helplessness, wanting to do something to help my men who were getting bloodied a few miles away; but there was little I could do but pray.

Dust-offs started unloading the wounded at the landing pads a few minutes later, suddenly transforming the place into a churning mass of turbulence. I was waiting in the triage area as the medical teams segregated the wounded according to need. The E.R. looked like a human slaughterhouse. Olive drab soldiers, soaked with red-black stains, were sprawled across wooden receiving tables amidst an assortment of stainless steel trays and cloth-wrapped bundles of sterile utensils. Plastic plasma bags were dangling from overhead hooks. Some were carried in with the shredded stumps of missing limbs, some with sucking chest wounds frothing with tiny pink bubbles, some were disembowled from gut wounds, some with shrapnel and gunshot punctures, while others were bound with bloody compresses around their heads.

The carnage was enough to make you recoil in horror. It was everything I could do to maintain my composure in the midst of that butchery. Floors were smeared with crimson splotches which men were slipping on. Anonymous body parts were discarded on abandoned stretchers. It was a grisly scene of bloody snapshots. Soldiers were in shock; others were writhing in pain or crying for more morphine. Nurses were rushing to patients with bags of whole blood and I.V. hook-ups, adjusting tourniquets or sucking out trach tubes. Here and there, orderlies were frantically cutting away muddy jungle fatigues and boots, while field surgeons in splattered green smocks were trying to stop the bleeding or desperately pounding on the exposed chest of a young soldier whose heart had arrested.

I was doing my best to comfort the wounded and help out where I could when one of the surgeons turned to me and said, ''Chaplain, there's a guy lying over in the corner who wants to see you. I don't think he's going to make it. He stepped on a land mine which blew away his legs and genitals. I think he said his name is 'Sully'." At the mention of that name, a torrent of thoughts rushed through my mind. There was no vindictiveness or judgmental thoughts, only compassion and regret. I headed to his stretcher thinking, "That poor devil. If only he had lived his life differently. What can I possibly do now?"

I knelt before him and couldn't help noticing the bloodied liner lying strangely depressed where his legs should have been. He was a caricature of his former self. His face was gaunt, complexion an ashen grey, and his body torn and disfigured. But I'll never forget the look of stark terror in his eyes. It was the look of someone slipping off a great precipice into a dark abyss. He looked at me with eyes watering with remorse. "Chaplain, I am being punished by God for my sin. I'm so afraid to die." I had looked death in the face myself, but I had never felt such an awesome fear as I did at that moment. I knew that Sully's eternal destiny rested on what I was about to say. However, as I moistened my lips and started to speak, God's Spirit imparted a confidence to tell him that He still loved him and forgave him and would receive him unto Himself. He just lay there, anxiously grasping each word I spoke. When I finished, he repented and asked Jesus to come into his heart. It was like a brooding skyscape had been rolled back, revealing the light of the sun. A peace settled over his bloodied stretcher, and the icy terror in his eyes was suddenly replaced by a look of contentment as he slipped away. I'd been skeptical of deathbed confessions, too, but I rose up knowing that God had given him mercy.

There were other Sullys and Johns whose paths crossed with mine. There were private times at impromptu services in the field or private chats during cigarette breaks or when eating C-rats where an opening was offered to extend the grace of God, and there were times where I saw God's sovereignty in the way He subdued circumstances and providentially covered us.

The Tet Offensive was in full swing when my battalion was given the job of making contact with a regiment of main force North Vietnamese Regulars who had infiltrated the paddy lands about twenty miles northwest of My Tho — the provincial capitol of Kein Hoa Province. We started upstream in "mike" boats about 1 p.m. on March the 7th. The western horizon was just flushing with gray-greens when we beached along an open clearing beside the Mekong and started loading into Hueys for the airborne assault against the suspected location. There were not enough choppers to ferry our entire company to the LZ, so the C.O. divided us into two groups. Captain Delgado, the C.O. and my close personal friend, headed off with the first wave. We were to follow after the choppers deposited the first half. A half an hour later, we got word over our field radios that the first wave had landed in a hot LZ and were getting cut to pieces by small arms fire and mortars. They were trapped in a pocket with only fifty able bodied men, in danger of getting overrun.

I remember the cloud of apprehension which settled over the clusters of waiting soldiers when we got word that we would be inserted with the rest of the battalion near the contact point, so we could break through to save what was left of Bravo Company. Few can imagine what it's like facing the terrifying prospects of going into a hot LZ. There's a level of apprehension associated with final exams, taking a driver's test, or giving birth. But there are few fears in this life as disconcerting as hovering over an open rice paddy under a barrage of bullets and incoming mortar rounds — especially when you're strapped in the straitjacket suspense of a claustrophobic chopper cabin, unable to duck or dive for cover. All you can do is sit and hope and pray that one of those high velocity bits of steel doesn't have your name on it.

We floated nervously several thousand feet above the mosaic greens, occasional clumps of palm trees, and mustard colored ribbons en route to the hot LZ. On board, teenage soldiers unveiled the various faces of terror. Some sat with wide-eyed apprehension, nervously clutching their rifles like deadly pacifiers; others were gritting their teeth with lungs drawing deeply; some sat with eyes locked shut in private communion with their God, while others sat frozen in stoical silence. Most of those boy soldiers were fresh replacements who had never passed through a baptism of fire. I was an old man in comparison, twice their age, and thankful that I had already been exposed to combat. I remember cupping my hand around my mouth and shouting some fatherly advice to pray, under the steady clamor of the chopper motor. And I remember the comeback of one young man who said, "Oh, you don't have to worry, Chaplain. I have been praying for a long time!" His reply elicited a chorus of nervous laughter which momentarily eased the tension.

Our chopper made a tight spiral descent over the jade colored paddies covered by a broken mantle of grey clouds from the deadly blossoms of mortar rounds hitting across the field. We could see soldiers splashing across the clearing for cover or sprawled behind the shallow parapets of dirt dikes firing towards the tree line. We could hear the muted popcorn popping sound of small arms fire in the distance and the occasional "ping" of invisible ground fire puncturing the thin skin of the chopper hull.

The chopper was slowly skimming about five feet over the paddy water, which was rippling from the slap of the prop blast, when the signal to jump was given. But the men were riveted to their seats in fear. The crew chief was screaming at them to jump clear, while a brassy stream of 7.62mm casings spewed out of the ejection port as the doorgunner chattered away at the tree line a couple hundred yards away. It was not a time to hesitate. We had to act or get blown out of the sky. After some firm encouragment, the men jumped into the ankle deep mud and promptly dove into the stinking muck face first.

The next few minutes were a confused collection of sights and sounds. I remember dripping with black slime, as we slogged across the shallow paddy in a crouched position, and the erratic mortar blasts which splattered the surrounding field with mud and shrapnel. I remember the pall of slate grey smoke drifting lazily across the field and the sporadic geysers which spurted around us from small arms fire. I remember the deafening "crump! crump! crump!" of incoming and the menacing tree line to our front which shimmered in the afternoon heat. I remember soldiers stumbling and falling from hits and the desperate line of men hiding behind the dikes in a state of confusion. I was in a strange detached state — like I was watching a slow motion movie of myself.

I was suddenly jolted back to reality by an infantry officer who bravely rose to his feet and shouted the order to run for the tree line. I started to balk at what appeared to be a suicidal command when I realized it was the right thing to do. We had to break through the barrage which was scything through our ranks and reach the cover of the tree line. Men, more afraid to stay than move, rose to their feet and surged over the dike, spraying the tree line with automatic fire on the run. When we penetrated the jungle, our situation only marginally improved. The bursts were exploding in the jungle canopy, showering hot shrapnel all around us, while small arms fire slashed through the undergrowth. We were engulfed in dense foliage which obscured the direction of incoming and added to our mounting sense of confusion.

I was embracing the earth, praying that I wouldn't get hit, when I was overcome by a tremendous impulse to get up and run forward. With bullets slashing through the vegetation overhead, I thought that it was crazy, but the urge was so overpowering that I sprang to my feet and tore through the jungle for about ten yards before throwing myself to the ground. No sooner had I hugged the dirt when the ground lurched from the impact of a 122mm rocket which cratered the jungle floor behind me. It hit the exact spot where I had been lying a few seconds before and where another soldier, who had taken my place, lay in a twisted heap on the smoke cratered dirt.

It's difficult describing the conflicting emotions I felt at that moment. On one hand, I felt the pang of guilt that I had escaped when the other soldier hadn't; on the other hand, I felt a strange elation that God had intervened on my behalf. It was a sweet and somber moment of laughter and tears.

Just then, a runner touched me on the back and said, "Chaplain, you're wanted immediately at the battalion headquarters. The C.O. wants you to take charge of the wounded. He said the med-evac chopper got shot down, and we'll have to carry the wounded out.''

When I reached the makeshift field headquarters set up inside the pockmarked rubble of a former farm house, I found out just how serious our situation was. The battalion was consolidated in a tenuous position, dangerously close to being overrun. We had no choice but to pull back.

What transpired next was incomprehensible to me. The captain in charge told me he was going to leave the wounded who were huddled together behind a wall of the farm house. To say I was shocked was an understatement — I was livid. His statement was unconscionable. The American Army never left their wounded for the enemy, no matter how hopeless the situation. With all the atrocities they were inflicting upon the wounded who had been overrun in other battles, we might as well have shot them in the heads ourselves. Chaplain or not, I felt like laying another kind of hands on that young officer and beating some sense into him. I got in the face of the captain and told him, in no uncertain terms, what I thought of him or anyone else who would dare consider such a despicable act. I would die with them, if I had to, but there was no way on God's earth that I was going to leave those men to the NVA. At that point, the captain snapped out of his shock and said, ''All right, Chaplain! You do whatever you must to get these men out; I'll do what I can to help you.''

I immediately broke the thirty or so wounded into two groups — the ambulatory and those who would have to be carried out. Some of the men improvised stretchers out of rifles and poncho liners, while I begged and borrowed and stole what men I could to serve as litter bearers for the seriously wounded. I remember squinting from the glare of a low slung sun as we pulled out. We were told to follow the tail-end of the column as they evacuated the area. The jungle was dark, damp, and dripping wet. The only light was from the periodic orange bursts of V.C. mortars. I remember groping blindly through the lush vegetation, tortuously dragging the stretchers up one slimy embankment and down another. Occasionally, we'd break through the dense undergrowth into an open stretch of rice paddies blanketed by knee-deep water.

The last man in the lead column was suppose to maintain contact with us as we snaked through the nearly pitch black night, but we lost contact with each other and found ourselves lost and disoriented in the darkness with Charlie all around us. With all the noise from the creaking litters and thrashing through the thick undergrowth, I didn't see how we could continue undetected.

We had few able-bodied men who could fight if we stumbled into an ambush. We were lost, not knowing where the battalion was, where Charlie was, or where we were; but the worst part was that everyone was depending on me for answers. One of the corporals summed up the feeling of desperation when he said, "Chaplain, which way shall we go? Tell us!"

I was looking to someone else for answers. In the blackness, I silently prayed for God to guide us. Without knowing where I was I said, "Go that way!" Our backs were so up against the proverbial Red Sea that I had no recourse but to simply trust that He who makes a way where there seems to be no way would lead us safely out of the snare. I felt like I was blindly leading a column of handicapped men through a mine field, but I pressed forward, trusting that God would not forsake us. Fifteen minutes later, we wandered into our own battalion perimeter dug in around the low-lying dike of a rice paddy. I'll never forget the sense of relief that overwhelmed us when we reached our line. The whole experience had been a walk through the "valley of the shadow of death" under the guiding hand of the Great Shepherd.

Our men were still straggling in when I discovered the added blessing that my good friend, Dick Delgado, was alive and well. Indeed, when I heard his wry battlefield humor, "Where were you Chaplain? You know, you can get hurt out there!" I almost cried.

I walked out of that experience with my faith in God's providential protection reinforced. Yet, the extent of His care would be driven home even more profoundly through what lay ahead.

The length of Vietnam was in the death throes of the Tet Offensive when our battalion received orders to clear out a village in the infamous Ben Tre area. The objective was a suspected staging area for a V.C. battalion. None of us relished the thought of operating in the vicinity of this treacherous V.C. stronghold. The entire battalion was on edge as we waited to saddle up.

I took advantage of the lull to catch up on some Bible reading. I pulled out my pocket Bible, which I kept safely tucked inside my helmet suspension, and opened the pages. My eyes fell upon the words,

> *Surely He will save you from the fowler's snare and from the deadly pestilence. He will cover you with His feathers and under His wings will you find refuge. His faithfulness will*

be your shield. . . . You will not fear . . . the arrow that flies by day . . . nor the plague that destroys at midday. A thousand may fall at your right side, ten thousand at your right hand, but it will not come near you. You will only observe with your eyes and see the punishment of the wicked (Psalms 91:3-8).

The words seemed to leap right off the page. They were speaking directly to me, saying "You will make contact with the enemy, but I will be with you and, as you trust in Me, not a single bullet will hurt you."

When I shared that promise with Captain Ron Pease, a good friend and fellow Christian, he took the bold and seemingly presumptuous step of telling all the men in Echo Company that God had promised to shield them in the coming battle.

However, as we headed out, those words seemed hollow and sermonizing compared to the flesh and blood realities confronting us. As we penetrated deeper into enemy territory, the landscape provided ominous tokens that we were encroaching into Charlie's heartland. All the outward circumstances argued against the promise God had given me that morning. The V.C. had actually posted signs in English warning certain death to trespassers. Miniature V.C. flags were painted on pieces of tin and nailed to trees notifying us, in effect, that "You are entering Communist country — proceed at your own risk." When we reached the outskirts of the suspected village, we were shocked to find a V.C. flag fluttering over the city gate in blatant defiance of our intrusion. Even the women and children were hostile. The kids would usually flock around us with wide-mouthed grins and beg us for tins of C-rats or

cigarettes, but not here. There were only the taunts of
"G.I. number 10!" and a battery of cursing. You could
see the cold contempt for us in their eyes. The hate was
palpable. Except for some old papa sans, the village was
devoid of men.

After leaving the backside of the village, we entered
an alien world of shattered trees and abandoned rice paddies inundated with dirty brown water. Repeated bombings had disfigured the surrounding countryside into a
blighted moonscape of flooded craters. We were making our way down a dike footpath overgrown by heavy
undergrowth from months of disuse and disrepair. There
was an almost unearthly look and feel to our situation.

We knew they were waiting for us. We could feel it.
About a half mile beyond the village, the V.C. opened
up with AK's and carbines. The air was alive with the
popping of automatic weapons. We ducked into a
bombed-out house whose plastered walls were peppered
with bullets and shrapnel from previous battles. Rounds
were cracking into the rubble around us or ricocheting
away with their parting whine. Our platoon was pouring
frenzied bursts of fire towards the muzzle flashes of the
V.C. dug in along the dikes. The reserve platoon of Echo
Company was running up to us under a barrage of bullets
which were whipping the air and kicking up dirt all around
them. I remember questioning myself, "How can those
men live through this? How can any of them survive this
hell?"

We called in for an urgent fire mission to relieve the
pressure. A few moments later, a spotting round of white
phosphorus exploded to our front with a burst of orange,
followed by an almost graceful umbrella of burning white

streamers. The 105 batteries on our floating artillery platform in the delta fired for effect. However, the shells started falling dangerously close, sending shrapnel splinters cutting through the air overhead. The shrill scream of incoming was terrifying. One of the rounds hit a few feet away, sending a piece of metal slamming into my helmet. I was stunned but, thank God, my helmet was only dented by the glancing blow.

I was hiding under some brush, so scared that my teeth were actually chattering and my knees knocking. In the natural, there was no possible way God's promise could hold up under the pressure. Still, my spirit held out a faint ray of hope.

When the barrage lifted, the C.O. ordered Echo Company forward in a flanking move to outmaneuver the V.C. who were pulling back. The rest of us moved forward cautiously. I was looking for any wounded along the trail. I had just passed a crater covered with mottled green algae when the crack of a sniper round sent me plunging into the crater, thinking it was a shallow depression, only to sink up to my face in the swampy muck. It had the foul-smelling stink of decaying matter and was probably a breeding pool for every known form of bacteria and leech. I clawed my way out of that fetid hole, dripping with green slime and reeking like something that had been left out in the sun too long.

When the firefight finally ended, I was overwhelmed by the reports that followed from some of the soldiers. A number of the men had been hit but, miraculously, no one had been wounded. One trooper said, "Chaplain, I took a round in the stomach, but my belt buckle deflected the bullet!" Another was rejoicing, "Praise

God! I got shot in the chest, but my bandolier of magazines stopped the bullet!'' Still another was dumb-founded by his discovery: ''I can't believe it, Chaplain. The shrapnel was so thick around me that a chunk severed my radio antenna next to my head, but didn't touch me!''

God had kept His promise and showed Himself strong on our behalf. Lessons such as that are worth the impact of a thousand sermons on God's loving care. Yet, I learned something more.

After months in my combat classroom, I began wondering if I was the only pastor in Vietnam who was experiencing such things. But, as my path crossed those of others, I discovered God had been performing the same sorts of miracles on their behalf. I also learned, in a much deeper way, that He was not just a God of the Americans but the God of the Vietnamese, as well.

During my tour, a Navy Chaplain attached to the Mobile Riverine Force told me about the exploits of a native Vietnamese pastor who had escaped from numerous near-death encounters at the hands of the Viet Cong. Pastor Hi was a courageous young man who lived in an area bordering a V.C. sanctuary outside of the pro-vincial capitol of My Tho. He was seriously undermin-ing V.C. recruitment drives through his successful outreach to Vietnamese teenagers. The Viet Cong militias were always looking for warm bodies to fill their ever-depleting ranks and viewed Hi as a direct threat. Conse-quently, they had targeted him for assassination.

After hearing about this man, I felt like I had to meet him. I finally tracked him down at a large missionary or-phanage in My Tho. He had to be one of the most energetic young men I had ever run into. He was beaming with the love of God and couldn't stop talking. After sharing some stories of how God had spared each of us, Pastor Hi told me this story.

Late one night, a squad of V.C. came to his house and arrested him. After blindfolding him and tying his wrists behind his back, they led him off into the darkness to be tried by a people's tribunal on the charge of being a C.I.A. agent, working covertly for the U.S. government. After stumbling and being pushed along, not knowing where they were taking him and fearing the worse, he arrived at a hidden rendezvous deep in the jungle. It was a large hooch filled with scores of black pajama-clad V.C. sitting on their haunches, Vietnamese style, around the inside wall. By all appearances, the V.C. had been summoned to this kangaroo court to witness his trial and inevitable execution.

Under the dim lighting of gas lanterns, what appeared to be a V.C. officer launched into a lengthy harangue of ridiculous accusations against Pastor Hi. They were obviously trumped up charges, intended to elicit the death penalty. To substantiate their charge of his being a C.I.A. agent, they produced an American copy of the R.S.V. Bible with maps of the Holy Lands which, they said, were military maps.

Although he was convinced that they would murder him, they afforded him an opportunity to give a rebuttal. However, he was so overcome with fear and resignation to his eventual death that he thought to himself, "Why not just let them do what they're going to do anyway, and get it over with?" But, if for no other reason than to buy time, he decided to say something — anything. Before he spoke, he prayed, "Father, I don't even know what to do. You know they have already determined to kill me and that any defense I give will do little good. Father, please help me and strengthen me. Show me what to say." At that point, he said, the Lord impressed upon him the confidence, "Fear not, for I am with you. Don't worry, just tell them about Me."

He then stepped to the center of the hooch and, for the next two hours, he related how he had been gloriously saved from his sins, how he had been called into the ministry, and how the Lord had used him to bring the gospel to countless young people. He rambled on until he had nothing left to say and was actually hoarse from speaking. But he was filled with the inner peace that God would watch over him no matter what the Viet Cong decided to do with him.

When he stopped, there was only silence. He looked around the room and, through the dim glow of gas lanterns, he could see the V.C. soldiers crouched on their haunches, looking intently towards him with moist eyes that glistened in the light and tears running down their cheeks. A V.C. captain brusquely led him to the door, pointed off into the darkness in the direction from where he'd come and said, "Get out of here and never look back." God had delivered him from the lion's den.

I never saw Pastor Hi again, but I continued to hear reports of his exploits among the Vietnamese. I heard how God prospered his ministry and how multitudes of teenagers came to the Lord through his efforts. I wonder, of course, whatever happened to him. I wonder if he survived the war and lives today in some underground church in Vietnam. But I have every confidence that no matter what happened to him, God's will was accomplished through his life.

In November of 1968, I returned home. I returned home to a nation divided over a war they didn't want and a war they didn't understand. It probably goes without saying that I returned a different man. I returned somewhat chastened by the things I had seen and the suffering I experienced. I also returned more sober in my view of war. I saw the horror, the brutality, and the sinfulness of a nation raped by it. I witnessed war as the ultimate breakdown of human morality. Nevertheless, I returned home with a greater understanding of the Lord than ever before. I discovered that, regardless of man's sin and rebellion, we are not at the mercy of an impersonal God. We are not subject to chance or fate. Regardless of circumstances, despite the tragedy, He is very much in control.

David Knight returned to private practice after his return from Vietnam. He is married and is the father of five children and grandfather of six. David is presently serving as the Senior Pastor of the King's Community Church in Spokane, Washington.

Phil J. Huss
Boatswain's Mate 2nd Class, U.S. Navy
50 Cal. Machine Gunner - Swift Boat
COS RON 1 COS DIV. 12
June '68 - May '69

4

River Rat

After my arrival in Vietnam and processing at Cam Ranh Bay, I was flown north to Chu Lai and assigned to my swift boat as part of the "brown water navy." During my tour as a "river rat," I would be running patrol duty and monitoring the inland waterways and coastal traffic for contraband. Essentially, we were waterborne traffic cops with orders to search anyone and everything for medical supplies, weapons, ammunition, currency, and gold leaf which were being smuggled or illegally secreted to the V.C. Those not possessing proper identification would be detained for further questioning or turned over to intelligence officers for interrogation.

Every day we moved along the waterways searching basket-boats, sampans, and junks. Our job was often a river "shell game" of hide-and-seek, search-and-destroy. It was also a nerve-wracking job fraught with the constant potential for sudden death. You never knew if the next boat you boarded would result in the tripping of a booby trap or a mid-river shoot-out. You never knew whether an ambush waited around the next bend in the river, or who was hiding with an RPG or AK pointed at you from the thick jungle which often rose like a lush green wall from the water's edge.

It wasn't the intensity of actual battle that was the worst part; it was the God-awful waiting to make contact. At least in a firefight, there was a sense of relief at firing at the enemy, even if you couldn't see him. But the waiting was like being strapped into a straitjacket of fear — not knowing where, when, or how it would take place was a constant war of nerves. Even though you were so scared at times you felt like wetting your pants, you tried, at first, to look cool so everybody would think you had a lot of guts. But after a season, the sobriety of combat leveled everyone into the conscious recognition that we were all just as scared as the next guy. The only ones who weren't were dead or crazy.

In that pressure cooker suspense, you learned to depend on each other on that floating island. You learned to cover each other's blind side, especially in the heat of a firefight. Each crewman not only knew his own job, but also another's area of responsibility in case he got hit. For example, in a firefight, my primary job was to man the combination 50 cal. and 81mm mortar, while the engine man made sure that I was fed a constant belt of ammo or a mortar round with the correct amount of bag charges. In the event I got wounded but could still function, we would switch positions or I would trade off with someone else on board to take up the slack. Because of the constant risk of death, we were all forced to be versatile. After a while, we all got so proficient that our duties became second nature.

But in spite of the ever-present threat of enemy contact, most of our duty was a mind-numbing monotony of well-worn procedures. The countless boardings and hours upon endless hours of searching, sifting, and identification checks were physically and psychologically exhausting. The never-ending undercurrent of nervous tension, waiting for the deadly inevitable, also took its toll. With nothing to break the boredom for days on end, you got to a trigger-happy place, oddly enough, where you half hoped that the shooting will start. The hardest thing to maintain, as we floated on the waterways, was our alertness. The heat, humidity, and repetitious grind tended to dull the cutting edge. But you couldn't afford to loosen up. To do so might mean sudden death for yourself and the others who were depending on you.

Occasionally, the boredom was interrupted. On one patrol along a canal in the Mekong Delta, we intercepted a suspicious boat and ordered it to stop. When we pulled alongside, the rest of the crew trained their guns on the boat with nervous anticipation, waiting for suspicious movement. I, in turn, went aboard to check out I.D. cards. While searching under bags of rice, baskets, and bundles of clothing, I uncovered some false deck plates concealing a container filled with medical supplies and gold leaf.

When I saw the treasure, my first thoughts were to waste all the Vietnamese on board and split the gold with the rest of the crew. I found myself conveniently justifying the murder by writing those gooks off as V.C. sympathizers who were supplying the enemy with much needed medical goods. But my momentary dreams of instant riches quickly evaporated in the river heat when I realized that we would never be able to sneak so much gold through customs back in the States. It also dawned on me that the passengers probably had vital intelligence information. After some preliminary questioning, we turned the people over to the proper authorities. We later found out that the detainees had confessed during extensive interrogation that the medicine was indeed intended for Charlie. They also provided valuable information about V.C. troop movements, strength, and objectives in that area. The news of that intelligence bonanza helped sooth the pain of also learning that the gold we had discovered was valued at $480,000!

Most boardings were not as exciting; the majority were uneventful, but occasionally, our slow motion drudgery was suddenly shifted to high speed suspense. One such situation involved those boats which tried to evade us. When we spotted boats trying to escape our dragnet, it was open season. We would fire a few warning shots over their bow and shout through a huge loud speaker, "Lai-dai!" If they didn't give up after the second round of warning shots and surrender shouts of "Lai-dai!", we would simply blow the boat out of the water any way we could.

Besides the all-pervasive boredom, there was the underlying awareness that your job had little redeeming value. You could always console yourself with the fact that you were intercepting the enemy or stemming the flow of contraband which gave aid and comfort to the enemy. However, we were not endearing ourselves to the hearts of the people. You could always see the hate and fear in their eyes when we trained our guns on them and ransacked their possessions. To most of the Vietnamese water people, we were unwelcome intruders disturbing their way of life. The Vietnamese peasants couldn't care less if we were liberating them from the Communists.

About two months after arriving in the country, we were patrolling a few miles south of Da Nang. It was August, and we were all miserably hot, drenched with sweat, and anxious for something to happen to relieve the boredom. Suddenly, shots cracked by followed by the shout, "Sniper!" We couldn't tell where the fire was coming from, but some gook was taking potshots at us. The gunner's mate in the forward gun tub opened with the "boom-boom-boom-boom!" of his twin 50's, spraying the river bank on our starboard side. The rounds were chopping up the bush and blowing geysers of sand and water all along the river's edge. I, in turn, was feeding bursts of automatic fire into the beach along our port side. After five minutes, we rested the guns. The sniper had also stopped. Whether we tagged him or simply wasted a couple thousand dollars worth of Uncle Sam's ammo will never be known.

No sooner had the action ceased when we picked up a frantic distress call from an army and ARVN unit which had walked into an ambush. As our radio operator got their coordinates, we moved upstream in the direction of fire. As we drew near, the river bank opened up on us. Bullets were ticking into the boat and hitting the water all around us; some were whizzing by overhead. We, in turn, responded with everything we had: twin 50's amidship, two guys with M-16's, and myself slugging away with the aft 50.

Through the near deafening sound of automatic fire, I heard the helmsman screaming that the ground unit wanted us to drop in 81mm mortar rounds near their position. As he hollered out the coordinates, I started dropping rounds down the tube, followed by the distinctive "thoomp!" Trying to adjust the levels and fix the coordinates with an overdose of adrenaline pumping through your system and incoming fire crisscrossing the deck was almost impossible. But after the return fire stopped, we had blown away 30-40 V.C. and recovered some weapons and important documents. Fortunately, we had taken no casualties.

As the adrenaline rush ran its course, we began to settle down. Nothing is as intense as a firefight. When it was over, I remember congratulating myself on how lucky we were. That was a long time ago. Today, I know beyond a shadow of a doubt that Christ had placed His protective hand around us and, as stupid as it may seem, I wouldn't be surprised if His guardian angels had been on the deck shielding us.

May 25, 1969, is a day I will never forget. We had begun a patrol up the Hoi An River and its tributaries. We spent the morning moving gradually upstream searcniug the usual sampans, fishing boats, and junks for contraband.

Our skipper had prearranged a rendezvous with another swift boat in the area to discuss some maneuvers and plans of operation. The meeting was to take place at a village along the river. As our boat officers were discussing the details of the day's operation, two friends from our boat and I, along with a couple of "swifties" from the other boat, slipped into the local village to find a gin mill to drink some Tiger beer and temporarily unwind.

During our conversation, one of the guys from the other boat mentioned in passing that a couple of days before they had been drinking beer in the same place with the crew of another swift boat while their officers also compared notes. Later that day, their boat was ambushed and had taken heavy casualties. At the moment, we were all enjoying the respite from our river boredom too much to seriously consider the news, so we just shrugged it off as one of those things that just happens. But after we returned to our boat, the nagging thoughts of our conversation kept coming back to me.

At first, the day unfolded like so many others — the usual uneventful boardings, I.D. checks, and sifting through the boats' contents. It was the typical mixture of monotony mingled with a subtle blend of nervous anticipation. Late in the afternoon, our radio operator picked up a distress call from some grunts who had stumbled into an ambush upstream. They were calling for us to give them covering fire with our 81mm mortar. We pumped in a few rounds and helped take the heat off their position. As we moved upriver, I still couldn't shake the foreboding sense of trouble generated by the conversation earlier in the day.

Around dusk, we were again called upon to provide fire support for some ground units. It was near the same spot where the 101st Airborne had taken a bloody mauling trying to retake one of the strategic hilltops that was so important to security.

Around 9 p.m., our boat and another moved into an ambush position under the cover of darkness. We had received intelligence information that enemy troop movement was expected in the vicinity. I remember that it was pitch black and so ominously quiet that you could have heard a pin drop. Waiting there in the darkness tended to heighten the nervous anxiety. The routine activity of the day seemed to numb the suspense, though it still lurked beneath the surface. However, the darkness of the night intensified my secret fears and stood as a harbinger of things to come.

The river where we set up our ambush was about 50 - 60 feet wide, a little too narrow for my liking. Suddenly, the locomotive sound of projectiles passing overhead disturbed the quiet. Our ships out in the South China Sea were firing their big guns in support of ground forces in the area. The distant thunder of exploding shells rolled across the landscape like a freight train passing in the night. The barrage lasted only a few moments, then the silence returned. I remember thinking, "With those big guns doing their thing, Charlie is sure to stay put."

We all welcomed the dead of night and hoped the day would end on a quiet note, but the radio crackled to life once again with an urgent call for support from an outpost which was taking heavy fire. They were on the verge of being overrun by V.C. sappers and desperately needed help. We immediately scrubbed our plans for the night ambush, started the engines, and headed about a mile downriver. I had a terrible feeling in the pit of my stomach, as we moved into firing position, that something bad was about to happen. What made it even worse was the fact that I only had fifteen days left in my tour.

I remember that moment as if a picture has been frozen in my mind forever. The gunner's mate was manning the twin 50's; I was standing ready at the aft 50 mounted on the 81mm mortar tube. Then, the curtain of the night was suddenly torn open with a blinding flash, a loud explosion, and my body was hurled into the air like a rag doll. It felt like a gang of people was beating and kicking me in one vicious stroke.

Instantly, my entire life passed before my eyes. I saw vivid images of my childhood, the confused impressions of adolescence, and the memories of adulthood. I had heard of others claiming to have experienced such a phenomenon in near-death encounters, but I had brushed those testimonies aside as something they had overly dramatized. But it was true; visual images of my entire life rushed by in an instant replay.

My overwhelming impulse was to get to my feet and reach my machine gun, but I couldn't move. There was excruciating pain in my legs. They were still attached, but they had been shredded by shrapnel. They just hung there in limp suspension. My hands, arms, and face felt like they were on fire. My eardrums were blown out by the concussion of the B-40 rocket which had landed four feet from where I was standing. I was badly shaken, but not in shock.

I pulled myself forward to the side of the boat with my arms, leaving a trail of blood smeared on the deck. "I think I'm hit!" I yelled to the skipper. "Oh, my God!" he gasped, looking at me as if I was some grotesque creature. In the dazed aftermath of the explosion I didn't really know how badly I had been hit, but the shock in his voice drove me to the edge of panic. "Can you make it, Phil?" he asked. I wanted to shout back, but I couldn't; I was too weak. My left arm was hanging in shreds. My hand looked like ground hamburger. I felt utterly helpless laying there with my life draining out of my body. The crossfire of automatic weapons punctuated the night. Bullets whizzed by my head, ripping into the boat all around me, and all I could do was lay there and hope I didn't get hit again. Finally, after agonizing minutes, the shooting stopped.

One of the navy ships out in the South China Sea had been monitoring our radio frequency and called to offer assistance. A Marine ground unit in the vicinity also radioed in not to shoot for fear that the ship's guns would be off-target. The captain of the ship asked the Marines to link up with our boat and give us assistance.

As I lay there in the darkness, soaking in my own blood and lingering on the threshold of a far greater darkness, I was terrified. I found myself praying harder than I had ever prayed before. I cried, "Lord, please don't let me die! I don't want to die! I'm too young! I promise if you let me live through this, I'll always to go church and Sunday School. I promise I will never miss a Sunday!" God, how I wanted to live at that moment. I had so much to live for.

Our officer had put in a call for a med-evac, but we were told that a chopper didn't want to risk coming in because the area was too hot and crawling with Charlie. None of the choppers wanted to come in without a gunship to cover them.

While I waited to be evacuated, some South Vietnamese friendlies and the guys on board tried to put me on a stretcher to carry me off the boat. In the process, they stumbled and accidentally dropped me overboard into the bacteria-infested water. It wasn't much different than being dunked in an open sewer. My wounds were immediately soaked in the filth. My body felt like I'd been branded by hundreds of red-hot pokers.

A couple of guys jumped into the water and managed to drag me out of the river. When they got me to shore, they tried to pull off my flak jacket. The pain was so unbearable that I was screaming at them to just cut the side straps of the jacket and put it under my head. Wounds covered the length of my body. My fatigues were ripped to pieces and my body was pockmarked with bloody gouges. The shrapnel from the blast had blown chunks of flesh off my arms and legs. Only my chest and back had been protected by my flak jacket. We all hated to wear those cumbersome jackets in the heat and humidity, but I'm so glad that I did that night.

The crew did the best they could to patch me up with compresses to stop the bleeding. They tried to give me a shot of morphine, but the needle kept bending as they attempted to inject it into my thigh. I asked for a cigarette, one of the worst things you could do when you're as badly wounded as I was. I must have smoked an entire pack waiting for the med-evac chopper to arrive.

Under normal circumstances, it should only have taken fifteen minutes to get a chopper in and out, but over an hour passed before the Huey finally floated in. When they lifted me into the chopper, I felt like the darkness was closing in around me. I was afraid to close my eyes for fear that they would never open again. I remember telling the medic I was freezing — freezing wet from my plunge in the river and the fact that my fatigues were drenched with blood from head to toe. His blunt prescription was simply, "Do you want to freeze or die?" The answer didn't take long to register: "I'll freeze!" Still, the trauma was taking its toll. I was drifting close to death, but fought to stay awake. I wanted desperately to close my eyes and sleep, but I feared the darkness. As we flew back to Da Nang, I kept praying that God would not let me die.

When our dust-off touched down at the 95th Evac Hospital, about eight medics and nurses ran towards the chopper. I was still conscious, but the events around me raced by in a confused blur of impressions: the prop blast, the sound of the rotor blades, the sweet smell of kerosene from the engine exhaust, the bright lights, the prick of the I.V. needles, the gurney team carrying me into the hospital, the rapid fire barrage of medical instructions, and the pain. As they rushed me into the makeshift hospital, they were cutting off my clothes and boots.

By all the frantic action around me, I could tell I was in a pretty serious condition. All the time, I kept thinking, "Please God, I don't want to die! I'm too young!" When they got me inside, I saw the rows of cots with wounded men who had recently arrived from some firefight. Some were screaming, some were groaning, others were crying. Looking at our wounded lying there with their bodies torn open overwhelmed me with fear. I tried to maintain calm but found myself asking the nurses and doctors, "Will I live?! Will I live?!"

After they stabilized my condition, I was wheeled into another room for X-rays to determine the extent of my injuries. I later learned that the bones in my left arm and hand were shattered by slivers of shrapnel. The skin was blown off by the force of the blast, along with large chunks of flesh. The length of my bloodied body looked like raw meat.

When the doctors finished examining my X-rays, I was taken into surgery to clean out my wounds and sew me back together. I know the medical team was fighting a desperate battle to save my life. As they were preparing me, I can still remember thinking, "I don't want to go under anesthetic because I might not wake up." I was fighting hard to the end to keep awake. As I was going under, I was still praying under my breath that I would live.

The next day, I came to with an I.V. stuck in my right ankle. It was the only place left on my entire body where they could freely insert it. A group of doctors stopped by on their rounds and asked me how I was feeling. "Just great!" I replied. My body looked as if it had been forced through a meat grinder, but I was just glad to be alive. They told me that it was a miracle that I was. As they left, I couldn't help feeling that the Man upstairs had heard my prayers after all!

In a few days, I was loaded onto a C141 Starlifter for a med-evac flight to a hospital in Guam. I spent two weeks gaining back some strength, then I was flown to Japan, to Alaska, and then to Scott Air Force Base back in Illinois from where I was finally transferred to Great Lakes Naval Hospital outside of Chicago. It was June of 1969.

They sent me to Ward 3 South, the contamination ward. Everyone in that ward had some serious staph infections — some due to arms and legs being blown off, others because of napalm or phosphorus burns over large portions of their bodies, and still others who were terribly maimed by booby traps.

There were about fifty patients on the ward. It was the only specialized ward set up in the hospital to treat such serious infections. Just after being wheeled on a gurney to the main desk of the ward, I asked when I would be able to go home. My question ignited a hearty round of laughter from the nurses and corpsmen standing around. The head nurse just looked at me and said, "You're going to be here for quite a while." I missed the humor in my question, but a profound sense of thankfulness came over me that God had spared my life.

During several weeks in the hospital, confined to a bed, with my entire body wrapped with layers of dressings, my arm held upright at my side with an I.V. tube feeding me, I had a lot of spare time to think — a lot of time to try and put things into perspective. It was true that my life had nearly been cut short. It was true that I was laying there in a mangled condition. But it was also true that I was alive, and I had an unshakable awareness that God, in His great mercy, had let me live.

That confidence gave me strength to trust in Him to heal me. It was that hope which sustained me and prevented me from succumbing to the deadly cycle of self-pity. As I lay there, I remembered my mother, who was a Sunday School teacher in the Lutheran Church, telling me as a child, "Remember to pray, because Jesus will heal you." The childhood memories of my mother's simple encouragements to pray gave me renewed hope. It's a proven fact that most people die from their injuries, not so much from the trauma itself, but because they simply lose the will to live.

One afternoon, I saw a corpsman wheel a patient down the aisle and put him into a bed across from me. As he was going by I said, "What's happening, man? How ya doin'?" He just rolled by without saying a word. I thought he must not have heard me. I could tell he'd been hit pretty bad because his right leg was missing just above the knee. Later that day, I heard him putting down everything anyone said or tried to do to help him. I could tell the guy was filled with bitterness and anger. I figured he was really feeling sorry for himself. I understood how easy it was to feel that way. Just one look around the ward and you could see dozens of excuses for self-pity. I'd felt the same way after I got hit, so I just let it slide. But this guy had a rotten attitude and just kept on griping about everything. After a while, his negativism got on my nerves, along with the other guys on the ward. We were all in a lot of pain, and we didn't need some jerk constantly reminding us about how miserable we were. It was like someone putting salt in our wounds, and none of us liked it. I found out that the complainer was a Navy Seal by the name of Micky Block. Back in 'Nam, he had picked up the nickname "Pervert #1." At the time I didn't know why, but if his attitude was a contributing factor, it was a fitting title.

His folks came to visit him one day. After they arrived, we could overhear a lot of cussing, arguing, and complaining. I could tell his mother was crying. It was a very ugly scene. The parents seemed like nice people, and none of us appreciated him taking out his frustrations on them. It was bad enough for them seeing their son laying there with no leg, let alone emotionally crippled. A Marine sergeant who'd also lost a leg and I tried to act as peacemakers. We came over to Micky's bed to give him some words of encouragement. We wanted to comfort his parents who seemed pretty upset. But Micky retaliated with a verbal thrashing. All we could do was return to our bunks and try to ignore the guy.

When his parents were leaving, his father stopped by my bunk. At first, I thought he was going to chew me out for butting into something that was none of my business, but instead he thanked me and Sarge for saying what he couldn't bring himself to say.

After months of painful recovery, I was medically discharged on July 20, 1970. I decided to stay in the Chicago area because the employment opportunities and pay looked better than in my hometown of Fremont, Ohio. I looked for work as a truck driver, but nobody was hiring because the trucker's union was on strike.

After a few fruitless weeks of having doors shut in my face, I went home to Fremont to apply as a policeman. Even though I had been rejected elsewhere because of my injuries, I thought I would have a better chance with my hometown police department. The fact that my dad had been on the force for nineteen years wouldn't hurt my chances either. However, when I applied to take the Civil Service exam, all they said was, "Sorry, you don't qualify." That blew my mind. I'd just come back from Vietnam, nearly gotten my life blown away permanently, still had the scars from serving my country, and that yokel was telling me that I didn't qualify? It was bad enough that the Vietnam vets were being taunted as baby butchers and labeled as morons for going to Vietnam in the first place but, my God, this was my hometown and my dad was a dedicated cop. I knew I could do the job. After all, back in 'Nam I was responsible for million dollar equipment, knew how to react in life-and-death situations, and could take orders. Surely, they'd make an exception. But all I got was a flat, "You don't qualify!"

I guess it triggered the pent-up frustration and unresolved rage simmering inside of me because I blew up and started cussing out the clerk and saying a lot of things that I later regretted. After that, I started feeling sorry for myself in a big way.

When no doors opened in Fremont, I drifted back to Chicago and started hitting the bottle day and night. My family and the girl I was going to marry were pretty upset, but I really didn't care. I was so disillusioned, I'd just about given up. I was trying to drown the past year and a half in alcohol, but it didn't do any good. As drunk as I got, I still couldn't completely soothe the inner pain. I was out of control and spent a reckless year on an endless merry-go-round of drinking and running around. Things didn't get better — they just got worse. I had an uncontrollable temper with a very short fuse. I'd snap somebody's head off for the slightest reason. My nerves were shot, and I didn't care about anything or anyone — not even myself.

After my sustained binge, my life started to settle down. In 1972, I married a beautiful Christian woman by the name of Toni in Fremont, Ohio. She had three little children from a previous marriage. I really loved her and those kids. Our union seemed to bring a fresh sense of meaning back into my life which I so desperately needed. However, after a few months, the deep inferiority complex which I'd picked up from 'Nam and the rejection that followed began to take its toll. I felt like I was failing miserably as a father, a husband — even as a human being. I couldn't control my nerves, my emotions, or my temper. Though I didn't understand what was happening to me at the time, I was suffering from post-Vietnam trauma and had all the symptoms. I couldn't explain what was happening — I didn't even understand it myself. Only now do I realize how messed up my head really was. My wife didn't understand the inner conflict which was tearing my life to pieces either, but she didn't give up — she just kept praying that God would touch me.

After a massive blow-out with my family, I finally reached a place where I recognized that my life was falling apart. Finally, on November 12, 1972, my wife's perserverance, no doubt coupled with my prayers back in 'Nam, brought results. The night I was hit, I'd pleaded with God to let me live. I meant physically, but God took it one step further. I fell on my knees in my bedroom, bawled like a baby, and asked Jesus to come into my life.

I was on a spiritual high for a few months, but the euphoria began to wear off. I was trying to run on the energy of my initial conversion, but there was no commitment on my part, no follow-through. I didn't attend church, read the Bible, pray, or try to cultivate my new-found relationship with Christ with any consistency. I was still drifting. I guess the seed had been planted, but not in the best of ground. I still needed more cultivation before the seed would bear fruit. So, for ten up and down years, I lived a life of religious hypocrisy: on again, off again.

In 1982, I attended a week of schooling for my job. I returned home on a Friday night and met my wife at church for an evangelistic crusade she wanted me to attend. I agreed to meet her there if I got back in town in time. When I arrived at the service, my wife wasn't sitting in the usual place — she was up in the front row. The message that night seemed like it was directed right at me.

Even though I had been born-again, a lot of painful memories about Vietnam kept surfacing. I was having a difficult time coping with guilt. I knew about the scriptural assurances that once we accepted Christ into our hearts, our past sins are forgiven and forgotten by Him. I knew this in my head, but appropriating that truth in the gut level of my life was another matter. However, that night as I sat riveted to the words of that particular sermon, the truth of God's mercy and forgiveness finally hit home. Because I had not fully accepted God's love, or even understood how He could have compassion for a guy like me, my Christian walk had been stunted and stifled. Until that evening, I had drifted along as a lukewarm Christian, but the revelation of the depth of God's forgiveness radically changed the course of my life from that night forward.

In June 1984, my family and I attended a special series of meetings at our church. During one of the services, the preacher confessed that he had a special burden for Vietnam veterans and that the Lord had given him a vision about an outreach ministry to them. I remember how profoundly moved I was by that statement. It seemed like something clicked inside of me — like all the gears were lining up just right. I could really relate to that kind of a vision, probably because I was so acutely aware of the deep-seated problems which so affected the Vietnam vets. I knew how much I had hurt, and everything in me was saying, "Yes, that's it — that's it!"

The following evening, an evangelist by the name of Dave Roever, a former Navy Seal who had been horribly scarred when a bullet blew up a phosphorus grenade in his hand burning over 90% of his body, was scheduled to minister at our church. I was asked to go along with our youth pastor to pick him up at the airport. After we picked him up, we all decided to get some dinner at a restaurant. As we were riding there, Dave began to share his experiences as a born-again Christian in Vietnam. In the course of our conversation, he was joking about a guy who was part of his Seal team back in 'Nam who they called "Pervert #1" — alias Micky Block, who was now a part of his ministry team. Since I had been released from the naval hospital in 1970, I had completely forgotten about that guy, but the mention of his name hit me like a ton of bricks. I had a momentary flashback to the same bitter young man I had confronted fourteen years ago, the same guy I tried to reach out to with understanding, the same guy who told me to get lost!

In a stunned sort of way I blurted out, "I know that guy!" Then I proceeded to recount my encounter with him when we were both on Ward 3 South. I was blown out by the knowledge that the bitter young man of my memory was now a strong Christian working in an outreach ministry to Vietnam vets.

As the special meetings progressed and Dave Roever shared how God had miraculously put his life back together for His service, the burden for reaching out to vets began to consume me. I didn't know if I was too emotionally wrapped up in my own Vietnam pathos to see objectively, or if it was really something God was impressing upon my heart. I didn't want to get involved unless it was really God's will. As I sat there in the pew with a torrent of emotions surging through me and my heart pounding in expectation, I closed my eyes and prayed, "God, I need to know. Is it just me, or is it You who wants to use me in this ministry? If it's just me, I don't want to do it. Please God, somehow, some way, You have to let me know!"

No sooner had I lifted my head from praying that my wife tapped me on the shoulder saying, "Phil, he wants to pray with you." The first time she said it, I was still so caught up in the questions warring inside of me that I didn't hear her. But she nudged me harder: "He wants to pray with you!" "Pray with me?" I thought. "What does he want to pray with me for?" My wife and I were

called forward, and the preacher read a passage from Pro-
verbs which he felt impressed to share with me:

> *Trust in the Lord with all your heart, and*
> *lean not on your own understanding; In all*
> *your ways acknowledge Him, and He shall*
> *direct your paths. Do not be wise in your own*
> *eyes; fear the Lord and depart from evil.*

Those words were like getting a direct telegram from God.
It was an instant answer to my prayer. I was overwhelmed
with joy, but I was really amazed that God actually
wanted to use an ordinary guy like myself to touch the
lives of others who were shattered and broken.

A few months later, I was standing in the airport in
New Orleans. I had come to see the new Micky, to learn
how to reach out to other veterans with the power of
Christ. I was standing by the baggage carousel waiting
for my luggage to come up the chute when I heard a voice
behind me say, "Excuse me, can I help you?" I thought
it was one of the airport porters so I just half-turned
around and said, "No, thank you." However, the voice
had a familiar ring. I turned around and did a double
take. It was Micky Block standing there smiling at me.
Instantly the warmth of that unspoken brotherhood, that
quiet comradery that Christians and many vets alike seem
to commonly share filled the air. We were like two long-
lost friends just standing there amidst the hustle and bustle
of a busy airport, looking at each other with a sense of
understanding that you can't really put into words. After
fifteen years, our paths had miraculously crossed again.
We'd each taken a different fork in the road, but God
had led each of us to the same glorious destination —
full circle to the same mission: just two former soldiers

who reenlisted in the Army of God.

Phil Huss is happily married with three children. He is an insurance salesman for Prudential Life Insurance Company in the Chicago area. Phil is also the founder of Vetwork, a successful outreach ministry to Vietnam veterans and their families in Palos Heights, Illinois.

Bill H. Baldwin
E-4, U.S. Army
Field Artillery Crewman
27th Field Artillery
Feb. '69 - Feb. '70
E-4, U.S. Army
Combat Radioman
1st Battalion 11th Inf.
5th Inf. Division
Aug. '70 - Aug. '71

5

Dinki-Dau

After three miserable months of hacking our way through the thick jungle highlands bordering the DMZ and Laotian border, we were physically and mentally shot. Living like animals out in the bush, enveloped in dense jungle greens, not knowing what month much less what day it was was like living in another world without time and space. After sweaty weeks without showers, clean fatigues, or hot chow, we were finally pulled back to LZ Mary to stand down. Operation Dewey Canyon II was finally over. During those long months of slogging through dripping jungles, we lived at death's edge, harassing Charlie, setting up ambushes, and interdicting his infiltration routes penetrating the Vietnamese side of the border. While we provided a blocking force, ARVN units crossed the border into Laos to stem the never-ending flow of men and materials heading south along the Ho Chi Minh Trail. It was the last major U.S. offensive before Nixon's de-escalation kicked into high gear. After two years in 'Nam, my bush duty was coming to a melancholy end.

I emerged from my bunker on our first night back, lit up a cigarette, and scanned the familiar nightscape illuminated with the hissing glow of parachute flares and chopper lights, probing, red rivers from mini-guns and the distant orange flashes from artillery explosions. I had gazed into that same Vietnamese night countless times during those two years, pondering the course of events that had brought me to this place. Sitting there, cupping the cigarette in my hand, I considered my life again. I mused to myself about the desperate prayer that had opened my door to Vietnam in the first place. I saw it as a miracle, even though most rational people would have labeled me "dinki-dau" (crazy) for pleading with God to send me to 'Nam, when so many back in the world were doing everything in their power to stay out. Some were manipulating college deferments, fleeing to Canada, going A.W.O.L., or faking 4-F classifications — anything to prevent them from seeing a Vietnam night.

Sitting on that sandbag bunker, my mind drifted back through the last three years of my life in the Army. My first tour in 'Nam in '69 was served with the crew of an eight-inch, self-propelled gun. I remember the incoming scream of rockets and the terrifying "crump!" of V.C. mortars walking across our fire base at night. I remember the V.C. probes in the pre-dawn darkness, night tracers, and young sappers tangled in the snarled strands of perimeter wire. I remember the belching guns and the 24-hour concussions of outgoing artillery. I remember the frantic calls for "fire support," the race to ready guns, the ramming home of rounds, the peal of distant thunder, the call to "cease firing," and the rotten egg stench of burnt powder after a fire mission.

I, too, had memories of returning home to Indiantown Gap, Pennsylvania after my first tour was up, where I was assigned to train R.O.T.C. cannon fodder for their turn in 'Nam, giving infantry firepower demonstrations and being called the best M-79 grenadier that side of the Cumberlands. But I was not at home back in the world. The war's unpopularity had stigmatized returning vets. We were social lepers in the eyes of an unsympathetic society which viewed us as moral misfits who had participated in something unethical and infamous.

The spit and polish, by-the-book regulations of stateside duty were unbearably oppressive to soldiers who had known the depth of intimate, honest relationships with other men — relationships that were forged out of the rarefied atmosphere of fire, heat, and war. Duty in the States offered little social satisfaction to soldiers due to the unpopularity of the war. They were hard times for men and women in uniform. The social register from which all young soldiers had been extracted had hopelessly alienated them from anything tainted with military service. Our civilian contemporaries, sometimes even our best friends in the world, viewed us as a symbol of a war which was despised by the majority of mainstream America. So, whether knowing it or not, those civilians were compelled by the turbulent pressures of the times to put distance between themselves and us. To extend warmth and comfort was the same as giving support to what was seen as an unjust cause. Consequently, the G.I. was often an outcast in his own country.

But, in a time when love, peace, and the universal brotherhood of men were being extolled, we found ourselves a painful part of an unwanted minority, segregated from love and acceptance. We found ourselves caught in the midst of an impossible dilemma which was tearing apart our very hearts and souls. For the soldier to exist, he was forced to play two roles. You had to play by the petty rules of the military if you wanted a discharge with a clean record. On weekends you had to play the chameleon and sanitize your army image if you wanted to preserve your social sanity outside the gates. There was something half comical, half pathetic about seeing teenage soldiers slicking down their hair during the week so they could let it down on pass or donning peace sign paraphernalia to fit in. But playing two roles meant living both for and against yourself. You were forced to suppress your convictions and deny your integrity.

I found it impossible to dance to the tune of this musical schizophrenia. Society and I mixed like oil and water. I couldn't play the shallow games any longer. I just didn't fit. The only slice of society that eagerly embraced us was the scuzzy side that just wanted to take our money.

In short order, the warmth and sense of belonging which I had known in 'Nam began to beckon me back. I was drawn by an irresistible need to recapture the love I had known in war — to rejoin my brothers in arms, to return to the one place I was truly accepted and needed. I tried to find that sense of belonging during my first time back in the States, but trying to lay hold of such relationships seemed as elusive to me as grasping the wind, so I returned to 'Nam — this time as a combat infantryman.

Many sights, sounds, and impressions of my second tour have become as intimate a part of me as the rhythm of my own heartbeat. Many are precious — others unbearably painful. That night on the bunker, I pondered the vivid reminders. I still heard the agonizing screams for God from a friend whose body had been strewn for yards by a land mine, and the whimpering cry of a scared soldier calling for "momma" in the blackness of the night. I still heard the rasping, chainsaw sound of aerial Gatling guns and the earth-splitting "whoom!" of 122mm rockets ploughing into the red clay a few yards away. I heard the terrified voice of a soldier a few klicks away crying over the radio transmitter because his armor platoon was being systematically wiped out by RPG's. I'll never forget his chilling frustration because the enemy was yelling out the names of the tank crews and their tank numbers before they sent each fatal round ripping through flesh and steel. I remember the tomb-quiet nights, pulling guard in my foxhole, drenched with sweat, waiting for Charlie to emerge from the darkness. I still smelled the gut-retching odor of decomposing flesh, and the invisible sense of danger which hung in the air. I remember the sickening sensations that settled over me as I monitored the grave radio transmissions from our mortar platoon getting slaughtered at an isolated fire base, and I remember the sheer exhilaration of payback when we quietly called in a massive air strike on top of the V.C. rocket battery when we spotted it from our jungle covering.

I thought about the three lonely weeks on a fog-shrouded hill we called "starvation mountain," cut off from food and water because the choppers couldn't fly with zero visibility. We spent those gray days hunkered down on that mountain crest under layers of thick fog, straddling a major V.C. supply route. Each day we sat behind our machine gun, waiting for unsuspecting Viet Cong, NVA, and even Chinese medics to break through the mist so we could cut them down. Our only food was the rice balls we had taken from the enemy dead and the bark from the surrounding Beetlenut trees. Our only water came from the ponchos we had stretched out between trees as lean-tos to catch the thick evening dew which trickled into our canteen cups.

I remember being inserted by choppers into the jungle blackness at night where it was so dark you couldn't see your hand in front of your face. I remember the sweat and 125 degree heat that cooked your brain by day in the lowlands, and shivering from the 45 degree chill in the mountains at night. I remember the constant fatigue of humping for hours through a suffocating greenhouse, carrying 100 pound rucksacks which dug into your shoulders, and burning peanut butter rations to keep warm at night. I remember the torrential downpours which soaked you for weeks on end and the endless hues of green. I remember drinking mud and burning black leeches off of my body with the glowing head of a cigarette. I remember pressing my ear to the ground and hearing the ominous rumble of mechanized armor reverberating through the earth as Russian reconnaissance tanks overran a Vietnamese outpost along the DMZ, and the napalm and artillery strikes which lit up the sky with such savagery that it seemed as if the whole war had been compressed into one, violent convulsion. And I remember the strange sense of safety I felt that night, sheltered in the green womb of the jungle miles away.

But most of all, I remember looking into the face of my best friend as we were drinking rations of coffee in a foxhole one night and telling him that I loved him, only to lose him the next day to a sniper's bullet. He was the first man I ever said that to. His loss was emotionally devastating. We had joked and laughed together. We had reminisced about home and talked about our observations of life — from what happened after death, to how butter melted together with syrup on hot pancakes. We had soothed each other's fears in the night and found a safe harbor in each other's companionship. It was a relationship of self-sacrificing love and loyalty which embodied the highest virtues in humanity. And it was a kinship which many a man found over there.

That night before his death, we had put our arms around each other and made a sacred pact of brotherly love. He had asked me to be the radioman on his patrol the next day so we could be together, but I had to decline because I had just come in from a patrol with the CP. The next morning, he died a few meters away from me in his radio operator's arms. Not being able to be there at his wounded side, in his final moments just beyond the ridge, only a sound of a gunshot away, was a pain which tormented me for years. In fact, when I returned home, the trauma of his death, coupled with the silent suppression of a despised war, actually erased the memory of his name from my mind — still forgotten to this day.

My friends offered me comfort, but the reality of the loss of my buddy had not yet taken its toll. The chopper took out his body without my being able to see him one last time. A month later, we were allowed to come into Khe Sanh for a few hours to resupply. It was there at that battered fire base that I honored his death. I gathered his helmet, boots, and rifle the battalion had kept for me and performed the melancholy, military ritual for the fallen dead: I turned his rifle upside down, with its bayonet piercing a sandbag, with his empty steel pot resting on top of his combat boots next to the sandbag. Some of the guys took their M-16's and fired a twenty-one gun salute in tribute to his passing. As I stood there with gusts of red dust kicking through the ranks, I spoke a eulogy over my best friend's possessions. With tears coursing through the grime on my cheeks, I uttered those painful, last words with heartfelt remorse that he hadn't at least died in my arms — that the love for him in my eyes was not the last thing he saw before he slipped into eternity. It had taken him fifteen agonizing minutes to die that day, and those fifteen minutes were an eternity in both of our hearts.

Such was the joy of friendships and the heartbreak of countless Vietnam veterans, and all veterans of war, who touched and loved a brother and then, in a moment, never saw him again. It was a loss that I felt could never be replaced.

The night sky was still alive with lights as I crushed out the last glow of my cigarette on the sandbag. In spite of it all, I was thankful that I'd come to 'Nam. There was a sense of belonging I had found here that I had never known before. In some strange way, I guess I knew from the very beginning that I was needed in Vietnam, even before I left the States. No matter what the war protesters or politicians thought, I knew that I wanted to fight for my country.

I shook my head and laughed at myself as I considered the chain of events that had brought me full circle. I was amused by the fact that the Army had once labelled me as a "vegetable" and wanted to keep me stateside, harassed and hidden beneath petty duties until my service was over. Shortly after basic training, I developed an epileptic condition which threatened to keep me out of 'Nam forever. But, in spite of my illness, I knew I belonged overseas. At first, my medical condition broke my heart and seemed to slam every door in my face that would lead me to Vietnam, but that was three years ago.

I couldn't bear the drudgery of desk duty, bound behind a typewriter, for the duration of my enlistment.

Besides, I was a miserable excuse for a clerk. My failure, coupled with my frustrated desire to serve in 'Nam, subjected me to a continual barrage of mockery and mental cruelty. I became an object of ridicule and scorn which reached a point of such severity that my N.C.O. finally hauled me in front of a company of trainees and told them that I was an example of what a soldier was not supposed to be.

After months of depression and insufferable harassment because I wanted to fight and couldn't, I appealed to God for a miracle. I couldn't take the abuse any longer. Something had to give. At about 2:00 a.m. one night, I got up and walked over to the all-night chapel across from my barracks. The chapel was empty as I entered and knelt in the shadows of the sanctuary before a large silver cross at the head of the chapel. I had never prayed with such heartfelt fervency. My spirit was broken. I pleaded with God that if He didn't let me go to Vietnam, I didn't want to live, and I meant it.

After sobbing in the chapel darkness for a while, I felt a great sense of courage sweep over my soul. I knew God had heard my cry. I got off my knees with a renewed determination to pursue my goal. I ran back to my barracks and started hunting through a phone book for the address of my Company XO. After finding it, I wrote it down and decided to go A.W.O.L. to find his off-post apartment. I crawled under the wires and walked for miles in the dead of night before I found his address. I was exhausted but still determined. When I found his apartment, I drew a deep breath and knocked on his door. Stumbling to the door half asleep, the XO looked at me in shock and disbelief and said, "Baldwin, what the

HELL are you doing here — at this time of the night?''
I felt a sudden surge of do-or-die courage. I drew another
deep breath, looked him in the eye, and said, "Sir, if I
don't get to fight in Vietnam, I'm going to go crazy and
die!'' Suddenly, the countenance of his face changed from
infuriation to one of compassion and respect. He told
me to sneak back into camp and get some sleep. I wasn't
sure of what to expect the next day.

The following morning, I didn't wake up until 10:00.
I was surprised that no one woke me up. I walked into
the office where I had always received my daily orders
and daily harassment, but this time there were no words
— just a respectful silence. The XO approached me carrying my 201 Personnel File, and all the N.C.O.'s turned
their backs as if they didn't see anything. In an un-
characteristically soft voice, he told me that I could have
my file for one hour. Under normal circumstances, a
soldier is never to look into his personnel file but only
carry it to a new duty station. He knew what I was about
to do. I took my file behind the barracks and removed
all medical papers pertaining to my epilepsy and burned
them. I removed my physical profile paper and burned
it, too. Now, no one knew I was an epileptic except God
and the Pentagon. I then went to the reenlistment office
and handed them my file and reenlisted for immediate duty in Vietnam. Less than thirty days later, I
was landing in Disneyland East. During my entire two
years in country, I didn't experience a single seizure, and
my condition was never uncovered. Looking back, I can't
justify the ethics or methodology of my participation in
this answer to prayer, but God seemed to overrule my
actions to draw me to Himself in a roundabout sort of

way.

My final tour in 'Nam was over. I was returning home the second time, with my term of service complete, to find my place in the world I'd left behind. However, I soon learned that nothing much had changed in my absence. I also returned to national rejection. The world I had come home to was the same world that had shunned me as a soldier after my first tour in 'Nam. That time, I was able to flee to the secret fraternity of brothers on the battlefield of Vietnam. But now, I had to stay. I couldn't go back. We were forced to take our Vietnam experiences and burn them like a witch at the stake. So I did. My vanity compelled me to do whatever was expedient, to assume any identity that would guarantee my acceptance. So, I buried my past, grew my hair to my shoulders, my beard to my chest, and entered into the Hall of Mellow Freaks — a musician, a freak, with a "floating" identity.

Vietnam had accelerated my maturity in many realms of my life but still left me socially immature. I returned stateside as socially retarded as before. At best, all I could do was play the games and mimic what others were doing around me. Yet, I was camouflaging the real me and my real emotions. I found myself empty and longing to reclaim the relationships I had left in 'Nam.

But the longing I craved so deeply within my soul was God's doing. He had permitted me to touch something special in that brotherhood of men that I would never want to let go. He let me leave behind the comradery and companionship to return to the shallowness and superficiality of relationships built on games and pettiness for a reason. He did so because, in His all-knowing way, He knew that my all-consuming desire for the friendship and love which I had experienced in 'Nam would eventually lead me back to Him and that self-sacrificing communion between Christians which even transcends the depth of relationships which were dependent upon the circumstantial pressures of war to hold them together.

Bill Baldwin, his wife Becky, and their two sons live in Tulsa, Oklahoma. Bill has a degree in Horticulture and works for the city of Tulsa giving music workshops to the city's poor. He is also an evangelist and Christian musician with an independently produced album entitled "Crossover".

Clebe McClary
1st Lieutenant, U.S.M.C.
Reconnaissance
1st Reconnaissance Batt. 1st Marines
Aug. '67 - Mar. '68

6

The Last Patrol

I was a proud Marine lieutenant when I arrived in the Republic of Vietnam in the autumn of '67. Only a few short months before, I had been newly wed and newly commissioned as a 2nd lieutenant. It was difficult leaving behind a loving family and what I considered to be a marriage made in heaven to my adoring wife Dea to fight in an unpopular war half a world away, but I was eager for action.

The undeclared war — a controversial conflict which eventually cost the lives of 58,000 U.S. servicemen — was in high gear when our Braniff jet touched down on the tarmac at Da Nang. The military activity was picking up, particularly in the northernmost section of the country where I would be assigned.

I was directed to the First Marine Division's First Reconnaissance Battalion five miles from the Da Nang Base. In short order, we new arrivals were debriefed and assigned by the general in charge of Marine operations in I Corp. During the debriefing, he asked if any of us wanted to volunteer for "recon" duty. Recon (short for reconnaissance) was a known synonym for suicide. This unit, which I consider the Marine Corps' best, operated covertly behind enemy lines. It was made up of a small team of men playing a dangerously sophisticated game of hide and seek with the enemy. In spite of the memories of my wife's pleas to stay out of recon, I jumped at the chance. After a few warm-up patrols, I was given command of my first platoon.

We worked the territory within a 45-mile radius of base

area and became a thorn in the enemy's side. We had to go no further than the first hill to fight. Helicopters transported us to and from our assignments in the mountains and the jungles where we spent from four to twenty-six days conducting reconnaissance and surveillance operations to detect enemy troop movement or possible arms infiltration. Our purpose was to gather information on the enemy's location, situation, actions, and number of troops.

Some patrols were little more than a leisurely walk in the woods, but most of our forays were "close calls" with our team just a heartbeat from death, saved by the miracle of timing. I found that recon teams either completed their mission safely or were badly hurt. Seldom was there middle ground. Confrontations with the enemy occurred with dreadful results. We killed only when we had to and avoided contact as much as possible.

As patrol leader, I usually took a 12-man team into the bush. We became known as "Texas Pete and the Dirty Dozen." Behind enemy lines we were hunters, stalking a deadly prey. We chased him through impenetrable jungle, hacking our way through and across mile-high mountains, lugging 110-pound packs on our backs, sometimes pulling them behind us through vegetation so thick that we had to crawl. Using movement as a defensive tactic, we snooped and hid, making it hard for Charlie to find us. When we had to fight, we usually hit and ran. We neither picked fights nor dodged them. A firefight was sort of like a ballgame: whoever shot the most the fastest won, and whoever got off the first shot lived. A skirmish didn't bother me at the time, but I was a little shaken afterwards, thinking of what could have happened.

Sometimes we were assigned to areas where an upcoming operation was planned, perhaps a campaign to sweep a valley clean of Communists. In a normal war, our troops would have kept sweeping and chasing the enemy north, killing and capturing them along the way; but this war had so many regulations that we weren't permitted to be too aggressive. Therefore, our goals were different.

As the chameleon changes colors to blend with his surroundings, we painstakingly camouflaged ourselves to be absorbed by the jungle greens and browns. While we smeared our faces with camouflage makeup sticks, Pfc. Ralph Johnson — a good-natured black Marine from Charleston, South Carolina — grumbled, "Lieutenant, I'm black enough! Why have I gotta put that stuff on me?" It was necessary to dull the shine of the skin. We didn't wear rings that could sparkle in the sun, and even my Marine Corps watch had a black face and band. Anything that rattled had to be taped down. We found that helmets and flight jackets made too much noise in the jungle; a bandana with leaves stuck in it or a canvas camouflage hat served better. All supplies were painted brown, green, and black.

Charlie was also a master at camouflage. Waiting for us to come by, the V.C. sometimes buried themselves straight up for 48 hours, breathing fresh air through a straw; or they sat covered in a hole called a "spider trap" for weeks with only a handful of rice to eat each day.

Trails and roads were rarely used. Instead, we followed the animal paths or cut our way through the vines and sometimes traveled in rivers and streams. Movement was often slow; some days we traveled several miles and other days only a few hundred yards.

The order of march placed the point man first to scout for mines and booby traps. He usually carried both an M-79 and an M-14, effective at long range. We changed the point man about every two hours because if he became fatigued and careless, we could be killed. My position was second, the primary radio man behind me, followed by the "Doc" (Navy Corpsman), M-16 riflemen, auxiliary radio man, and, finally, "tail-end Charlie" who covered our trail by smoothing footprints and pulling vines and leaves over our path. If he suspected we were being followed, he set out booby traps and claymore mines.

Walking single file, we were careful not to step on the same rock as any other man in the team. The fourth or fifth man likely would knock it loose and slide down the hill making too much noise as well as suffering injury. If we heard anything, everybody froze. Thumbs down signaled that it was the enemy. Coming to a bomb crater, open place, or stream, we stopped and let the first man cover the second man and so on until we all passed safely. When we made noise by hacking vines or cutting trees, we froze and waited to see if Charlie heard and was making a move to reach us. Even putting a poncho on in rainy weather became an art simply because even the slightest rustle might give our position away.

Settling into our harbor site (camp) before dark, we placed claymore mines, booby traps, and trip flares around our position to give us ample warning if Charlie hit. On occasion, he disconnected our mines and slipped to within a few feet of us to leave Communist propaganda for harassment.

Darkness was our disadvantage, and Charlie knew it.

He usually hit around midnight or just before daybreak. Throughout the night, we received H & I fire from artillery around our position. These intermittent artillery barrages not only made the enemy a little leery of coming too close to us, but also kept artillery warmed up and hitting on target if we needed it to counter an enemy assault. We avoided movement at night — not even visits to the privy were allowed. We took turns sleeping, but often we were on 100 percent alert: everybody awake. We formed a 360 degree circle with a string running from my leg to each other man's leg. Lying on the ground beneath the stars, we made friends with the jungle creatures. By morning, the birds and monkeys thought we were one of them and had adjusted to our presence.

As we chased Charlie, we waged small-scale warfare against other enemies — insects, heat and disease. Mosquito repellent kept these annoying pests under control pretty well in the jungle, but leeches attached themselves to the waist, wrists, and ankles unless we tucked our shirts in and tied our pants at the ankles and our sleeves at the wrists. As temperatures soared, we took salt tablets almost daily. On Sunday, we took our yellow malaria pills to ward off the fever. In addition, we received routine shots to combat disease in the tropical climate.

Because there were many teams sent into the bush, my team rarely received as much ammo as requested on my report submitted to the ammo bunker prior to patrol. There was sufficient ammo for the teams to have a mediocre supply, but if one team took everything it wanted, another team would be weak.

My troops were tough and gave their best. They obeyed patrol orders almost to the letter and pulled us through some life-or-death encounters with Charlie. I watched teenagers molded into men by the harsh realities of war. The medals they won were earned by gallantry — not the eloquence of the poet's eulogy but the pain and anguish of blood sacrifice. In my opinion, they achieved combat efficiency as defined by the Marine Corps: the ability to accomplish an assigned mission in the shortest possible time with the minimum loss of life and waste of material.

Recon was, by this time, covering twice the area with half as many teams as when I arrived in Vietnam, half of the men having been sent to the northern area of the country as activity there intensified.

The news reports described to troubled America an ominous scene in Southeast Asia. Immense anxiety showed in letters from home. Mom and Dad wrote in early January, "We continue to pray and worry from one letter to the next. The news on TV and radio and in the papers seems worse every day. Please use every precaution."

The Lord admonished us in Matthew 6:34, "Don't be so anxious about tomorrow. God will take care of your tomorrows, too. Live one day at a time." That's the way I lived in 'Nam, one day at a time — not worrying about the threat of tomorrow or even the danger at hand — just doing my job to the best of my ability and entrusting my safety to the Lord.

I sensed that God was leading me and my men for a special reason. When our choppers safely straddled mines that should have blown us away, I knew we were in divine custody. Family and friends bombarded heaven with prayers for my safekeeping. More than one church had me on its prayer list.

I did what was expected of a Christian. I attended chapel services when in base area and served as battalion layman officer, filling in if a chaplain was unavailable. I recognized God's protective hand on my life and concluded that He must have some definite purpose for me, perhaps to work with youth. Preaching even occurred to me. I even felt a sort of "calling," and I wondered what service He had in mind.

Time raced by. Many troops complained about how long they had been in 'Nam and counted the days they had left. I was so busy that I hardly noticed. I put in long hours, but I liked my work. I appreciated the discipline and the challenge of military life and thought seriously of becoming a career Marine.

I couldn't put a price tag on the experiences I had had in the Corps up to that time. I'd been through a lot that I hoped I'd never see again; I expected to endure much more before leaving that battle-blemished land. All in all, it had been a sound experience and a practical education. During my year and a half in the Marines, I probably learned more than I had in four years of college and three years of teaching and coaching. Serving in a combat zone spawns maturity; my daily decisions had life-or-death consequences. "Think like a man and act like a man of thought," goes a quotation attributed to Goethe. I was a man of thought; I planned almost 24 hours a day. I tried to imagine what Charlie would do if he were me, then I did something else.

My men were well-trained and cooperative. Their performance was superior and their morale was outstanding, despite the anti-war sentiment at home. Some men in my outfit had protested and demonstrated against the war while in college. When they came face to face with the Communist threat in Vietnam, they came to believe in our cause — a struggle for freedom.

As the war ground on, the battle activity accelerated. A truce for the Vietnamese observance of Tet — the Buddhist New Year — was like intermission in a war movie: time out to catch our breath. My platoon received permission to take gifts to Vietnamese families on Phuoc Ly Hoa Minh, a village of 232 in Hoa Vang District, Quang Nam Province. The village chief had me at his table for hot tea, rice bread, and cookies while my men were served rice wine and Tiger beer. This pleasant interlude was just the calm before the coming storm. In early '68, all hell broke loose. The enemy launched a major counteroffensive during Tet, hitting all of the major cities in South Vietnam except Da Nang.

I had been in Vietnam for five months now. In a few days, I would be on an R & R flight to Hawaii to meet my wife. It would be ten days short of a year since we had been married back at Quantico. In just a few days, I would be soaking up the sun on Waikiki. I had one last patrol to pull between my reunion with Deanna and my last bush assignment in 'Nam. After R & R, I expected to be promoted to Company Commander. I had delayed R & R until I could tell Dea that my bush fighting was behind me. I was saving this good news for the celebration of our first anniversary in Hawaii.

I had already completed eighteen hazardous recon patrols deep into enemy territory without serious injury, but not until the nineteenth patrol, the last and longest, did I look death so closely in the face.

I never thought I'd be hit. It was not arrogance but rather confidence — in myself, in my men, and in God who had seen us safely through danger time and time again. I had no dark premonitions about the mission to Hill 146, a stationary combat observation post deep in enemy-controlled territory. In five months as patrol leader, I hadn't lost a man, and I didn't expect to this time.

My 13-man team included some veteran troops: Pfc. Ralph Johnson, Pfc. Tom Jennings, Pfc. Rod Hunter, and Cpl. Bob Lucas. Most of the other men were new, including Lance Cpl. Thomas L. Jones, Pfc. H.G. "Henry" Covarrubias, Pfc. Burkhart, and Navy Corpsman Shawn Green. Most of my regulars had left the bush for office assignments.

Hill 146 measured roughly 75 meters from east to west and 50 meters from north to south. As our chopper hovered in a cleared area for us to jump out, the propellers stirred up dirt that had concealed three box mines. Pfc. Jennings hit the deck and cut the wires to the mines. My radio man and corpsman dug a foxhole to my left, and three other men took cover in a foxhole to my right; the remaining eight were at the western end about fifty yards behind me around the perimeter of a bomb crater which was about twenty feet deep. We were in an excellent position to fight. I felt a nagging uneasiness. We guessed the enemy was up to something, something big. Through two tense days and nights, we watched and waited. I had an ominous intuition that we were going to get hit.

The silence of the third day warned us to get ready.

We were aware of the NVA's ability to move silently through even the most rugged terrain. Usually, they knew the exact shape of the position they intended to attack and where the patrol leader would be. The hill was terraced into what was almost a stairway up the sides.

Lieutenant Barta radioed us to see how things were going. I told him that enemy rockets and mortars indicated we were in for a long night. Reminding me that we were to meet our wives in Hawaii in a few days, he cautioned, "Take care, Clebe."

The darkness settled heavy with foreboding. We looked and listened. It was just after midnight, March 3, 1968, my wife's birthday, when we were hit.

The men to my right cried out as a grenade fell into their foxhole. Johnson jumped on it, smothering it with his stomach to protect his two buddies. He died a hero and later received the Medal of Honor posthumously. One of the pair, Jennings, was struck by shrapnel. The small wound apparently severed an artery, causing him to bleed profusely; he lingered moments from death. Seven others, including our corpsman, Shawn Green, and our radio man were wounded in the initial assault. My whole team was about to be overrun. We had to keep fighting. I moved from one positon to another, directing our desperate defense.

By this time, my left hand had been blown off by a fragmentation grenade.

Another grenade came in. I saw it in time to throw up my right hand to protect my face. The pain! As if an axe had split my head! The left eye was torn out, the vision in my right eye blurred by blood. The blast had burst both eardrums and mutilated my right hand.

I remember thinking, "If I can just reach the safety of the bomb crater. . .," when another grenade showered my legs with hot shrapnel.

Death looked me over — a helpless heap of bleeding flesh and splintered bones.

Suddenly, there was movement behind me. "Lieutenant! Lieutenant!" "Chief! Is that you?" I gasped. "Yes, sir!" It was Pfc. Hunter. Kneeling by my feet, he began picking off the enemy as they charged up the hill.

Corporal Lucas had bolted from the bomb crater to search for me when he saw an NVA ready to shoot me in the head. Lucas shot him first, causing the enemy bullet to pierce my arm. Having saved my life once, he knelt by my head and returned enemy fire.

I told Lucas to take over the patrol and call for helicopters to come in after us. He radioed the pilots; they told him that because of rain and fog, they couldn't come until daylight. "Forget it!" he told them. "Nobody will be left at daylight!"

We had been issued only five grenades per man, though I had requested ten. In no time, they were used up. My men then lobbed rocks down the side of the hill, hoping the enemy would think they were grenades and pull back.

The chopper pilots reconsidered and decided to come in immediately.

Meanwhile, we called in two "Spooky" units — World War II cargo planes that flew at night, equipped with Vulcan guns that harnessed enough firepower to kick up dirt every square foot for 100 yards. They were reserved for whoever was getting hurt the worst. I had requested them on other occasions but never got them. They could have been on the other side of the country, but the Lord sent them to us. Their red tongues of tracer fire were the only thing that kept up our morale while we waited for the choppers to come in.

If the NVA had followed up their initial assault, we would have been wiped out. Attacking from three sides — north, east, and south — they had avoided the western side where our machine guns were set up. Thus, it became impossible for us to fire the M-60's in the direction of their assault without hitting our own men.

Creeping silently to within 15 to 20 yards of our position without being detected, they had disconnected all our mines and booby traps. With ten of our thirteen men dead or wounded, we would have been an easy conquest if they had followed through. Perhaps the suicide squad killed more of themselves than they expected, or we killed more than they thought we would. It must have taken awhile for them to reorganize at the bottom of the hill. Whatever the reason, it helped save our lives by buying us precious time.

Doc Green regained consciousness and began fighting to save my life. I believe that God used those many years of athletic training to keep me alive. My pulse rate was 36 beats per minutes; the average is 75. Had my heart beat at a normal rate, I could have bled to death. My left arm, severed just below the elbow, did not bleed as much as it would have if amputated above the joint. The arteries appeared to have been seared shut by the hot metal from the grenade. Doc put a tourniquet on the stump of my arm and started to tie off my left leg which was shredded like hamburger. Knowing that I would lose it for sure if a tourniquet was applied, I kicked him away. Because I had sustained head wounds, morphine could not be administered for pain.

The first chopper to land on the hill about 1 a.m. was loaded with the wounded, dead, and dying. The rest of the men piled into the second chopper, all except Lucas and me. The chopper crew thought I was dead and urged Lucas to leave me behind. He ignored their plea and risked his own life to save my life a second time. Grabbing me under the arms. Lucas dragged me 50 yards to the chopper, lifted me aboard, and held me, my legs dangling out, as the helicopter took off. Immediately, some one hundred and fifty NVA stormed the hill in force. A delay of just minutes and not one of us would have left that hill alive.

The pain from the wounds and the cold air proved almost unbearable by the time we landed twenty minutes later at Marble Mountain Hospital near Da Nang. Attendants hustled me onto a stretcher and began cutting away my blood-drenched clothes. "Don't cut my boots! They'll be ruined!" I objected feebly. They snipped them anyway as I'd seen them do to dying troopers before, while the doctors and corpsmen started cursing and slapping me. "Why did they bring me this far to beat me to death?"

Aching and angry, I tried to strike back. The tactic worked. Most of my veins had collapsed from loss of blood, but the slapping and cursing made me respond, reviving a vein in the temple. I felt the prick of a small needle, and as the life-sustaining blood began to flow, mercifully I lost consciousness.

Jennings died half an hour after reaching the hospital. Burkhart, suffering multiple shrapnel wounds, was medevaced out of the country. Five others were treated for minor shrapnel wounds and released.

For days I lingered closer to death than life. I was vaguely aware of a frantic effort to keep me alive. Tubes protruded from my torn body like hoses from a car engine. My anguish was equal to a taste of hell.

Before they med-evaced me out of the country, the men of my platoon paraded by, one at a time, for a last look. Lieutenant Barta cried like a baby. "Top" Barker refused to come. He said he wanted to remember me as I was because I was the only lieutenant he ever knew "worth a cuss".

While I was fighting for my life, my wife's joyous expectations of meeting me in Hawaii were suddenly shattered by the delivery of one of those ominous telegrams from the Commandant of the U.S. Marine Corps. It read:

A REPORT RECEIVED THIS HEAD-
QUARTERS REVEALS THAT YOUR
HUSBAND SECOND LIEUTENANT
PATRICK C MCCLARY III USMC SUS-
TAINED INJURIES ON 3 MARCH 1968
IN THE VICINITY OF QUANG NAM
REPUBLIC OF VIETNAM FROM A
HOSTILE GRENADE WHILE ON A
PATROL. HE SUFFERED TRAUMATIC
AMPUTATION OF THE LEFT ARM
AND SUSTAINED SHRAPNEL
WOUNDS TO ALL EXTREMITIES.
PROGNOSIS POOR. OUTLOOK DIM.
YOUR GREAT ANXIETY IS
UNDERSTOOD AND YOU ARE AS-
SURED THAT HE WILL RECEIVE THE
BEST OF CARE. YOU SHALL BE KEPT

INFORMED OF ALL SIGNIFICANT
CHANGES IN HIS CONDITION.

I finally arrived by med-evac flight at the U.S. Army 249th General Hospital at Camp Drake, Japan. I was in critical condition and not much to look at. Where my left arm had been was now just a stump, my left eye had been torn out by the grenade explosion, my right hand was mangled by the blast when I tried to shield my face, my right leg was full of shrapnel, the left one shredded, my feet were black from jungle rot, and I was fighting against gangrene in my left leg. Besides the physical torture, the mental anguish over my condition, the mounting concerns for my loved ones back home, and my inability to adequately console them was unbearable.

However, as I gradually regained my strength, I found myself able to thank God for the fact that I was still alive and still had a loving wife. I hurt, but I was not a bitter, broken man. All I wanted was to go home. The flood of condolences and words of encouragement poured in, but I desperately needed to see my wife and family myself and help pick up the pieces. By the end of March, arrangements were finally made for me to be transferred to Bethesda Naval Hospital in Maryland.

As the days passed, however, my emotional condition took a temporary turn for the worse. I knew enough about God not to question His ways. I could not imagine what purpose He had in my experiences, but I tried to sound convincing as I encouraged Dea on a tape, "The Bible teaches that everything happens for the best for those who love the Lord. I look at my arm, and I think about my eye, and I wonder . . . but I guess you shouldn't question the Bible. At least I'm living."

But, inevitably, the time did arrive when I asked, "Why me, Lord?" Taking a good look at myself and remembering how beautiful Deanna was, I began to think she would be better off without me. I became so depressed that I gave up. I lost my desire to live. People had teased me by asking good-naturedly what a beautiful girl like Dea was doing with somebody like me. I quipped, "It's my personality and Southern charm!" but suddenly it wasn't funny any more. I wondered, too, and wished I could die.

After an agonizing month of waiting, I made the long med-evac flight home to be reunited with my wife. As she entered my hospital ward for the first time, my words to her were "Dea, honey, it's me. Baby, I know I'm not a pretty sight, but I'm happy to be alive and home."

There I lay, a pathetic 115 pounds, with bandages covering the left eye and both ears, head shaved, face full of stitches, stump of the left arm bound, right arm in a cast and motionless, left leg open and draining with the bone exposed, and the right leg covered with shrapnel wounds.

"You're beautiful!" she cried. Running to me, she gently wrapped her arms around my frail form, afraid of hurting me. "Don't worry," she assured me. "We're going to make the best of everything."

Several operations followed to remove metal from my head, gums, forearm, legs, and feet. One eardrum was reconstructed, using the lining of a vein in my temple. The other eardrum was rebuilt in later surgery at Philadelphia Naval Hospital. After the reconstructive surgery, my hearing greatly improved. Most of my teeth had to be capped. Surgery was also performed on my left eye to remove the damaged tissue. I received an artificial eye but eventually adopted a black patch instead.

All my plans for a promising military career had been blown to bits that night on Hill 146, and I didn't know what the future held; however, I was pretty sure that it would be a long road back to anything resembling what I then considered to be a normal life. The road to rehabilitation and reconstructing something meaningful out of the ashes of what had been had all the built-in fears and insecurities one would expect of someone in my condition. But things would not turn out as I anticipated; God had other, long-range plans for my life.

When the smoke of battle clears, the bodies are buried, and the peace treaty is signed, then the rebuilding starts. For me, the war was over. The challenge facing me was to rebuild a devastated life. Little did I know, at the time, that God wanted to cooperate.

During my first leave from the hospital in Florence, South Carolina (Dea's hometown), an evangelistic crusade was being held at the football stadium where I had thrown and caught many touchdown passes and coached many teams. It was sponsored by the Fellowship of Christian Athletes. I read in the newspaper that Bobby Richardson, former second baseman with the New York Yankees, and Vonda Kay Van Dyke, former Miss America from Arizona, were to participate. While coaching in Florence, I had once invited Bobby to speak at my school. I said to Deanna, "I'd sure like to see Bobby Richardson"; and of course, any Marine would like to see Miss America! So we went to the stadium on the night of July 26, 1968.

We heard Bobby and Vonda Kay give brief testimonies, sharing what the Lord Jesus Christ had done in their lives.

Then came a message that God used to change my life. The crusade was presented by Billy Zeoli, President of Gospel Films, Muskegon, Michigan. His father, Anthony Zeoli, accepted Christ in prison and had become a powerful evangelist. He was called the "walking Bible" because of his knowledge of the scriptures.

Billy preached to us about some of the great men of the Bible who had become "fools for God." He spoke of Noah, who likely was labeled a fool by the people in his community when he built an ark at God's command. He told of Joshua, who must have been ridiculed by his soldiers when he announced God's battle plans for Jericho. He mentioned others who obeyed God, though it seemed foolish to men. He said that if they were fools, they were fools for God. He said there are two kinds of fools in this world: fools for Christ and fools for others. The greatest fool of all, he added, is one who hears God's plan of salvation and rejects it. "Whose fool are you?" he asked. "Whose fool are you?" Those words dug into my soul like red-hot slivers of shrapnel.

His question seemed to slap me in the face. I realized whose fool I'd been all of my life. I never drank or smoked, in order to become a good athlete and to impress people. I was a good person, playing the role people expected of me. I grew up in church and believed in the right things — the Bible, tithing, good morals, and clean habits — but I had never invited Jesus Christ into my heart as Savior or let Him become the Lord of my life.

When the invitation was given, I stood. To my left, Dea also stood. With my left eye gone and hearing poor in the left ear, I was not aware that God had touched us both until we walked forward together to receive Christ as our personal Savior. We had difficulty finding someone to counsel with us; everyone thought we were Christians who had come to assist with the counseling! Finally, the Rev. Sam Anderson, a Presbyterian minister from Hemingway, South Carolina, led us to the Lord.

My heart was changed that midsummer night, but my life did not change noticeably. For years, I had tried to live the Christian life; the difference was that now Christ was living in me. When this Marine surrendered to the Lord, it was not defeat but rather victory. In the Marine Corps, I had sought only to serve my country. At last, I joined the greatest army that has ever marched — the Army of Jesus Christ.

God's purpose became clear: He spared my life that I might find abundant life in Him. I did not know it at the time, but through my experiences, He was to touch countless lives.

The crusade leaders asked me to give my testimony publicly the night following our commitment. I don't remember what I shared because I didn't know how to describe what had happened. New life! Abundant and everlasting! A child of God! I couldn't explain it, but I knew it was real. It was the beginning of a ministry that was to take me across the United States numerous times, as well as abroad, sharing the miracles God had performed in my life.

Months of painful therapy followed, but it involved more than just physical recovery. God began to adjust the steps of my life and direct them into His service. He planned to redeem my experiences in Vietnam for the benefit of others. He had enlisted me into His service. Opportunity after opportunity presented itself to share my testimony and the life-changing power of Christ.

Finally, in September 1973, I felt the Lord leading me into full-time evangelism. After much prayer, Dea and I organized the Clebe McClary Evangelistic Association. This unusual ministry as a layman has taken me throughout America to every state — and most of them more than once — including Alaska and Hawaii. We have witnessed in churches, evangelistic crusades, civic organizations, prisons, and over 500 high schools. I have been invited to speak to numerous groups, including the Fellowship of Christian Athletes, Campus Crusade, Youth for Christ, and Word of Life, as well as in many churches around the country.

The nightmare of Vietnam is not easily forgotten. The horrors of that midnight on Hill 146 will never be erased. Daily I am reminded of the high cost of liberty by the price that I paid — 100 percent disability. But even saddled with such a discouraging label, I have found it exciting to look ahead and see what can still be achieved. I am not bitter or angry, but grateful in the profound revelation that though I paid a heavy price in flesh and blood, Christ paid a far greater price by laying down His life for me — a reality that I was forced to appreciate that desperate night on Hill 146 when Ralph Johnson gave his life to save his two buddies — and it is with this recognition that I have dedicated my life to His service.

I am a living testimony, what you might call "living proof," of the power of Christ to bring good out of bad, meaning out of meaninglessness. Even as the great assurance of Romans 8:28 reads, "And we know that all things work together for good to those who love God, to those who are called according to His purpose," God has redeemed the pain and suffering of my experiences in Vietnam and caused it all to work together for good — not only for myself, but for thousands across this country.

Clebe McClary, his wife Deanna, and his two daughters Tara and Christa, live at Pawleys Island, South Carolina. Clebe travels extensively throughout the United States speaking in prisons, campuses, military bases, V.A. hospitals, local churches, prayer breakfasts, athletic groups, and motivational seminars. Besides his many speaking engagements, he has authored a book on his Vietnam experience entitled *Living Proof*, which testifies of his determination to give what it takes and press on in spite of the odds. Gospel Films also released his story in a film entitled, "Portrait of an American Hero." He recently received the Gen. Omar Bradley Award at the Independence Bowl and plans to place the award at the foot of the Tomb of the Unknown Soldier in Washington, D.C.

Col. Myrl Allinder
Major, U.S.M.C.
Helicopter pilot
HMM 365
Oct. '64 - Jan. '65
F-4 Phantom pilot
Marine fighter/
Attack Squadron 122
May '69 - May '70

7

Major Who Loves Us

I was driving my jeep across the sandy road to the Marine Air Station at Chu Lai in October, 1969. It was eleven at night, and I was absolutely exhausted. I'd gone to bed at midnight, was roused out at 2 a.m. for a combat mission, briefed for nearly two hours, launched at 5 a.m. leading three other Phantoms on a bombing mission, returned at sun-up for breakfast, worked in the hangar with my maintenance crew overhauling some F-4's, and flew a late afternoon mission flying fighter cover for a B-52 strike. I'd finished out my duties around 8 p.m. when I drove over to check-up on the 200 Montagnard orphans that I'd helped rescue in a move down from their mountain village to the safety of one of the Marine barracks on the beach of the South China Sea.

Heading back in my bone-weary condition after risking my life for my country and putting my career in the Corps on the line for those kids, the voice of the Holy Spirit stopped me dead in my tracks. It was only one word, but it struck me so hard that it felt like someone had slapped me across the face. I jammed on the brakes and skidded to a stop. Hot tears of frustration and loneliness coursed through the dust and grime on my cheeks, and I began to cry out in wounded indignation, "God, how can you say such a thing to me? I've risked everything!" One well-chosen word jarred my whole life on that black night in Vietnam — that one word was "HYPOCRITE!"

Not that I'd been a stranger to hypocrisy. I'd spent a

lifetime perfecting that art. In many ways, my entire life, my whole career, had been a sham — a self-serving show. As an ambitious jet-jockey, I had lived out my cocky version of the "Great Santini" — parties, flying, parties, flying, drunkenness, flying. Through it all, I maintained just enough religiousity to qualify as a first class phony. I moved with the crowd and did whatever the crowd was doing, whether that was being knee-walking drunk on Friday night or church-sober on Sunday. But underneath the facade, I was a moral tumbleweed going whichever way the wind blew. This was my condition when I received my first set of orders for flight duty in 'Nam.

I was already a seasoned fighter pilot, but the immediate demand was for chopper pilots. After several months of retraining, I joined a Marine observation squadron at Camp Pendleton. In July '64, my unit was sent to Vietnam to provide support for the South Vietnamese Army. I went with naive notions of combat, heroics, and medals! However, the gung-ho, follow-the-flag images of guts and glory soon vanished amidst the carnage of Vietnam.

There was nothing romantic about that dirty little war. Running resupply runs into blistering LZ's, blindly navigating fog-shrouded mountains, flying through the night with tracer fireballs floating upwards around you, running dust-offs, or landing troops under a hail storm of small arms fire was nerve-racking to say the least. But spiraling down for a landing in a small clearing under a barrage of bullets, kicking out some ammo crates, or lifting out two or three wounded was easy in comparison to hauling out a load of waxy-looking bodies. They were often a ghoulish grey-green, frozen in grotesque positions, with blank eyes which seemed to look right through you when they were stacked on board for the return flight to the morgue unit at Da Nang. The former glamour of being a jet-jockey quickly evaporated in the presence of a cargo load of dead soldiers.

It was at those moments that death seemed very real — very close. I could even smell it. The gnawing fear in the pit of my stomach drained all energy, emotion, and thought. It took all the concentration I could muster to focus on flying, performing under stress what the Marines had drilled into me.

Perhaps the worst part was not in flight but back in the solitude of the barracks where I had time to replay the vivid images of warfare over and over in my head: the thought of the day's missions, the dead corpses, the devastated families back home. Were those men in heaven or in hell? What about me? What if one of those grey-green bodies was mine? Where would I end up — heaven or hell?

It was these sobering reflections that led me to cry out to God for help, and He heard me and gave me a profound sense of peace which passed the daily terrors of the war which surrounded me.

It was in this frame of mind that I finished my first tour in 'Nam: at peace with my Maker in the midst of war and deprivation. However, it was only a circumstantial peace. Another peace waited to be settled in my heart.

God had, indeed, met me, but I hadn't changed all that much. I just returned with a cosmetic overhaul — a sanitized version of the Great Santini. I was still playing the same old hypocritical role. I returned to the comfort of my family, the luxury of easy living in Monterey,

California, and a promising career in the Marine Corps. As I labored diligently six days a week for an advanced degree, my presence began to make ripples in the upper echelons of the Corps. Oh, it's true that I woke up one morning and didn't cuss all day, and another day I tried to take a drag off a Camel and it tasted like one. My buddies were surprised when I lost my taste for whiskey and cleaned out my liquor cabinet. It's also true that I began to be a big man in the church, but instead of wooing men to Christ, I was thumping them into the self-styled image of Myrl with a guilt trip which boasted, "I don't cuss, spit, or chew — how about you?"

In the blinding glare of my own conceit, I subtly assumed that I'd achieved my new-found success through my own strength, through my own understanding. In self-righteous deception, I secretly gloated in how far I had come and it was in that frame of mind that I launched a personal crusade to tell others the message of how I did it — the gospel according to Allinder.

However, my pride would soon be humbled, and the mask of hypocrisy which I had worn so well would be ripped from my face. It happened at the Marine Corps Headquarters in Washington, D.C. in 1968. I was walking down a corridor when a big, tough, honest Marine blocked me in the hallway, poked his iron fist into my chest, and said, "Hey, Allinder, I hear you're pretty religious, ain't cha!" He just stood there facing me down, laughing cynically as my face flushed with embarrassment. I'd been caught like someone had suddenly exposed some dark secret. But it wasn't such a secret after all. In spite of all my "airs," I reeked with self-righteousness and hypocrisy.

I stood there naked, trying to regain my composure, looking for some clever comeback. I started to say, "Well, I don't cuss, spit, or chew, how about you?"; but those words seemed so hollow at that moment. Finally, after a few agonizing seconds, I stuttered a lame, "I'm just as bad as you, sir! I'm just as bad as you!" But in my heart, I knew I was really worse. At least he lived his life openly, while I lived out my phoniness behind a veil of self-righteous contempt. The cosmetic polish job on my spiritual brass — "I don't cuss, don't chew, don't run with those that do" — had looked so impressive in the sterile confines of my church, but it had suddenly tarnished in the hallway of the Marine Corps Headquarters.

Devastated by the revelation of my shallowness and self-conceit, I went home that night to commence a several month ordeal of painful soul-searching. It was a gut-wrenching period of personal inventory, of prayer, scripture, and constant mental anguish. I was groping for some meaningful way to tell that Marine about Jesus — to put things right.

After months of depression, I was reaching a breaking point. On one restless night, I got up and started reading from the Gospel of John. I had a weekly prayer breakfast to attend in the morning at the Admiral's dining room, so I didn't want to get to bed too late. However, the scriptures weren't giving me any comfort. Instead, a certain verse had inflamed my temper — that verse was John 14:12: "Truly I tell you, he that believes in Me will do the same things that I do, and he will do even greater things because I am going to My Father!" I couldn't even tell a Marine about Jesus, let alone do a miracle! I wanted to rip that page right out of the Bible. My problem was

I couldn't rip it out of my heart. It was three or four in the morning before I fell into an uneasy sleep.

My alarm rang at 0600. I pulled myself together, drove to the base through bleary eyes, and stumbled into the Admiral's dining room in a lousy mood at 0700 along with 30-40 other officers who had come to pray for P.O.W.'s. About 0720, we were getting ready to pray when I noticed a Navy chaplain I hadn't recognized before. I thought it would be a nice gesture to ask him to read a scripture before we prayed.

"Hallelujah!" he shouted. "I've just been talking to Jesus, and Jesus just spoke to me!" Oooh, my head! A sense of panic swept over me. I actually began to rise in my chair to escape from this fanatic who was unlike any chaplain I had ever met. But Chaplain Linzey dropped me in my tracks with his next statement: ". . . and He just gave me a scripture for you!" All the fight suddenly drained out of me. I broke into a sweat and began to tremble. I knew what that scripture would be: "Look at John 14:12."

The months of frustration finally overwhelmed me. In desperation I cried, "How is it possible to do the things of Jesus? I couldn't even tell a tough Marine that Jesus loves him!"

The chaplain looked at me with understanding and said, "You need the baptism of Jesus." I fell on my knees to the floor, not knowing what he was talking about, but the words just seemed to fall from my lips on their own: "What's to prevent me?"

"Nothing!", the chaplain laughed, as he laid his hands on my head and all the other officers in the room gathered around me to pray. I know it sounds crazy, but his hands were like branding irons! My body was swept with heat from the top of my head to my feet. I was bathed in the presence of God. At that moment, I was so conscious of my sins before Him that I recoiled in terror crying, "Oh God, get away! I'm a failure as a man, a husband, a father. Please God, get away!" I had never spoken such words to myself, let alone confess such things before a room full of my fellow officers.

The sensation of His love for me was overpowering but still I wept, "God, I'm a failure in the Marines as well! I'm full of vanity and lies and walk over people to get ahead! Oh, God, I'm a filthy man!" Just then, I sensed His voice stilling my soul: "You have not chosen Me; I have chosen You."

My tears of terror turned to tears of peace and adoration. My hands began to come up in a very military gesture — the raised hands of unconditional surrender. At that moment, the war that had raged in my heart and had made Vietnam look tame in comparison suddenly ended as my hands went up in the Admiral's dining room.

By '68, the war had reached a boiling point. Because of the steady demand for pilots, I received my second set of orders for Vietnam. I wouldn't be flying H-34's on my second tour but Phantoms. After several months of re-qualifying with F-4's at Cherry Point, I shipped overseas and was assigned to the air base at Chu Lai.

When I wasn't pulling ground duty as the Maintenance Officer, I was flying F-4's in a variety of roles. These included close air support for our ground units, bombing strikes on the strategic infiltration routes heading south through Laos, and combat air patrol missions protecting B-52's who were flying bombing runs against Route Pack

1 — the Hanoi/Haiphong complex on the Red River Delta.

In between combat duties, I was busy organizing impromptu prayer meetings, passing out tracts and Bibles, holding spontaneous song services on the flight line or in the hangars, and testifying to base personnel. After we finished our duties, a group of us would often drive to the outlying hamlets to build schools and orphanages. Off base, our guys were also handing out as many Vietnamese Bibles and hymn books as we could get our hands on. We couldn't seem to pass them out fast enough.

The crowning achievement of our efforts involved the wholesale movement of 200 Hrey Montagnard children from their villages seventy miles west of us in the mountains bordering Laos. Most of their parents had been killed resisting the Communists. A few months before, I had met an aged medical missionary from Australia named Dr. Stuart Harverson. When he told me about his work with the Hrey and the desperate need to evacuate their war orphans to the safety of orphanages on the coast, I volunteered my services.

Some Army C-7 pilots agreed to land their short take-off-and-landing cargo transports in a clearing near the mountain tribe and fly out the 200 children to Chu Lai. The immediate problem which confronted me at Chu Lai was finding a place to house them, food, and the medical support to take care of them. However, when a Marine unit was suddenly transferred, I unofficially requisitioned their empty barracks. None of the other loose ends had been cleared up, but with at least a roof to cover their heads, I called Dr. Harverson and the army pilots to "Bring out 200 on Wednesday!"

I still had no idea where we would get the food, clothing, shots, and X-rays, but I figured if God could take care of Moses and three million, feeding Dr. Harverson and 200 would be a snap! I simply put the word out among the Christians on base that we needed help to pull this mission of mercy off.

Right on schedule, the children were picked up and flown back to Chu Lai. When the transports landed, they each spilled their load of fifty laughing, shouting, awestruck children who were discovering civilization for the first time. They immediately rushed in screaming waves across the runway to their new Marine, Army, Navy, and Air Force "big brothers." The only problem with Chu Lai's newly adopted family was the fact that my commanding officer had not been notified of my unauthorized invasion. However, within thirty seconds after their landing, the startled Base Operations Officer was on the horn to MAG-13, who in turn was on the phone to the Wing CG and Wing Doc demanding to know "the meaning of all this!" When they finally discovered that the sole perpetrator of this unorthodox airlift was one Major Allinder, there was an official warrant for my hide. After all, this was a war zone, not a nursery!

As it turned out, I had previously directed members of my staff to brief the Group Commander on our new "Operation Orphanage," but unbeknownst to me "events of war" sidetracked the intended briefing with our colonel. It had to be a providential slip-up, for the colonel later confided that if he had know of the scheme — even if he had discovered what was happening as the transports were circling to land — he would have countermanded the whole plan and forced them to turn away — if necessary, to return their "cargo" to the mountain jungles. But God had other plans for those kids and me.

Now, faced with a "fait accompli" of 200 children on their way in trucks to "their barracks" accompanied by a seemingly like number of baby-sitters, all the colonel could do was chew me out — which he did rather thoroughly! I left his office with his resounding order ringing in my ears to arrange for their soonest "onward transport to an ultimate destination other than Chu Lai"! In other words, "Get them out of here — I don't care where, but just get them off of this base!"

I responded to his order with a prompt "Aye Aye," for that was the original plan of Dr. Harverson — to eventually build an orphanage and school on the north side of Da Nang's Half Moon Bay, move the children there as soon as possible, and then bring out hundreds more.

Miraculously, the care and shelter began to appear on the evening of the first day for the children of Chu Lai! The Wing Flight Surgeon immediately began to chew on what was left of me after the Group Commander finished! "What about shots? X-rays? Food? Clothing? Bedding?" I still to this day don't know how it all came about but, miraculously, supplies began to appear. We found enough serum to innoculate the kids for every kind of disease the doc could think of! Somewhere a navy chief heard of our plight and brought an old, outmoded X-ray machine, but he had no X-ray film that would fit it. From somewhere else, an army sergeant brought some old-type X-ray film his outfit couldn't use — and it just fit our outmoded machine! We completed chest X-rays at once. Cots began to appear. Children who, moments before, had arrived wearing only a dirty loincloth and a smile, were soon frolicking on the beach in oversized dungarees and boots. Our toughened men turned their eyes away, blowing their noses.

Later that evening, I broke down weeping. The occasion was the first Chu Lai evening meal — the first in complete safety and peace for most of the children in their entire lives. The "menu" consisted of one huge pot of boiled rice — that was it. The children had lined up according to age, the youngest first, and the first two two-year-olds dutifully brought in their one metal bowl loaded with rice, placed the bowl on the concrete floor at one end of the empty barracks, and squatted down, one on each side of the bowl. They folded their arms across their knees, but they weren't eating. I went up to the two two-year-olds and urged them in English and with hand motions to eat, but they just smiled at me and waited. The other children followed suit until there were two rows of children facing their row of bowls. When they were all seated, the oldest, who was 16, led the children in singing from the Psalms of David that they had memorized, gave a magnificent prayer to God in thanks for all His wondrous provisions of the day, and then, with one accord, they began to eat!

I was totally wiped out. But I wasn't the only one crying. The other men about me were no longer just "blowing noses"; they were bawling their eyes out.

When I brought out my guitar after the supper of rice, the children surged around. We sang choruses, interspersed with so many of my "I love you's," that one of the children named me "Major-who-loves-us." My new name caught on. In the following days, every time I would drive up to the barracks, I was welcomed with choruses of gleeful children chortling "Major-who-loves us! Major-who-loves us!" I would sweep them up in my arms while others pressed around and swarmed over my jeep. "Major-who-loves-us! Major-who-loves-us!" There is no way to express the depth of emotions I felt for those waifs, so simple and open, so loving and beautiful. In some ways, they meant more to me than my own four children at home. Maybe it was the contrast they presented in the midst of war-torn Vietnam. The beauty of the whole experience was intoxicating.

That was the state of my heart and mind that black night when the Holy Spirit spoke "Hypocrite!" It was like a hydrogen bomb vaporizing my Eden! The echos of "Major-who-loves-us!" were still washing gently over my soul when God's thunderous "Hypocrite!" turned Eden into a Sahara. "How can You say that to me? Don't You see how I've poured myself out for those kids?"

The last rosy glow of "Major-who-loves-us" was now displaced by a vision. All the beautiful faces of the loving children faded, and only one of the 200 children filled my view.

He was about 13 — and the ugliest, stinkingest human in Vietnam. His knees were knocked and knobby and swollen, he was pock-marked, his teeth were rotten, his belly swollen and distended, and his breath was horrible. In a word, he was repugnant. The vision began to play back every single encounter I had had with this young lad over the preceding days, for he had called me "Major-who-loves-us" also. But each time the child had started to come near, God had stood by with a camera, and now He was replaying the "film" of my facial expressions — and my heart expressions — as this wretched lad had reached out to me for some of this "love" that I had found so easy to share with the beautiful looking children. In the "movie of my mind," eyes had narrowed, brows wrinkled, heart stiffened — and the pitiful little bag of humanity felt the devastating crush of my rejection, the invisible wall of my aversion, and had never gotten closer to me than about five yards. My suppression of the child was so complete that I did not even consciously acknowledge that he existed until that sobering moment of confrontation with God's convicting power.

The hot tears of anger and frustration now became tears of abject humiliation and shame. "If you don't love this one, Myrl, you really don't love any of them." God said it so softly, so gently, but it rocked me harder than His first thundering word.

"God, You're right! I am a hypocrite! I have rejected and pushed this boy away. I've despised that boy. He is the rottenest thing I have ever seen. I feel no love or affection for him whatsoever. But I tell you the truth. Tomorrow, as soon as I'm free, I will be back at their barracks, and I will tell that little boy that I love him. But Father, You have to make it happen. Up to now, my words have been lying and hypocrisy. You will have to make my words be true, for I only feel revulsion for him and not love. Oh God, please forgive my sins of hypocrisy!"

I don't remember the next day's military duties too well; I was lost in the depth of God's dealings. I think I flew three missions and worked on some aircraft maintenance problems. What I do remember is that around 4 p.m. I told my Master Sergeant Maintenance Chief that I had some chores to do and would be gone for awhile, jumped in my jeep, and headed for our "orphanage" barracks.

As I drove up, the kids were in their usual romp on the beach. Kids were laughing and frolicking in the surf, playing mock battles, and chasing a soccer ball. As one group noticed my jeep and began to cry out "Major-who-loves us!", others picked it up and soon it seemed the whole chorus of kids was swarming around. This time, however, I didn't grab them up and hug them and swing them as I usually did. I scanned the group intently, looking for one special knock-kneed 13-year-old.

When I finally saw him, I was so intent that my stare froze him in his tracks about 15 yards away. I'm sure he thought he was in trouble and I was going to punish him. He wanted to flee from me, expecting the same rejection which I'd manifested in days past. But my eyes held him — he couldn't move. As I stood there riveted on that child, I could see the fear welling up in his eyes. Ever so deliberately I raised my hand, pointed at the child who so wanted to flee from me, and, choked with emotion, I enunciated as clearly and distinctly as I could, "I . . . LOVE . . . YOU!!"

At first there was shock, then disbelief as he glanced quickly about to see if there wasn't someone else to whom I was speaking — and, at last, realization that indeed I was speaking to him alone! His eyes grew wider and wider, matched by the joy of his upturned face as his lips found it impossible to hide the ugly teeth and hide the biggest smile all at the same time! The poor child gave a squeal of joy as his arms flew open and he made a dash for me.

And, all at once, I saw my second vision in the space of 17 hours: the boy's ugly face with its crooked grin transformed into the face of Jesus Christ! I was looking into the face of Jesus! A groan escaped me, and a shock of love flushed over my entire being as I grabbed up the woebegone little boy and pressed him to my breast. The tears of love, mercy, and compassion swept me into the heavens! I felt hands on my head again! The chaplain's hands were burning on my head again! Only this time, they were the hands of Jesus!

In an instant, He melted my miserable heart of stone and gave me a heart of flesh — a heart of compassion. I really, really loved the boy! The genuine love of God surged through me to comfort this crumple of a child! As I held him to my breast, I remembered the words of Christ: "For as much as you do it to the least of these, you do it to Me!"

What will you hear about Vietnam? Of Christian meetings in the midst of combat every day of the year? Of the marines, airmen, sailors, and soldiers who were saved? Of the thousands of Bibles and song books passed out? Of the servicemen who left the military to return to Vietnam as missionaries? Of the orphanages and schools they built? Of the cross of Jesus Christ painted on Phantoms going into combat? Well, all this is true.

But I will tell you, rather, of how a raggedy Montagnard Indian boy let me see the face of Jesus Christ, and how my life was changed forever.

What mystery! What warfare!

Col. Myrl Allinder and his wife Martha reside in Clearwater, Florida, and have four grown children, one of whom is a Navy lieutenant. He is still on active duty in the U.S.M.C. Since his last tour in the Republic of Vietnam, he has held a variety of key positions, both in the States and overseas, as Squadron Commander, Fellow Chief of Naval Operations' Strategic Studies Group, and Head of Planning and War Games at the Naval War College. He presently serves as Chief of Plans in the Joint Deployment Agency, under the Joint Chiefs of Staff.

Jere Fullerton Sr.
Corporal, U.S.M.C.
Parachute Rigger
Marine Air Group II, 1st Marine Airwing
Feb. '67 - Mar. '68

8

A Place To Run

I grew up in the little town of Whitman, Massachusetts, in a happy, middle-class family. I was the fourth of eleven children. Eight of us kids were to serve in the U.S. armed forces, but I was the only one who would serve in Vietnam.

In 1964, after high school and a brief stay in college, I entered the U.S. Marines. It took four trips to Boston before I finally passed the required physical. I had some sort of malformation of the eyelids for which they kept shooting me down. Maybe on my fourth try the Marine Corps decided my persistence was more important than irregular eyelids. More than once, when undergoing the grueling training at the Marine Corps Recruit Depot in Parris Island, S.C., I wished they hadn't made that decision. However, when I finally completed training, I was a proud "boot" and was absolutely convinced that I had been molded into one of the best fighting men this country had to offer.

Since I had enlisted in the Marine Corps with an aviation guarantee, I received some specialized training at Parachute Riggers School at Lakehurst, New Jersey, and then served in a series of aviation squadrons until I finally received orders for Vietnam. I landed in Da Nang, South Vietnam, in February 1967. As the 707 touched down, I realized I would finally do what I had been prepared to do: fight for my country. However, I soon found that the day-to-day reality of a war zone was markedly different from what I had envisioned. I had once thought that my basic training at Parris Island was hell; but after a short time in Vietnam, I knew how mistaken I'd been.

At the end of February, 1967, the Viet Cong launched their first attack of the year on the sprawling air base at Da Nang. It would be the first of many. Da Nang represented a prestigious symbol of American military power and influence in the northern province of Vietnam. It housed thousands of American support troops and hundreds of aircraft there to protect some 300,000 civilians in the area, as well as support American and ARVN operations in I Corps.

In typical fashion, the surprise attack came in the predawn darkness of February 28. The rockets and mortars were launched from an area some five miles southeast of the base. The V.C. had targeted the U.S. Army 37 Signal Corps Battalion, but the majority of the rockets and mortars landed off base in the village of Ap Do. Fifty-eight civilians were killed, scores were wounded, and over 150 buildings were leveled in the densely populated area. Although American casualties were light, the V.C. were giving us notice that even the huge air base at Da Nang would pay a high price for the support we provided Vietnamese and American ground units, as well as the bombing sorties launched against strategic targets in North Vietnam.

This attack marked the beginning of a new phase of escalation in the war. We soon became familiar with the new term "rocket belt." The rocket belt was the area around the base where the Viet Cong gunners could effectively launch their rockets to cause maximum damage, demoralize the U.S. and Vietnamese troops at the base, and frustrate our ground forces who were constantly running security patrols searching for the rocket firing teams.

In the following months, the alarm "Incoming!" became a familiar addition to our vocabulary.

On March 16, fourteen Soviet-made 140mm rockets slammed into the air base. The rocket barrage lasted only one minute, but with devastating effects. Charlie had launched them just a third of a mile from the previous site they had used in the February attack. Marine ground units, dragon ships, and tactical aircraft immediately responded. The V.C. made a desperate attempt to escape but were neutralized by our overwhelming firepower.

With the stepped-up tempo of attacks, we were forced to throw a larger number of ground units into the bush to keep the V.C. off-guard. But Charlie was usually able to keep one step ahead of us. After these hit-and-run attacks, they generally evaded us by fading back into the sanctuary of the jungle. We seemed unable to prevent the rocket attacks and were totally defenseless once they were airborne. Once they began their lethal arc into our perimeter, it was just a matter of seconds before they gouged a crater in a runway, gutted some aircraft, shredded some building, released thousands of searing hot splinters tearing through everything near their impact, or landed harmlessly in some unoccupied area. To second-guess their trajectories was an exercise in futility. At best, you hoped you were not in the right place at the wrong time.

The relentless determination of Charlie to hurt us manifested itself in their willingness to suicidally sacrifice themselves in order to gain the propaganda value of demonstrating to the world that the largest American installation in Vietnam was vulnerable to their attacks.

On March 23, the South Vietnamese police captured

a V.C. cadre officer in the marketplace of Da Nang. He had received his training at an NVA intelligence school in the north and was carrying a detailed map of our air base installations, as well as harbor piers. Upon interrogation, he confessed that the Viet Cong were planning an all-out attack on the air base in the near future.

The news of this discovery caused an atmosphere of eerie uneasiness to settle upon the air base. We found ourselves sweating out the nights, waiting for the "whoosh" of incoming rockets and the inevitable "whoommm!" that followed. The nights seemed longer as we watched the star flares floating down continuously around the base, casting distorted shadows across the landscape. It gave the impression of being in a dark dream — a bizarre twilight zone between reality and unreality.

One night in the middle of this grinding war of nerves, I was standing near the flight line watching the air traffic taking off and landing. I happened to glance over and catch an A6A Intruder taxi into take-off position then roar past. I knew it was one of our birds because of the call sign Delta Tango. The jet was bristling with ordinance. It was carrying a full compliment of 500 lb. bombs plus rocket pods. It was overloaded in its pregnant condition, and ate up most of the runway in its attempt to attain enough velocity to get off the ground. As it reached the end of the runway, a C141 cargo plane accidentally veered directly into its path. Just then, the crew of the A6A blew the canopy, scrambled out on the wings, and dove from the 100 m.p.h. jet. The jet hurtled on and crashed broadside into the C141. The cargo plane was carrying 14,000 pounds of highly volatile acetylene as part of its cargo. There was an enormous explosion as an orange and black fireball engulfed the plane, incinerating the flight crew of the C141.

The visual impact of that catastrophe triggered an intense depression and only compounded the nerve-fraying suspense of waiting for the incoming rockets. At least in the bush you were able to aggressively stalk Charlie, but locked behind miles of tangled concertina wire, anti-personnel mines, trip wires, claymores, machine gun bunkers, observation towers, and perimeter patrols, we still felt helpless with no place to run. We seemed like the proverbial "sitting ducks" waiting for the commencement of hunting season, not knowing if the next rocket had our name on it. After weeks of anxious waiting, we began to console ourselves that the worst was over, but our wishful thinking was premature.

On the night of July 15, I received my baptism of fire. I remember in high school reading Stephen Crane's *Red Badge of Courage* and fantasizing about how I would react if I ever had to face my own baptism of fire. That Civil War novel struck a deep cord as I secretly identified with the inner tug-of-war between cowardice and courage which lurks in the recesses of every man. I feared the role of cowardice and preferred to envision my response as one of cool, collective heroism under fire. However, my night of baptism would not be so glorious. It could better be characterized as terrorized pandemonium.

I was working the graveyard shift, ferrying flight crews back and forth from the compound area, when the rocket vigil ended. Shortly after midnight, I heard a strange whistling sound screaming overhead. It was the first of many 122mm Katusha rockets which rained down upon us that night.

I was standing just inside the hangar bay, waiting for the "whoomp!", when the first rocket hit just above the avionics shop. I watched as a gaping 10 ft. hole was ruptured in the hangar wall, blowing men away in the flesh-ripping concussion. The shrapnel clanged and rattled as it ricocheted through the hangar, like nails tumbling down a metal chute.

Through the deafening roar and blizzard of flying shrapnel, I could hear the screams of airmen writhing in agony on the hangar floor. I ran dazed in search of cover, but another rocket tore through the roof and the force of the explosion hurled me into the road. A lieutenant who was running by helped me toward a bunker. Just then, another round whistled close overhead before plowing into a trailer a few feet in front of us, but it didn't go off. It it had, I wouldn't be telling this story.

Lying battered and bruised in the darkness of that bunker, I realized that I had escaped serious injury. Still, I wanted to run somewhere — anywhere. I wanted to do something, but we were all so helpless, so trapped. We could do nothing but wait and hope and pray. The only place to run was to God, the instinctive, universal response of men under fire. Huddled there in the midst of fire and pain, I prayed in desperation that God would spare my life. I promised Him that if He did, I would live for Him. I swore I would do whatever He wanted me to do. He would keep His side of the bargain, but I wouldn't.

The toll from the V.C. attack was staggering: 184 of our people were killed or wounded, 50 aircraft destroyed or damaged, the runways were pockmarked with huge craters, the base bomb dump was demolished with a direct hit, and the entire base was strewn with twisted wreckage from the overnight barrage.

After that savage rain of rockets, I weathered eleven other attacks. The nightly rain of rockets became a commonplace event. Living with the constant fear of incoming fire intensified the "wait and see" war of nerves. Many times I prayed that God would turn the pages of my calendar faster, but deep in the pit of my stomach, I couldn't seem to shake the constant fear that I wouldn't come out alive. I felt like a helpless square on a bingo card waiting to be called. As the weeks dragged by, I found myself seldom straying from the shelter of the bunkers.

Another sobering incident that helped compound the growing sense of frustration and anxiety was the unexpected news I received from the Red Cross. They notified me of my grandfather's death. We were very close, and the news of his passing overwhelmed me with grief. He had been a godly Christian, and I desperately wanted to attend his funeral. I went to my commanding officer and requested emergency leave. I was denied because, in my C.O.'s words, he "couldn't stop the war for everyone's grandfather who died." I was furious. When I left his office, I slammed his door so hard it almost ripped off its hinges. To make matters worse, my C.O. was shot down by a surface-to-air missile the next day on a sortie over North Vietnam. I never saw him again. I not only had to suffer from the guilt of not being able to say goodbye to my beloved grandfather, but I had to live with the compounded guilt over my last words to my C.O.

Besides the ever-present specter of death which haunted us all, the sights and sounds of Vietnam could unexpectedly shift from the black and white drudgery of daily routine to the technicolor reality of an unearthly hell in a matter of moments. Duty in 'Nam consisted of extended gray periods of intense boredom, interrupted occasionally by the grim episodes of war. It was an emotional roller coaster which fluctuated between monotony and high intensity terror.

On one such occasion, I was driving my truck across the Da Nang River Bridge when I passed a long line of Vietnamese in black pajamas and conical hats. They were streaming by on the opposite side of the road just beyond the riverbank. Some were crying and wailing hysterically. I pulled over to the shoulder of the road, put on my helmet, and grabbed my M-16 rifle. I remember how unbearably hot it was climbing out of the cab. I walked across the street and headed past the line of Vietnamese, not knowing what to expect. As I drew closer, the sickening smell of decaying flesh suddenly hit me. Pushing my way through the onlookers, I discovered the source of attention. The ditch to the side of the road was littered with the bodies of dead Viet Cong the Marines had killed. They had obviously been dropped there by one of our patrols as a grisly object lesson to the Vietnamese traffic that passed by of what the Marines did to the Viet Cong and their sympathizers.

The pungent stench of those mutilated corpses bloating in the midday heat cannot adequately be expressed in the English language. Somehow, adjectives like revolting, gruesome and nauseating don't seem to capture the stark reality of that scene.

Several had been burnt by napalm. Their charred bodies had been decomposing in the tropical sun for several days. The image of the first corpse will be forever seared into my memory. It appeared to be a young boy about 14 years old. His body was twisted in a rigor mortis position to one side. On his chest were five small holes neatly stitched in a diagonal line across his robin's egg blue shirt. Where the bullets had exited was another story. As if under pressure, a rubbery mass of intestines and organs were ballooning out of a gaping cavity which had been blown out his back.

Even though I nearly vomited on the spot, a morbid curiosity drove me on. Further down the ditch, I came upon an even more revolting scene. A torso was lying there and nothing else. Everything from the waist up was missing, and everything below the knees was gone. What remained had been burned to a crisp by napalm. What was once a living human being was now just a charred hunk of rotten flesh.

The blunt brutality of that experience shattered my sensibilities. Billy Graham speaks of three kinds of hell: first, there is hell on earth, then there is a private hell in your heart, and finally, there's eternal hell. As I returned to my truck in shock, I now realize that I had witnessed the first two dimensions of hell. I left that sun-baked ditch by the Da Nang River Bridge emotionally crippled and bitter at the bestial insanity of what I had stumbled upon.

On January 31, 1968, the eve of the famous Tet Offensive, the V.C. opened their New Year's celebration by slamming forty rockets into the Da Nang air base. The seventeen minute attack started in the predawn darkness when the base was the most vulnerable. After the opening salvo, the V.C. gunners started lobbing in two or three rounds every 15 to 20 minutes. For nearly five straight hours, we endured the sporadic "Whoom, whoom,

whoom!'' which punctuated the night with terror. Again, we were totally helpless as we huddled in our bunkers listening to the indiscriminate explosions falling around us, wondering what would happen if we received a direct hit. With the Tet counteroffensive, our status was upgraded to "red alert.'' American intelligence had intercepted reports that the NVA were on the verge of launching a combined ground and air assault on the base. They would first pulverize the base with rockets and mortars, then follow up with an all-out ground assault.

All base personnel were split up into platoons and assigned specific fields of fire. At 2055 hours, the Air Force E.O.D. teams planned to set off random TNT charges at designated sites around the base to simulate an incoming umbrella of rockets and mortars. They hoped to trick the NVA into prematurely launching their ground assault. We, in turn, were dug in and waiting, loaded down with flak jackets, bandoliers of ammo, and grenades.

It was a total blackout as I laid behind my machine gun pointed towards downtown Da Nang. The suspense was electrifying. I could hear the clanking and rattling of tanks and armored personnel carriers maneuvering along the perimeter. Every few moments, I could make out the faint shadows of men scurrying into their ambush positions against the twinkling lights of Da Nang. The noise gradually died down until a worried silence settled over the base.

At 2055 hours, the night suddenly lit up with TNT explosions. We braced ourselves, tightened the tension on our trigger grips, and waited for the expected assault. My fatigues were soaked with sweat as I waited for something to happen. Seconds seemed like hours, but nothing moved. Our clumsy attempt to ambush Charlie had obviously been detected.

More than one of us thanked God that Charlie hadn't stormed our position. If they had, it would have been a bloody free-for-all. Still, the icy terror of waiting, wondering if my hole would be the point of contact, fearing what I would do if I were being overrun, dreading the thud of an incoming grenade, the methodic bursts of AK's, the sudden blast of a satchel charge, or a thousand other private fears exacted their toll. I was a casualty even if I hadn't taken a hit. Looking back, I honestly don't know what was worse, the pressure of waiting in the shadows for death's appearance, or facing it up front.

During my tour in Vietnam, I saw the war "up close and personal," to coin a phrase from Howard Cosell, and I saw much more than I wanted. It was not the sanitized war with its chivalrous codes of ethics or romantic notions of glory and honor, nor was it the edited celluloid version safely viewed at a distance on some television screen. It was a private exposure to the stark reality that war is, indeed, hell. Destruction and human suffering surrounded me daily. I cannot forget the smell of burnt flesh, the butchered bodies that lined the roadsides, the weeping Vietnamese, the maimed children, and the sight of mud-caked jungle boots protruding from the cover of a green poncho liner.

Finally, my time to leave arrived; the waiting was over! I survived the long night, but my private nightmare was not over. I returned home disillusioned and bitter. I felt we had been betrayed by a political expediency which did not have the heart to win a war that was unpopular. I was angry that we'd been sent to lay our lives on the line for a cause our government wanted to wash its hands of.

The emotional sensibilities of some are more vulnerable to the cruelties of war than others. Some men receive flesh wounds in war; others are afflicted with more subtle scars. Some come home with physical deformities; others return psychologically warped. Sometimes it's easier to diagnose and treat the obvious injuries affecting the body; to diagnose and treat the deeper wounds of the heart and soul is much more difficult. On the outside, all may appear normal, but inside is a festering abscess of guilt and pain — the pain of what we experienced, the guilt that we made it back when so many, more noble, did not.

I returned in just such a condition. Inwardly, I felt like one of those haggard, shell-shocked soldiers with the thousand-yard-stare straggling back to the rear after months of wearying combat. During the Vietnam War, there was a steady, unseen stream of men and women returning to America in this dazed condition. Some came home in aluminum caskets, some came home without arms, legs, or eyes, but countless thousands returned as I — to live out the private hell that had begun in Vietnam.

Psychologically shattered by guilt and bitterness, I vainly sought refuge in a liquor bottle which I lived at the end of for 16 years. There didn't seem any way out of my torment so I retreated to the numbing consciousness of alcohol. During those years, my life was steadily crumbling. I was unconsciously completing the deadly cycle that had begun in Vietnam. My marriage was falling apart, and my health was deteriorating. In 1975, disease caused the removal of cartilage in my right knee, and also in my left knee in 1979. In 1977, I suffered two heart attacks, followed by another in 1978.

I never considered myself a war hero — only a survivor. However, looking at myself in the mirror one day, I wondered if I was a survivor after all. At that moment of honesty, I looked like the walking dead. I was no longer living but merely existing as an empty shell of my former self. I had finally come to the realization that I had destroyed myself. There, looking at my face in the mirror, I reached out to the one physician who could heal me. Somehow, I knew in that supreme moment of pain where to turn. Trembling, I sank to my knees and asked God to come into my life and end the torment.

As I knelt before Him with an empty soul and a body wracked by pain and disease, I had no way of knowing that He would choose me as the raw material to fashion a miracle which would redeem my suffering and past experiences in Vietnam for His glory.

The constant feeling of helplessness back in 'Nam, huddled in the darkness of a bunker as death stalked the night, the endless days of terror, feeling trapped with nowhere to run, and the years of hopelessness and frustration which followed would now pass.

In the aftermath of that turning point, I began to take evening walks to think and sift through what had been the ashes of my life. It soon became a habit and, in time, my walking turned to jogging, and my short jogs became three mile runs. I seemed driven to run.

In June of 1983, I entered my first official race. It was 3½ miles long and I came in next to last, but I finished. In July, I tried again and covered 10 kilometers in 54 minutes. In August, I covered the course of the 8 mile Stowe, Vermont Road Race in 69 minutes and 8 seconds.

I was ecstatic. Finally, in September, I ran the Maple Leaf Half Marathon of 13.1 miles in 133 minutes. I had managed 10 minute miles.

It began to dawn on me that my compulsion to run was no accident — it was God-given. Since I had had heart attacks, I had been required to take beta blockers — medication that blocks signals from the central nervous system and impedes needed adrenaline from being released during threatening situations or exercise. However, as I trained, my body was growing stronger, I began losing weight, and my muscle tone and posture improved dramatically. Though I knew God was already allowing me to accomplish more than was humanly possible for a man with my track record, I felt He had something even greater in store for me. I trusted, prayed, and continued to train, not knowing where it would all lead.

When I learned about the U.S. Marine Corps Marathon to be run in Washington, D.C., God's will suddenly became clear. God understood the pain in my soul and my need to honor the brave men who lost their lives in Vietnam. I was to run the entire marathon of 26.2 miles and to carry with me the name of each man who had lost his life in the war that had so nearly cost me my own. It would be my contribution to the men and women who had given their all. I now had somewhere to run and a reason. I would be running to close my chapter on Vietnam on a positive note, and to testify of what God had done on my behalf. Upon completing the course, I would publicly thank Him and acknowledge the fact that my body, under normal circumstances, could not possibly withstand the physical stresses of a marathon, and that the honor of carrying the names of my comrades was strictly a gift from God.

The Lands and Records Section of the state of Vermont put all the names of the men who died on microfilm for me, and I packed that microfilm into two canisters which I could carry during the race. I began extending my distances and running with weights to simulate the weight of the canisters. Only 2½ weeks before the race, I was running 18 miles. I prayed that I would be able to complete the rigorous demands of 26.2 miles. I drew confidence from the scriptural promises "I can do all things through Christ who strengthens me," and "My grace is sufficient for you, for my strength is made perfect in weakness." By the end of the week, I completed two exhausting 23-mile training runs.

Though the physical training was intense, there were other problems to overcome. I began speaking to news reporters and on local radio stations asking for financial support for my mission. I did not have the money to make the round-trip to Washington or pay for my expenses so I called local churches and asked them to join me in prayer that I would receive the needed money. By the time I needed it, my expenses were covered — I even had a $300 surplus!

Finally, the day arrived. There were nearly 12,000 people at the starting line when the cannon went off and the runners surged forward. At about the eighth mile, Ted Koppel of ABC's Nightline and his daughter took up my pace. They said they liked my shirt. On the front was printed "USMC Vietnam 1967-1968 I put my trust in God," and on the back "Dedicated to the 57,661 (the count at the time) men who died in Vietnam." His daughter left us in the dust but we didn't mind — we just wanted to finish! As we talked about my mission, he asked if he could share my honor by carrying the names for a while and I allowed him to do so. With God's grace I did finish the race — I did so in 5 hours and 8 minutes. I had really run 26 miles 385 yards, and believe me I felt it! As I crossed the finish line, I knelt and publicly thanked God for the honor of serving Him.

I had planned to bury the canister beneath the Vietnam Memorial Wall, but bureaucratic red tape and park policy prevented me from doing so. Though I was somewhat disappointed, I was pleased when the American Legion asked to have the canisters for their archives which were being constructed in Illinois. After a brief ceremony at the Vietnam Vets Memorial, I turned the capsules over to a chaplain who would deliver them to the American Legion.

I was jubilant and so thankful that God, in His great grace, had enabled me to do what, without Him, would have been physically impossible. I felt like a privileged spectator to my own miracle.

News of my accomplishment soon reached the 700 Club which picked up my story and did a filmed interview which was broadcast to 15 million viewers in scores of countries world-wide with the message of hope that God can do for other suffering vets what He has done for me.

Since that run, God has continued to open miraculous doors of opportunity to share the redemptive, life-changing power of Jesus Christ with others who are still struggling with the unresolved mental stress, emotional trauma, and physical pain from Vietnam.

Jere Fullerton is married and resides with his wife Joan in Osterville, Mass. He has three children, including Jere Fullerton, Jr., who is a Marine embassy guard in Cairo, Egypt. Since running in the Marine Corps Marathon, he has had numerous opportunities to share his testimony through radio, television, civic clubs, Kiwanis, Full Gospel Businessmen's meeting, and church groups. Jere and his family attend the Osterville Baptist Church.

Lynn Hampton
Lieutenant, U.S. Army
Nurse
93rd Evac Hospital
Mar. '67 - Mar. '68.

9

The Best of Times - The Worst of Times

It was September of '67 when I arrived at the 93rd Evacuation Hospital at Long Binh from Tuy Hoa, where I had spent my first seven months in Vietnam.

The hospital at Tuy Hoa was built on a sandy beach. It was a troubled hospital, filled with internal conflicts and officers so preoccupied with their careers that everything else came second — including the patients. In the years following the war, observers found this to be very typical of Vietnam. Too much was built on sand.

Among other things, life had become a series of integrity tests — with human lives and health at stake. I arrived at Long Binh feeling like a tremendous weight had been lifted from my shoulders.

I was assigned to Ward Four. It was a large ward: four quonsets in the shape of a cross with the nurses' desk in the center. Two of the wings were for combat casualties, one was for venereal diseases, and one was psychiatric.

Although it was rainy and muddy and steamy and ugly at Long Binh when I arrived, I don't remember it that way. I remember a sunny Ward Four, maybe because from the day I arrived, I fell in love with it, and the love affair grew until the day I left. There were dear souls with true hearts working on that ward, and even though it was often unbelievably hectic, there was real teamwork and an overall feeling of satisfaction — of things being done right. Eventually there was a very deep "knowing," the kind of knowing that only comes from working with people under pressure — and an appreciation. I haven't forgotten a single face, or how they were, or what they meant. For me, so much of the good about Vietnam was at Long Binh, although you never could really escape the bad; they were always right there together in sharp contrast. It was truly "the best of times and the worst of times."

The psychiatric wing of Ward Four was something of a unit unto itself, with its own specially trained corpsmen and a male nurse during the day shift. There were two psychiatrists who were pretty nice fellows and not the least bit weird like the ones I had known in school.

Most of the psychiatric patients came in in a daze, filthy and ragged from the field, sometimes with leeches they were unaware of around the tops of their boots. They would be guided to a cot where they began several days of "sleep therapy," which was just that: sleep induced by drugs or the patient's own exhaustion. Most of them would probably have slept without drugs for several days; most everyone in from the field did. They would wake up long enough to drink something and maybe to eat, go to the latrine, and then return to a deep sleep. Finally, they would have a little time to talk with one of the psychiatrists and, after a few days, would be back in the field again. The army didn't officially recognize such conditions as "shell shock" or "battle fatigue." It was simply "situational trauma" for which they prescribed sleep and tranquilizers, then returned them back to the situational trauma.

Sometimes, they would talk with the nurses. Although the particulars varied, the problem was always pretty much the same: too much Vietnam, too much death and killing and horror and exhaustion — just worn out and worn down by it all. And, of course, there were always the unanswered, unanswerable questions about Vietnam which lingered in the air like an unseen stench.

The patients would usually have a radio playing, and it seems we were always hearing, "Slow down, you move too fast, got to make the morning last... and feeling groovy." I started feeling groovier than I had in a very long time. Long Binh was such a relief after Tuy Hoa — everyone was so civil. And yet the war was always with us. I think we were all vaguely aware that a lot of our joking was an attempt to keep our morale up. If something was too horrible to contemplate, we joked. If we were too tired to take another step and patients were still coming, we joked and took many more steps.

The stories that had been shocking my first few weeks in Vietnam were no longer even unusual. The "horrors of war," although not unimportant, became repetitious after a while. There are just so many things that can happen to human bodies: brains spilling out, guts spilling out, human limbs on trees, boy soldiers hurt really bad, confused, dying, and crying for their mothers.

So they slept, and told their stories, and went their ways; someone had understood. But we had all understood anyway, and there was nothing anybody could do about it. Sometimes I would watch them leaving and think, "It's not easy being cannon fodder." Most faced it like men, even though they were still too young to vote.

The patients on the urology wing usually had gonorrhea, sometimes syphilis, or lymphogranuloma venereum — a disease that causes huge, painful abcesses in the groin that had to be lanced. Every now and then, there would be someone in the agonizing throes of kidney stones, and some were wounded in areas that qualified them for urology, but primarily it was a VD wing. After a while, I started thinking of Ward Four as a microcosm of Vietnam — with those who were casualties of it, those who were overwhelmed by it, and those who were fooling around with it.

When I first arrived, we didn't even have running water to wash our hands — just basins. It was probably somewhat of a health hazard with so much infection on the ward and open wounds, too. But by then, dirt had definitely become relative. It seems much worse to me now looking back than it did then. We just got used to it after awhile. Later, Sgt. Howdyshell jury-rigged some jerry cans with spigots on them. It was such an "innovation" that they got them to work and installed them throughout the hospital! It always bothered me, too, that in an area as civilized as Long Binh, the hospital (of all places) was so primitive in comparison. But then, priorities in Vietnam often seemed strange to me. It wouldn't have had to be that way; luxuries abounded if the powers-that-be had been interested in "procuring" them.

One luxury we did have was a television set, and every evening the patients watched "Combat." At first, I couldn't believe my eyes — wounded soldiers finding solace in "Combat." Later, it made me a little sad as I realized something important was probably going on. Day after day, they watched Vic Morrow and his squad fighting their way across Europe, making progress. It all made sense. It was all so clear cut, without any of the ambiguities of Vietnam. There were the good guys and the bad guys — that simple. Those who died died for something. It was John Wayne and the movies all over again; something nice to think about even though we all knew in our hearts that "John Wayne and the movies" were somewhere in never-never land. I guess it was a little slice of madness that made strange sense over there.

There were a lot of insane things in Vietnam. I remember the day the general came to visit. We knew about it a week in advance and received orders to polish things we didn't even know we had. Since the psychiatric patients were the most able-bodied, they ended up doing most of the work.

The big day arrived. The ward was spit-polished, and the patients were proud of a job well done. The general entered with an entourage wearing starched jungle fatigues. However, apparently no one thought to tell the general that most of the patients on the urology wing had venereal diseases as he passed down the line congratulating them! I was really enjoying it. I had missed Bob Hope and thought this had to be the next best thing.

Except for those in sleep therapy, the psychiatric patients were all lined up in front of their beds, standing at attention. The general was making his way to their wing when the commander of the hospital whispered that they were psychiatric patients. He shook his head, "No," and abruptly left the ward, leaving the patients standing there with their faces falling. The rest of us were standing there more or less paralyzed in disbelief. I think we all knew it was a deliberate snub, meant to communicate that he thought they were cowards or something. I was thankful some of them slept through it.

One night about eight that same week, one of the

psychiatric patients flipped out. It always happened so fast. I looked up from some paperwork to see a pile of corpsmen and patients on top of him and ran to the medicine cabinet to get the usual big shot of Thorazine. No matter how many people pitched in to help, it was often a very unnerving matter of trying to hit a "moving target" and wondering if you were going to end up bending or breaking the needle and really hurting the patient.

In the midst of the chaos, attempting to cope with the moving target, needle poised in mid-air — STOP FRAME! I suddenly realized that this guy wasn't crazy — the system trying to restrain him was. He was reacting normally to Vietnam. He really knew what was going on. The rest of us somehow just hadn't quite let ourselves experience the intensity of that realization.

In a split second, I saw my chance and injected the Thorazine, leaving the moving target crumpled at the bottom of the heap sobbing out the anguish of us all. The patients and corpsmen were patting him, telling him it was all going to be better in a minute. But it wasn't going to be better in a minute, a year, or even ten years. I walked back to the nurses' desk with the empty syringe feeling extremely abnormal. I thought about how many of the patients looked when they came in: ragged fatigues, filthy, eyes staring blankly. Then I recalled the general in his starched jungle fatigues and wondered who was really in touch with reality and who wasn't.

But a ray of hope and meaning occasionally punctuated the madness. There was Baby Jane — half Vietnamese, half American, eight or nine months old — one of the children from the orphanage. She was there when I arrived and had been pretty sick — sick enough to have her spleen removed — and she had clubbed feet.

The movie "What Ever Happened To Baby Jane?" hadn't been out too long, and sometimes I wondered if we would ever think of her years later and say, "What Ever Happened To Baby Jane?"

She was sort of the ward mascot, and she was very important; I knew it then, but now I think she was even more important than any of us realized. In a situation with a baby like that, you really have to forget about being a nurse and become a mother. You can't hold back anything or the child won't develop properly. So we were all mothers — even many of the patients were. It wasn't the easiest thing to be doing in the middle of war, but it was the best. We were making a statement about the value of one human life in a place where death and dying were commonplace events, and life was one of the cheapest commodities on the market. We really put everything we had into it — at a time when forces that had no regard for the sanctity of human life were beginning to tear America apart. So, in the middle of a war whose unstated philosophy often regarded not only our enemy but also our friends as less then human, a very sick, discarded, "imperfect" Baby Jane was precious and loved and nurtured. "Combat" wasn't real, but Jane was, and very much in the here and now.

"Whomp... whomp... whomp... whomp!" went the med-evac rotors. It was frustrating yelling comforts to a dying soldier under the relentless beating of the chopper blades. He was gurgling and gasping for air through the slit in his throat. "I'm a nurse, I'm right here with suction, I'm watching every breath you take. Don't worry!"

He looked like a fat mummy wrapped with thick gauze bandages. His charred face was swelled twice its normal size without bandages. The patient seemed to have been reduced to nothing more than a monumental effort to breathe. He opened his lashless eyes momentarily in acknowledgement of what had just been said, then closed them again in abject misery, gathering what strength was left to blow a huge, thick, green glob out of his tracheostomy. "Slurp!" went the improvised suction. The smell was pervasive, the utterly sickening kind which you can almost taste.

There were two of them, burned to crisps — even their lungs. They were going to die, but slowly. I wondered how they had been burned, if they realized this was the end, if they had gone to Vietnam feeling that nothing bad would ever happen to them. Now they couldn't even talk, they were dying, drugged and helpless in a world of pain.

A few minutes earlier I had been taking it easy, enjoying my dust-off ride south to transfer some patients from one hospital to another, looking at the scenery and chatting with the corpsman. I'd had a busy morning. One nice thing about Vietnam was that nobody ever begrudged you a few minutes to take it easy if you could. They knew it wouldn't last long.

It soon became apparent that I was the only one on the chopper taking it easy. The crew was definitely "on duty," scanning the radio frequencies, seemingly preoccupied in responding to calls. I realized that I had thought about it all quite simplistically — take the chopper, pick up the patients, transport them to the hospital.

Before I knew what was happening, the corpsman was tapping me on the shoulder and yelling in my face, "Do you mind if we take a few extra minutes to pick up some casualties? I don't think it will be too dangerous.'' I yelled back, ''No, I don't mind.'' I always felt like nothing bad would ever happen to me. There was more talking on the radio; a tense, rather worried atmosphere prevailed. The corpsman was tapping me on the shoulder again, pointing out their smoke, when they changed their mind. By the time we got the stretchers loaded, the guys in the chopper seemed impatient, to say the least. There was more conversation on the radio.

Both patients had two I.V.'s apiece. Since I.V. fluids for burn patients must be very carefully monitored, I had just finished checking their charts, computing the I.V.'s in drops per minute, and counting each drop, when I looked up to see th corpsman turning them all wide open! I said, ''Wait! St .p! That I.V. was perfect. What did you do that for?''

What happened next is as vivid to me as if it happened only yesterday. I can still see the corpsman standing near the patients' feet. I can still see the olive drab canvas on the litter and hear the I.V. bottles jiggling, the steady whomp, whomp, whomp of the blades, and how he raised his voice because of the noise. He was tall and thin and looked very young. He said, ''I always turn all the I.V.'s wide open.'' But it was the expression in his eyes, even more than the blood on the floor and his boots or what he said, that caused me to really understand. They told a story that all the words in the world could never tell. They were utterly serious and kind of wild.

I could have given a ''mini-lesson'' on I.V.'s, but the only thing that seemed truly appropriate to say was ''Oh.'' He didn't need a lesson. After only sixteen weeks of training, he did a super job — "forcing" guys to live! Dealing with stabilized patients was just totally out of his context.

We all had the greatest respect for the dust-off people. Everyone said that you had a better chance of making it after being wounded in Vietnam, all things being equal, than if you had been in a traffic accident in the States. When precious seconds counted, they didn't lose many. When I got off the chopper, I'm sure they were glad — they didn't need complications. I left with something more than respect; not so much for minds like steel straps but for hearts and souls like steel traps. I'll always remember that corpsman and his utterly serious wild eyes. More than anything, I suppose, they were saying, "Die and I'll kill you."

By now, I had my own scrapbook of unforgettable memories: burned children, young men with limbs blown off, an old man the V.C. tried to castrate with a machete, a V.C. that reminded me of a dog carcass, and pregnant women with bullet wounds in their abdomens. Yet there was something else — there was another reality — not just in my eyes but in my heart. I had had the rare privilege of seeing some very good things in people. Not big, impressive things — just human things, very decent things. I could see patient after patient, most with long rows of sutures. Some were such characters — nothing ever seemed to get them down. I remember two guys who had removed their own sutures, and those who were in a hurry to get back to their units. Others were just nice, unselfconsciously minding their own business, playing the hand life had dealt them with a quiet dignity void of any complaining or self-pity. I realized that I owed to those boys who had paid so dearly with their flesh and blood the fact that my reality was not solely horror — they were the best patients in the world.

I had seen some melodramatic and rather depressing black and white scenes of military hospitals in old World War I and World War II movies and wondered if it was just that movies never quite got things right or if people viewed the world differently back then; and I was thankful for the atmosphere of real courage and optimism that prevailed where I worked.

I remember the ones so overcome with grief they could hardly talk, and all the noble things they must have seen in their buddies, and how they must have died. I remember the boys with awful-looking feet who could have screaming nightmares one minute and sweet, sleeping faces the next. I remember the fevers, and the chills, and how brave everybody was; and it seemed my heart would burst for the sheer love of humanity.

On the evening of November 22, I walked past the mess hall on my way to the nurses' quarters. The aroma of turkey dinner filled the still night air and brought warm thoughts of home and family and the meaning of it all to mind. Tomorrow would be Thanksgiving Day. I remember thinking how glad I was that Thanksgiving was an American thing — how "right" it seemed.

Early the following morning, we got word that casualties would be coming in — lots of casualties. Some new patients had already arrived during the night and, before long, the ward began filling up with more.

Around mid-morning, the supervisor came through talking with patients. The conversation seemed to be mostly about Thanksgiving and turkey. I was busy changing dressings and didn't pay too much attention until I overheard him griping because he didn't see a whole lot to be thankful for, being in Vietnam instead of home. His words struck me with such forcefulness that I did a "double-take." A few mouths dropped open in disbelief and one of the new patients said, "We do. We didn't think we'd live to see today — and a lot of our friends didn't." They were survivors from the 173rd Airborne Brigade who had fought at the battle of Dak To.

As the day progressed, a picture of the horror at Dak To began to take shape. Knowing they were terribly outnumbered, they had gone after the NVA anyway, well entrenched, in bomb-proof bunkers in the mountains around Dak To — Hill 875. It was something very close to a suicide mission. A fierce battle ensued that must have lasted for about four days. One patient said they had heard a general on the radio giving orders not to fall back for any reason. Even John Wayne in "The Green Berets" fell back! Air strikes were finally called in but the bombs fell short, hitting our own troops instead. Two companies had been virtually wiped out.

A sergeant came though the ward talking with patients and looking for men from his company. He said, "Every hospital between Dak To and Saigon is full — I've been through all of them. There are only two men left out of my company." I gave him some juice, and he drank it like he needed it desperately but wasn't even aware that he was drinking it. He sat there by the nurses' desk for a few minutes and left. What else was there to be said?

After seeing their wounds, the term "fresh casualty" sounded like a sick joke. The stories continued. If we had been blindfolded, the stories alone would have been enough to make you want to scream, faint, and throw-up. Many had been disorganized and cut-off in small pockets in the dense jungle and overrun. Helicopters were unable to get in; supplies had run out. Casualties could not be evacuated. Men died who would have made it even after a day, even after two, even after three days. They had fought on without water, without morphine. Living and dead alike were rotting together in heaps. They were tales of horror beyond belief. Helpless, they had heard the screams of wounded men being tortured and killed by the North Vietnamese.

At noon, when Thanksgiving dinner was served, some were awestruck at what was happening. Not long before, they had considered themselves as good as dead; now they were having turkey with all the trimmings. It was Thanksgiving, and the most meaningful Thanksgiving any of us had ever had. It was overwhelmingly obvious that life, "only" life, is cause enough for celebration; yet it was somber and sort of "numbing." There was a sense that we had witnessed something infamous.

No one noticed at first; but, after a couple of days, it became obvious that one of the patients was in a great deal of pain yet had never asked for a shot. He wouldn't even take Darvon, an analgesic not much stronger than aspirin. The thought of it actually seemed to make him feel sick — you could see it on his face. He had done a good job of hiding it, but something like that can't be hidden forever. I said to him, "I know you're suffering. You haven't fooled me for a second," and stood there looking friendly as if to say, "I'm not leaving until you tell me something." He didn't mind talking about it. He said, "I just can't bring myself to take anything. Every time I think about asking for a shot, it doesn't seem right, and when I think about Darvon, it really almost makes me sick.''

Then the whole story came out. He had been the ''acting medic'' at Dak To because all the corpsmen had been killed. He had been there for days with a lot of guys who were very seriously injured. They had run out of bandages and water and morphine. All that was left were 2″ x 2″ gauze squares and Darvon. He said, ''Every time we got people on the LZ to dust them off, we'd get mortared. I patched up the same guys three and four times just trying to get them out.''

He asked, ''Darvon is real strong, isn't it?'' Everything about him was begging me to say ''Yes.'' As convincingly as possible I said, ''Oh yes, Darvon is real strong.''

He wasn't playing some kind of a ''martyr-complex'' game — this was honest and deep. I think I may have decided to respect it and let him do what he felt he had to do. One of the advantages of being young and strong is that you heal up fast — physically, anyway. For sure he was suffering, but the physical pain, as bad as it was, was the least of it.

He needed so much to be done with it, to put it all behind him and say ''I did everything I could,'' but with memories like that, it was too soon. He was still fighting the fight with those he couldn't help, although he probably helped them more than he realized.

Darvon didn't stand for the relief of pain — it represented suffering. Maybe he had to endure for himself what it had been like for the others. Maybe if he could make it through being wounded with nothing for pain, he could look back on it and believe that it wasn't as bad as it had seemed or feel reassured that it was at least bearable. That night I cried myself to sleep.

Even then, I had a terrible sense of betrayal. But who of us could have imagined that in the end, after years of seemingly endless fighting and after future battles were fought and won and relinquished, we would simply give it away? I think I will never understand.

The Tet Offensive of 1968, was just around the corner; talk about the "worst of times" — a blur of death, dirt, vomit, courage, and paperwork; of patients diving for the floor and pulling their I.V.'s out, and lining up on the sidewalk for days; of running for the bunker, and resenting the V.C. for interrupting patient care.

Then, suddenly, home and back at Fort Campbell, Kentucky, trying to deal with the long term realities of the war and those career-minded glory-seekers again — with human lives in the balance again.

I left the Army in 1969, with conscious thoughts of having come through it all "smelling like a rose" — not because it had been easy, but because I'd kept my integrity thanks to a Christian heritage. I realize now that it was "nominal"; however, I was sincere and walked in what light I had.

In 1976, Jesus became very real to me. I gave my life to Him and experienced something so marvelous that I have compared it to skydiving: a letting go of life, trusting God to rescue, every bit as real as letting go of the airplane, trusting in a carefully packed parachute. Peace, joy, and love overwhelmed my soul.

But it wasn't until fifteen years after Vietnam that I wept over it for the first time. I returned to the States from a missionary stint in Haiti with an overwhelming burden to write about it all, to put it down on paper, to make some sense out of my troubled impressions.

But the writing dredged up far more than I could have forseen. I discovered a pain which I didn't know existed and found myself confronting a past I'd hoped was long forgotten. I was awaking to the sobering reality that I had dealt with absolutely nothing from Vietnam, and the blunted images and pent-up trauma were gaining on me rapidly.

Even though I'd been a contented Christian, the anxious specters from my past began to surface from deep within. As I struggled with buried conflicts, still unresolved and seemingly unresolvable, with unanswered questions, with the overwhelming sense of betrayal, and just plain old pain, a feeling of isolation settled over me. It was very subtle, and yet so real that I could almost sense a barrier between myself and the world around me.

There seemed to be a huge disparity between what I knew had occurred, and my perceptions of it at the time. I tried my best to break through to the reality of it, but couldn't. I suppose bewilderment best describes what it felt like — bewilderment mixed with anxiety. But I didn't know what I was anxious about.

A friend called me two or three times to say that she had seen something on T.V. about nurses from Vietnam having "delayed stress." She kept saying, "I think you've got it. Don't you think you ought to get some help?" And every time I assured her that I was "just fine," that I had gotten through Vietnam fine, and was still fine. I thought I was. I had never even heard of "delayed stress."

After a while, I stopped writing — creativity ceased. I heard about a rap group at the Vet Center in Orlando, so I started attending. At first, I simply thought it might help me get back to writing. I still didn't think anything was wrong with me, even though at times I felt physically ill. For weeks, I hardly said anything in the group; I couldn't get enough of a handle on what was going on inside of me to talk about anything. Sometimes someone else would say something that would seem almost overwhelming and I would think I was about to cry, but I never did.

I continued to feel like a "fish out of water." My Christian friends prayed but didn't understand. I think they thought I was falling away. Fellow veterans understood about Vietnam but often had no understanding of where I was coming from as a Christian. I seemed trapped in a no-man's-land which only complicated my feelings of isolation.

It was a long, dark night of the soul but not so much of the spirit. The prayers helped, the rap group helped, and Jesus was there through it all like a rock — with understanding enough for anything. His Word, that "stands sure forever," kept reminding me to rejoice — to hang loose!

I finally realized that one of my major problems was "psychic numbing" — the cause of the disparity I sensed in trying to write about Vietnam. I had pooh-pahed it when I first heard about it but finally realized that I still had some buried anger yet to resolve. My writing was the medium God used to force it to the surface.

One thing I have observed is that many Vietnam veterans are still having a great deal of difficulty with trust. They often feel betrayed by a country who wanted to forget about them and a government who sold them out. Often, they will only trust another Vietman veteran. And, although problems with trust can seriously undermine a person's entire life, I think I've come to the point where I can confidently say, in hindsight, that it can turn out to be one of the best things going for us. In my own case, I know it made me seek God in a way I might not have otherwise. I kept going until I found the truth — not content just to take someone's word for it or with something that wasn't logical — with someone else's watered down, secondhand religion. I finally found out that the only thing that can ever totally satisfy the human heart is a fresh, real experience with Jesus Christ. And I found that He isn't some quick and easy panacea — He's the answer to life!

Looking back, I think there is hope in knowing that scattered throughout the United States is a remnant of a generation who knows firsthand that something was terribly wrong with the road this country was taking. No doubt it's still a confused generation groping for answers, but thank God, at least still groping... and acutely sensitive to honesty.

I remember seeing a news segment back in 'Nam that had a lasting impact. It showed Israeli soldiers during the Six-Day War as the Wailing Wall was being liberated. They were running for it and weeping and praising God. I wanted to weep and rejoice with them, but I couldn't. I just sat there balancing on the end of my bench, shaken to the core of my being. They had obviously won over insurmountable odds. Just as in biblical times, God had fought for Israel. I sensed that something earth-shattering was happening! I think it did me more good than any church service I had ever attended. History seemed reconnected, and something had happened like it should have, for a change. I wondered if God was with America like He used to be. Maybe I should have wondered if we were with Him like we used to be. Maybe this is the ultimate question which remains.

It seems important to me to try to evaluate what it was that made America great. One man once said, "America is great because America is good." But what brought us so quickly to become a nation that one day could consider the inhabitants of another country sub-human, and the next, callously declare its own unborn children non-human? I'm convinced it's because we have forgotten who we are and where we came from. If Vietnam was anything, it was a painful barometer of the moral cancer spreading through the very fiber of who and what we are becoming as a people. I hope that its warning will not go unheeded. I pray that we will once again turn back to God and to the principles that once made us special and strong and good. If the tragedy of Vietnam can redeem even this, it was not in vain.

When the Vietnam Veterans' Memorial in Washington was dedicated, one of the reporters said something like, "Well, they finally got their monument; they built their own monument and held their own parade." My first impression of that commentary was that it was sad and unjust. But immediately I thought, "No, it's only right." Those who safely watched the war each night on the six o'clock news don't know the truth — maybe especially those. Only the veterans themselves really know. But we do know — for what and for whom.

We experienced the all-out assault on human dignity, the games, and the politics. We saw the mutilations and the terrorism and felt our country beginning to crumble beneath us — not to mention the war itself. We knew the pain first-hand, but we also know the good that was there.

Not in the clamor of the crowded street,
Not in the shouts and plaudits of the throng,
But in ourselves, are triumph and defeat.

- Longfellow -

Lynn Hampton has been a missionary to Haiti and has written, *One Look Back*, an account of her Vietnam experience. She has been a counselor at the Vet Center in Orlando, Florida, and, for the past two years, a missionary to El Salvador, working in the refugee camps and remote mountain areas. In the fall of '85, she returned to the States to join in the last battle of Vietnam — the battle for the P.O.W.'s still held prisoner in Southeast Asia.

John L. Steer
Sgt. E-5, U.S. Army
Rifleman
2nd Battalion - 503rd
173rd Airborne
Mar. '67 - Nov. '67

10

Hill 875

I arrived in Vietnam at the height of the war with that uniquely American blend of motherhood, apple pie, love-my-country patriotism, and the blood and guts, gung-ho, kill the bad guy mentality of John Wayne and "The Sands of Iwo Jima." I'd spent the last few months in airborne training, double-timing through the woods of Georgia screaming, "Kill V.C.! Kill V.C.! Kill V.C.! I want to be an Airborne Ranger, I want to live a life of danger!"

I landed with boyish fantasies of winning the war single-handedly and wasting as many gooks as possible. Chants of "Kill V.C.! Kill V.C.! Kill V.C.! I want to live a life of danger!" were still reverberating in the back of my mind when our commercial jet touched down outside of Saigon. Over the next few months, foolish dreams of a "life of danger" would take on a grim reality which would profoundly alter the boy-soldiers forever.

No sooner had the wheels of our jet screeched on the runway when the pilot's voice came over the intercom notifying us that the V.C. were mortaring the air strip. We were told to sprint from the plane for the safety of the nearest bunker. Under the barks of watchful sergeants and the scream of our departing jet, we were herded through a maze of sandbags and 55-gallon drums to the cover of a debriefing bunker. After our initial indoctrination and screening, we were piled onto olive drab buses with wire mesh screening the windows. I remember asking the driver, "Hey, why is there wire mesh on the windows?" "It's so the friendlies won't throw grenades at us." "The friendlies throw grenades at us?" I thought.

"If the friendlies are doing that, what are the V.C. doing?" I thought I came over to rescue the Vietnamese from the Red Peril and the friendlies are throwing grenades at us? It was a rude welcome to Vietnam.

After a couple initiation weeks at jungle school, I was assigned to the 173rd Airborne Infantry, 2nd Battalion, A Company, of the 503rd. My new unit was coming in from the field when I arrived at the company compound at Bien Hoa. They had just completed operation "Junction City One," the only battalion combat jump ever made in Vietnam. A few were busted up, but they were all glowing with the aura of victory. I was new but extremely proud to be assigned to that unit. It took a while to prove my mettle and earn their respect as a competent soldier; but, in short order, I formed a few close friendships.

During March of '67, our search and destroy sweeps were centered around the Bien Hoa area. We'd hump through the boonies for a few days, try to make contact with Charlie, then return to the beer and the bar girls. Occasionally, a guy would trip a booby trap or a few guys would get killed in a firefight, but, for the most part, it was the kind of acceptable attrition that I had expected. I remember standing at attention in the company area after each mission, watching some troopers receiving medals for valor. I can still hear the mournful sound of taps and see the rows of boots with the helmets of the dead propped at the butt end of M-16's in honor of the fallen.

As our unit moved further north, the operations became tougher and tougher. We had to operate in the field for longer stretches. I was growing harder also. Contact with Charlie became more commonplace. We were no longer fighting the local V.C. but crack North Vietnamese Regulars. They weren't peasant guerillas carrying vintage World War II rifles, wearing tire tread sandals, or sneaking around at night in black pajamas. They were fully equipped with uniforms, automatic weapons, pith helmets, and web-gear. They had been fighting in the jungle for many years and were a formidable foe.

I remember after one brutal firefight, I was sitting on top of this V.C. bunker with the bodies of approximately twenty dead Americans lying around, not counting the wounded. One of our platoons had stumbled into a Viet Cong ambush and was chopped down with automatic weapons and captured claymores. What was left of the dead were laid out on green ponchos waiting to be flown out to "Graves Registration." It was unbelievable what modern weapons could do to a human body. Pieces and parts were stacked upon the ponchos like scraps in a slaughterhouse. One of the choppers coming in to extract the wounded dropped off a replacement for one of the outbound dead. He had only been in the country for a few days, and his first exposure to the jungle was the mangled remains of the dead and wounded. I hollered at him to come over and stay in my bunker for the night since it was so late and he wouldn't have time to dig in. The cover of a foxhole was essential because we were getting mortared almost every night. He came over and introduced himself. I could tell he was partially in shock from the sheer savagery of what he had seen. Maybe my gesture of warmth struck a cord, because he began telling me about his home life and how only a few days prior to his coming to Vietnam, his mother had been committed to a mental institution. He just broke down and started sobbing. I just couldn't handle that. I had already begun to suppress my emotions. I cursed him and told him to shut up. I realize now that I had seen too much to cope with his crying. The bloodletting had already triggered that inner mechanism which learns to shut off any feelings which might awaken painful emotions. It was like wearing an emotional flak jacket. I guess I was afraid to let down my guard lest I start crying and couldn't stop, as well.

However, over the next few months, George proved himself to be more than a worthy soldier, and we became close friends. The last time I saw him was in a hospital in Japan where he was in a full body cast. I would give anything to get together with him today and just cry. The sacred communion forged in the crucible of combat was one of the truly redeeming experiences that many of us shared. It was a covenant which caused young men to selflessly sacrifice everything most precious and dear in this life to save a buddy under fire or simply to share a letter or a can of C-rations. Those were true friendships between men who really needed each other. They were relationships many had never experienced before and few since. It was an intimacy of understanding that still lingers today, though we only endured a few passing months of brotherhood on the battlefields half a world away.

I remember we had been humping through the jungle for several days and we were exhausted. The guy ahead of me stumbled into a large hornet's nest hanging from a vine. Within seconds, they were swarming all over him, stinging his face repeatedly. Immediately, his face swelled up with huge welts, then he went into shock. We set up

a perimeter, dug in, and waited for his dust-off to take
him to the hospital. I don't know what happened to him.
I suppose he died. After a dust-off, we usually never
found out what happened to them — departed friends
never to be seen again.

The jungles were awful places. There were snakes, mos-
quitoes, malaria, and ringworm. There was bamboo
poisoning on your arms, and it would be full of festering pus blisters. I mean ugly red pustules — not thin-
skinned, but big chunks of skin. We would have to take
a stick and scrape them off as we gritted our teeth and
watched the pus ooze out as we tried to wash it off.

One time I was tromping through the jungle with diar-
rhea so bad I couldn't go a half hour without water running down my leg. These were all common occurrences
out in the jungle. We were always wet; our feet were rotting, with big chunks of meat peeling off. We would wake
up with leeches in our noses or any other place they decided to fasten themselves.

To the dirt-eating grunt, Vietnam was an endless succession of bummers. Besides the never-ending fear of
death, we had to endure a host of miseries: merciless
humps through a sun-scorched landscape packing sixty
pregnant pounds, brain-broiling heat, hot house humidity,
dehydration, heat exhaustion, sunburn, red dust, torrential rains, boot-sucking mud, blood-sucking leeches,
steaming jungles, malaria, dysentery, razor-sharp elephant
grass, bush sores, jungle rot, moaning and groaning,
meals in green cans, armies of insects, fire ants, poisonous
centipedes, mosquitos, flies, bush snakes, vipers, scor-
pions, rats, boredom, incoming fire, body bags, and a
thousand more discomforts.

The night after the guy was med-evaced, I spotted movement in front of my position. I could make out the form of a North Vietnamese Regular in full camouflage with a Chinese machine gun. I opened up, with a soldier to my right, and dropped the enemy. I crawled out to check out the body, kicked off his soft cap, and to my surprise, a cascade of hair fell out. It was a seventeen year old girl. I was momentarily paralyzed. This was not like shooting at the pop-up silhouettes back at training in the swamps of Georgia. We had several choices when it came to a situation like this: you could go crazy, kill yourself, spit, curse, or just go on.

Another time, we swept through an area pockmarked by a massive artillery barrage. Dead and wounded North Vietnamese soldiers littered the cratered landscape. I was rummaging through the rucksack of a dead North Vietnamese soldier, looking for something to eat, when I found a picture of his wife and kids. All of a sudden I realized this was a man — not a dog or a gook — but a man. At that moment, the old "him-or-me" logic didn't seem so comforting.

By June of '67, we were working on company-size operations outside of Dak To near the Laos and Cambodian boundaries just inside of South Vietnam. On the previous operation, our company commander was shot. His replacement was an adolescent first lieutenant fresh from the States. The difference between him and the rest of the platoon was the fact that he was a typical "ninety-day-wonder" — green and dangerous. We had a lot more combat savvy than those "by the book" lieutenants.

On the night of June 21, we were informed we would be moving out in the morning to patrol a section of the

Ho Chi Minh Trail. Several of us cautioned the new lieutenant that we just didn't move on open trails because they were usually full of booby traps and potential ambushes. It was hard squirming through the gitcha vines and thorns, but it was safer than the trail. He said he had orders to get us from point A to point B in so many hours and had no choice but to send us down the trail. The night before we set out, we were all a little nervous. We all knew it was crazy, and somebody was going to get wasted.

As we sat around our positions and talked, I made friends with a guy named Strobilgon. I had never liked him before because he was young and a real smart-mouth. When I think about it now, he was just like me: insecure and a little scared, but a good soldier. Maybe that's why I half hated him at first.

The sun had not begun its westward climb when we saddled up. We were all apprehensive. Moving down an open trail was the height of foolishness — we all knew it except the lieutenant. The word was passed back, every so often, to keep a five-meter spread between us. The theory held that one enemy mortar round or booby trap would only blow away one guy, even though it didn't always work out that way. Shrapnel was blind and indiscriminate, and often strayed beyond predicted boundaries. After humping for a couple of hours, we halted along the trail for a can of C-rats and a short break. The trick was to stop by a tree so that it was easier to slide ourselves and our heavy packs gently to the ground. We could also use the tree to pull ourselves gently back up. It was really spooky. Everyone ate in silence. We were all anticipating trouble.

After a short break, we were back on the trail. After

humping another hour or so, I spotted some woven pieces of bamboo hanging like Christmas tree ornaments on the undergrowth. They were not real obvious, but my eyes happened to fall on them. I halted the company behind me and told the men to spread out. I was just about in the middle of the company, so I worked my way up to the lieutenant and showed him one of the ornaments and told him I thought we were heading into trouble. He ordered me and the rest of the men to forget about it and keep moving. A few mintues later, we heard the rhythmic crack of AK's up ahead. The lieutenant told us to keep moving forward — that it was only our own men reconning by fire. We knew the firing wasn't from American M-16's but had the distinctive sound of Russian AK's. However, we obeyed like mindless robots and walked right into a classic horseshoe ambush.

I was with weapons platoon trying to set up our 81 and 60mm mortars while the rifle squads formed a perimeter. Our platoon was on a hill in the middle of the perimeter. We were ready to fire, but we couldn't. The towering, 200 foot canopy was so thick that the mortar shells would have detonated overhead, raining red-hot shrapnel down on our own men.

We could hear the rippling of automatic weapons as our rifle squads braced themselves for the NVA assault. They charged screaming in fanatic human-wave attacks as our own men cut them down. They kept coming until we killed enough of them to stagger their assault and force them to fall back and regroup.

While the firefight was raging below, those of us on the top of the hill filled in gaps along the perimeter and cut down bamboo to make a landing zone for the helicopters to come in and take the wounded out. Then we helped the medic care for the wounded until the med-evacs could come in.

It wasn't long until I heard the urgent call for "ammo bearer!" They needed someone to carry M-60 ammo down the hill, right into the thick of the battle. I volunteered. I grabbed a case of ammunition and started sliding down the slimy hill. About halfway down, I reached a vantage point where I could see the North Vietnamese soldiers, and they could see me. Bullets started kicking up dirt all around me. I was scared but couldn't take time to shoot back — I had to keep moving or die. Further down the hill, they lost visual contact with me. When I reached the front line, I was shocked to find dead and wounded Americans lying everywhere. There was a sergeant still fighting even though a bullet had ripped through his face and had blown off two of his fingers. A good friend of mine lay there with four bullet holes in his gut. He was cool and calm. I lit several cigarettes for him while I waited to get my breath back. Many of the men were wounded, but they continued to fight courageously. I was getting ready to head back up the hill to rejoin my platoon when someone hollered, "Hey Steer! Take this guy back up with you." I threw the severely wounded soldier over my shoulder and started clawing my way up the slope. I was petrified knowing that, in just a few seconds, I would be fully exposed once again to the enemy snipers. I dug my fingers into the wet clay and pulled myself forward. About halfway up the hill, rounds started hitting all around me. I heard the sickening "thud" of a bullet hitting the guy I was carrying. At that instant, I didn't think either of us would make it to the top alive.

When I reached the top, I went back to helping give plasma to the wounded. I dreaded the thought of going down that hill again. "Ammo bearer!" The call shot through our position again. I thought to myself, "I've already been down there once. It must be somebody else's turn." My buddy Strobilgon said that he would go. They loaded him up with a case of ammo, and I told him where the hot spots were before he left. About ten minutes later, I learned that he'd been killed about halfway down the hill. I was devastated and overwhelmed with guilt. "Why didn't I go? Why didn't I go?"

The firefight lasted about eight hours. I was one of the last men to be extracted from the hill. I stayed behind to load the body bags and wounded onto the choppers. I was lifting one of the plastic bags into the chopper when a head rolled out and landed on the ground. All I could do was put it back into the plastic bag and try to keep it together. I don't know the exact figures, but our company started with a little over 100 men. Nearly 80 of them died that day. I was splattered and smeared with blood from carrying the wounded and dead. I didn't have any physical wounds, but I was torn to pieces emotionally.

When our survivors got back to Dak To, we were segregated in a roped-off area like a bunch of freaks in a circus sideshow. Soldiers from other companies would walk by and just look at us. General Westmoreland flew in and stood on the hood of his jeep like some kind of Patton and told us how brave we were and how we had kicked the hell out of an NVA battalion. Somehow his soapbox speech carried little consolation, especially for the families of the dead. That battle was a watershed for me. A part of me died, as well. I felt guilty for being alive, and for Strobilgon's death, and began to think I would never see the United States again.

My heart had grown as hard and cold as stone. I had learned to repress the last fleeting vestiges of my humanity. I was controlled by an insatiable hate, coupled with a suicidal urge to die. But when I did, I was determined to take as many of the enemy with me as I could. I guess I had just seen too much. Too many of my friends had died — some in battle, while others had ended their torment with a bullet. I had reached the borderline between sanity and a maniacal madness.

After one firefight, there were a lot of dead North Vietnamese soldiers lying around. Some of the guys were cutting off ears for neck ornaments. I never really got into that, but it didn't bother me — a lot of grunts did it. It was a ghoulish way of putting a proverbial "notch" on your gun. I remember sitting down next to this dead North Vietnamese soldier to eat my lunch, propping him up against a tree, opening his mouth, and sticking a bit of food in it. Then I started talking to that stiff like he was one of the guys. People say to me, "How could you do that? I could never do anything like that." I say to those people, "Unless you lived like a wild animal for a year in the jungle, you don't know what you're capable of."

As the months passed, it was the same old thing: move out at daybreak through the remorseless heat, beat the bush for Charlie, occasionally trip a booby trap, or take part in a firefight which would claim a few lives. By now, the hardening process was complete. Layers of thick callous covered my feelings. I didn't want to get close to anyone. I didn't want to see any more pictures of wives and kids and sweethearts. I couldn't bear hearing another family story or reading any more letters from home. I only wished I hadn't gotten so close to so many already. I couldn't stand the heartache of seeing any more men die.

When November arrived, I started entertaining a faint ray of hope that I might board the freedom bird after all. We'd survived a couple of months without any close calls, and now there were only a few months to go. Would I get to see the United States again? Then I remembered a short-timer named Sam. He spent his twelve months in hell and should have been pulled out of the field. He had "short-timer fever" and couldn't stop talking about going home. But one night about one hundred feet from me, an enemy mortar round found its mark dead center on top of Sam's bunker. It seemed so unfair. He had done his time. Why did he have to die? None of it made any sense. It seemed like every unit had a story like Sam's.

I had some conversations with God, but I talked to Him as if He were some distant being a million miles away. I wasn't sure if He could even hear me; I knew I couldn't hear Him. Like a lot of guys, I had attended Lutheran catechism classes on Saturday mornings and learned about tradition and our denomination, but I couldn't figure out why God let His Son die on the cross if He was so almighty. Maybe they had covered that, but, if they had, it never clicked. I had a little pocket New Testament, the one thing they give you when you go into the service. I tried to read it occasionally, but I couldn't read very well. A friend named George taught me to read a little in it, but I had difficulty understanding it.

On the night of November 19, we talked about our morning objective: Hill 875. It sat there right in front of us so serene and still — like the calm before the storm. There can't be too many of them up there, we hoped. They told us there were three companies of North Vietnamese soldiers dug into Hill 875. We hoped that our intelligence was wrong. When we asked for more men, we were told that it was not in the game plan.

Think about it. There were over 300 crack Regulars inside fortified bunkers just waiting for our move. They had little slits in their camouflaged bunkers to shoot the six foot Americans when we moved up the hill. There were steps cut into the side of the mountain inviting us to make a frontal assault into their waiting machine guns. It was like receiving an invitation to our own funerals.

We started up at daybreak. I was in A Company heading up the left flank. Everything was quiet. Maybe they had packed up and left? Then, all of a sudden, there was total confusion. There were bullets and RPG's coming from everywhere. Explosions were ripping across the slope. There was only one thing to do: we charged, running and screaming, right into a murderous hail of enemy fire. When we reached a plateau about halfway up the mountain, we dug in and formed a perimeter.

The hill was already strewn with our dead and dying. We had to get the wounded out or they would be more statistics. A landing zone had to be cleared to bring in the choppers, but all the trees were at least three or four feet in diameter. My company, or what was left of it, clambered back down the mountain and into the jungle to carve out a landing zone so we could get the severely wounded out. We fought our way back down, losing more and more men as we went. When we reached a suitable site, we set up a perimeter and started cutting a landing zone.

About that time, our C.P. received information that a large enemy force was moving down the Ho Chi Minh Trail straight for us. James Lozada, myself, and one other man grabbed several weapons and ammunition and moved to block the approaching enemy. We set up an ambush on the trail and waited. James and I were manning the M-60 which was well concealed in the foliage. The other guy on the radio was pacing back and forth on the trail. He knew this was a suicide mission and just kept repeating, "This is crazy. Everything is crazy." In moments, his pacing exposed our position to the oncoming enemy and drew a barrage of incoming fire which started hitting all around us. He just took off for the tree line and ended up with a silver star for his strategic withdrawal.

James and I stuck it out on the machine gun with James firing and me reloading, but they just kept coming. We were firing measured bursts, trying to keep the gun from overheating, when it suddenly jammed. I was trying to clear it when James hollered at me to kill a gook right in front of me, but I didn't see him. I was watching a lot of other enemy soldiers further back. Then, just in time, I saw him. He was lying about fifty feet away, in a prone position, with an AK-47 pointed right at us. I emptied a full clip into him, then managed to get the machine gun firing again.

Some of the guys in our company were screaming at us to come in, but we were pinned down and cut off. However, we knew we had to move or be killed. The enemy had already pushed past us on both flanks, so

James covered me while I dodged across the trail, then I covered him. He squatted down next to me behind a log. I started to yell at him to get down lower when I was jerked back by two AK-47 rounds that ripped through my shoulder and left arm. I screamed at James, "I'm hit!" but he couldn't hear me. The same rounds that tore through my shoulder hit James. He was slumped forward over the machine gun with most of his head blown away. I found out later that he earned a Congressional Medal of Honor for his bravery on Hill 875.

It was drilled into us to never abandon a machine gun to the enemy, but my left arm was hanging limp while I clutched my M-16 with my right hand. Still, I wasn't about to give it up. They were overwhelming our fire power, and it would only be a matter of seconds before I would be overrun if I didn't move. I scrambled back, half stumbling, half crawling toward our company as some of our men laid down a base of covering fire. About halfway back to our line, the radio man came in behind me tossing grenades behind us to cover our escape. When I reached our company, I was in a state of frenzy. I knew we could not make a stand here — there were just too many of them. It looked like someone had kicked over an NVA ants' nest and they were spilling all over us. They would cut through us like a hot knife through butter. Our only hope was to retreat back up the hill with the rest of our battalion. We pulled back, firing as we went, dragging our wounded with us. Some of the men were too terrified to move. I was scared, too, but if we didn't retreat, the gooks were going to finish us off. I started screaming and threatening, "Get up that hill, get up that hill or I'll kill you!!" Finally, we struggled back up the hill and reinforced what was left of our battered battalion. I moved from position to position encouraging the men after I realized my own wounds were not immediately life-threatening. When our water and ammunition started running out, ammunition cases were dropped by parachute, but they landed outside our perimeter. Of the three men who tried to retrieve the ammo, one got killed, one got wounded, and one came back with an armload of ammunition.

We didn't know it at the time, but we were not pitted against three companies in our battle for Hill 875, but three regiments of North Vietnamese Regulars. They outnumbered us many times over. They had been infiltrating south in preparation to launch the Tet Offensive when we ran into them.

The sun was sinking on the horizon, filling in the valleys and draws with pools of darkness. There were almost a hundred wounded inside our perimeter. As the night closed in, I was helping Father Watters administer plasma to fellow soldiers when the sky lit up with the hissing of illumination flares. They were floating down overhead like smoking stars, bathing our position with a lethal floodlight which silhouetted each of us to enemy snipers. I hugged the ground and pulled part of a poncho liner over me so I wouldn't be seen. In the next instant, a blinding explosion ripped through our position. When I came to, arterial blood was spurting out of my mouth and nose. There was so much that I was actually gulping it down. My ears were ringing from the concussion. My right arm was severed below the elbow, and my right leg was twisted grotesquely behind me, barely attached by fragile strands of flesh and sinew. Puncture wounds covered my body.

Pieces of flesh, splotches of scarlet goo, and severed limbs littered the ground. Men were screaming and dying all around me and, I sensed, I would soon follow.

I found out afterwards that the marking flares had been accidentally dropped by our own people. When the Phantom pilot saw the marking flares, he swooped in, releasing his deadly payload of two 750-lb. bombs right on top of us. There was no time to react — just one violent blast which hurled me through the air. One bomb exploded in the midst of our wounded, blowing them to pieces; the other was a dud.

When I came to, I surveyed the slaughter and just knew I couldn't live much longer. I had put a lot of guys in plastic bags who were not nearly as bad off as I was. I wasn't scared to die, but I was afraid of going to hell. My macho man, tough guy image was gone. I cried out to God at the top of my lungs, "God, don't let me go to hell! Don't let me..." I blacked out again, but, when I regained consciousness, all of my bleeding had miraculously stopped. Not only that, but I had a strange assurance that I was going to live. I called out for help, but there was no response. Everybody around me was dead or unconscious. God was the only one left to hear my cry. Father Watters, who had been just three feet from me when the bomb went off, was killed instantly. They only found part of his chest but knew it was him because of the cross insignia on his collar. He was also awarded the Congressional Medal of Honor posthumously for his heroism on Hill 875.

I couldn't use my left arm, that is, until my right arm was blown off — then it started working pretty good. I was nauseous and hurt like I had never hurt before in my life, but I dragged myself along the blood-drenched soil until I reached some bushes. I was looking for shelter from the enemy. It was only a matter of time before they overran us, and I had heard stories of what they did to our wounded. I found myself among a pile of American bodies. I drank one of the canteens of water that I found on one, then pulled two bodies over me, partly to keep warm, partly to hide from the enemy. I just lay there, half dead, half alive, lapsing in and out of consciousness for three days. All I remember between the blank spots are the blurred impressions of waking up and passing out, of the bright yellow ball in the sky, and the darkness. I remember hearing the desperate cries of the wounded crying for help from dead medics who couldn't relieve their agony, and I remember the random shots, the stench and the flies.

I later learned that the NVA had overrun a number of our units around Dak To and had mutilated and systematically murdered the wounded by shooting them or cutting their throats. I'll never know if I escaped the butchery because I was lying unconscious under a pile of bodies.

Seven helicopters were shot down in rescue attempts before they were ordered to quit trying until the area was secure. At last, another battalion of the 173rd fought their way to us and pushed the enemy back. I vaguely remember when they found me how brave they tried to be. They wanted to comfort me as best they could with assurances that the doctors would put my arm and leg back on, and I would be as good as new. "You'll see — you'll be as good as new." Many of them were retching their guts out at the sight of the carnage. They found me under a pile of decomposing bodies with gangrene already eating away at what was left of my shredded stump. Oddly enough, I felt compassion for them — maybe because I had been fresh and innocent once myself. Can anyone imagine the horror of 300 bloated, fly-infested American bodies, not to mention all the dead North Vietnamese soldiers? For four hellish days, the tattered remains had lain exposed to the elements alongside of the wounded.

One of the survivors walked into a meeting I was holding in Philadelphia last year. He was a tall fellow with a Bible tucked under his arm. He walked up to me with kind of a smirk on his face and asked me if I remembered him. I said he looked a little familiar, but I couldn't place him right off. I asked him if perhaps he had been to one of my meetings. He just asked me if the name Bob Gerber meant anything to me. My mind began racing back, back, back, nineteen years and eleven thousand miles from home. "Yes! Now I remember!" He was a friend of mine. We had served together in Vietnam. We embraced each other with a sentimental bear hug and moist eyes. I asked him when he had gotten saved, and he told me back in '75. He had seen an advertisement in his local paper featuring me as a speaker in his area. "I wondered if it could possibly be the same John Steer who served with me back in 'Nam. Then I thought, no it couldn't be. That John Steer was dead; he had to be dead." He remembered seeing what was left of me on a poncho liner and was positive I hadn't made it back.

I remember them rolling my bloodied body up in that plastic poncho and heaving me like a sack of potatoes into the Huey which was hovering about five feet off the ground. I remember lying on the blood-soaked floor of the chopper looking down, as we banked over the trees, at a swarm of North Vietnamese soldiers who had emerged from the tree line, blazing away at my freedom ride. Our door gunners were stuttering away with their M-60's as we flew off. I received a letter in Japan that said that our chopper had taken six hits.

After arriving at a tent hospital, I asked the doctor if I was going to live. He said, "Sure, sure, don't worry about a thing." They wrapped me up in what seemed like one long bandage. Most of my body was dressed in white gauze. I was then moved by stretcher to a chopper, then transferred to an ambulance. As the morphine took effect, I drifted into a detached state of numbness. There was not too much pain — only nausea and incoherence. When I arrived at the hospital, a lot of guys were ahead of me so I lay on a shelf for a long time before they moved me into surgery. Three surgeons worked on me for six hours. It was the first of many operations to follow. I remember waking with a fear of opening my eyes. I prayed, "God, let it all be just one bad dream." I was afraid I might wake up in hell. When I opened my eyes, I saw a white ceiling. As I looked around, I saw the trapezes, cables, pullies, and traction. There was a little Red Cross worker sitting next to me. She jumped up excitedly as if she was glad to see me alive. I looked like I was probably going to make it. I looked down and saw my right arm. It was gone from about three inches below the elbow. I remember a single tear rolling down my cheek. A white sheet was stretched tight from my chest down and, fearfully, I asked if I still had my right leg. "Yes," she said, "but they may have to amputate." My leg had been so badly blown apart and so riddled with gangrene that it looked like a huge piece of rotten flesh. The bone had been broken in several places from my thigh down to my foot. Still, I couldn't afford the selfish luxury of feeling sorry for myself when so many of my friends could no longer savor the simple fact that they were alive.

While I was fighting for my life, my parents back home received one of those dreaded telegrams from Western Union which read...

> THE SECRETARY OF THE ARMY HAS
> ASKED ME TO EXPRESS HIS DEEP
> REGRET THAT YOUR SON
> SPECIALIST JOHN L. STEER WAS
> PLACED ON THE SERIOUSLY ILL
> LIST IN VIETNAM ON 21 NOV 67 AS
> THE RESULT OF METAL FRAGMENT
> WOUNDS TO THE LEFT THIGH,
> CHEST, RIGHT WRIST WITH A COM-
> POUND FRACTURE OF THE LEFT
> WRIST AND SURGICAL AMPUTATION
> OF HIS RIGHT ARM BELOW THE
> ELBOW. HE WAS ON COMBAT
> OPERATION WHEN HIS UNIT ENGAG-
> ED A HOSTILE FORCE IN FIREFIGHT.
> IN THE JUDGEMENT OF THE ATTEN-
> DING PHYSICIAN, HIS CONDITION IS
> OF SUCH SEVERITY THAT THERE IS
> CAUSE FOR CONCERN, BUT NO IMMI-
> NENT DANGER TO LIFE. PLEASE BE
> ASSURED THAT THE BEST MEDICAL
> FACILITIES AND DOCTORS HAVE
> BEEN MADE AVAILABLE AND EVERY

MEASURE IS BEING TAKEN TO AID
HIM. YOU WILL BE KEPT INFORMED
OF ANY SIGNIFICANT CHANGES IN
HIS CONDITION.

After a couple of precarious weeks in intensive care,
I was med-evaced to a hospital in Japan. It was the most
painful experience in my life. At one point, while I was
wating to be attended to, a doctor asked me how I was
doing. When I begged him for a shot of morphine, he
started tearing off the bandages covering my stump for
a closer look. The pain was so unbearable that I started
screaming, "You... mother! I'll kill you! I'll kill you
You... !" I was cursing with the last of my strength.
"God, it hurts! Oh God, it hurts!"

I get a kick out of rehearsing all those war stories. You
know the ones about the doctor telling the patient that
his leg will have to be amputated, and the patient telling
the doctor that there was no way they were going to cut
off his leg. The macho soldier tells the doctor to get lost
and leave him alone. Then, in two weeks, the guy walks
out of the hospital with barely a limp. His departing words
are, "See, I told you you would never cut my leg off."
It didn't usually turn out that way in real life, but I was
an exception. Eventually, the flesh on my leg started turning pink again, and I kept my leg.

I spent a couple of agonizing months in intensive care
in Japan: weeks of removing painful dressings, of scrub-
bing off dead tissue and gangrene, of surgery and sutur-
ing on my stump, of probing damaged nerves, of one injection after another, of skin grafts, and traction and
draining sores, of sweat-soaked nightmares of Hill 875,
and screaming like a terrified woman. What is more, I

had to struggle with the psychological hell of feeling like my life was over — as if I should be thrown out on the dung heap — an eighteen year old armless, nearly legless, freak.

When I was well enough, I made the long trip back to the States to begin a lengthy shuttle from hospital to hospital. I went from Great Lakes, to Fitzsimmons, to Minneapolis VA Hospital, to Denver VA Hospital, and finally, to Little Rock VA Hospital. I spent the first eight months as an in-patient, and most of the next year and a half in and out of hospitals.

In short order, I married a wonderful girl from Brekenridge, Minnesota, and immediately commenced to make her life miserable. I lived in constant suspense, always expecting some gook to jump out of the bushes and start shooting at me. I carried a gun everywhere I went. I was totally paranoid and felt I had to prove myself. I suppose this was partly because my right arm was gone. I guess I was over-compensating for my disability.

I was fitted with an artificial arm with a hook, which I wore proudly. However, I remember my physical therapist sarcastically telling me, "Steer, you wear that hook more like a medal than something to be ashamed of." I said, "That's right, lady." I would go into a bar with my emotions fluctuating between bitterness and fear, depression and rage — yes, especially rage. I'd walk into a bar and people would be talking about football or boxing. "Don't they know there's a war on? Don't they know I still have friends back in 'Nam struggling a day at a time just to stay alive? Don't they understand?" Some news footage on Vietnam was playing on a T.V. behind the bar when some guy yelled, "Change the channel! Get that Vietnam stuff off there. See what the scores are on channel 9."

But it wasn't that easy for me. I couldn't turn it off. I couldn't forget. I had to remember. Who else would remember those boy soldiers who barely had a chance to live?

I went to a VA hospital, and they sent me through a revolving door of shrinks and four frustrating years of psychiatric care trying to unravel the tangled web of hate, despair, and fear. They placed me in group therapy with some hippies and "peaceniks" who spent one hour making fun of my silver and bronze stars. I ate Valium like candy to deaden the torment. I wanted to go back to Vietnam to help my friends. I wanted to win the war. Vietnam was real, but I was no longer sure if America was.

My wife would say, "Why do you cry yourself to sleep? You're always talking about the men who died. Can't you just forget it? Why do you want to die? Don't you love me and your daughter?" I did, but I loved those guys I left back on Hill 875, too. I was eaten up with guilt — guilt that I was still alive, and they weren't. Why was I still alive? I was a prisoner to Hill 875. It haunted me with its memory. The guilt was driving me to a secret determination to share the long sleep besides my fellow comrades.

Did anybody understand? People were rejoicing when Nixon got us out of Vietnam. Why wasn't I rejoicing? I wonder if the 2500 that were left over there were rejoicing? People would say to me, "Vietnam — that was a waste." You mean to tell me that the 58,000 men that died in Vietnam and 60,000 that died of suicide or other violent deaths in America all died in vain? People often ask, "Why are you telling us about the Vietnam veterans and their problems? We didn't do anything."

I spent five years living in dark bars, searching for some elusive answer. I had ruined my life and made my wife's a living hell. I'd brought Hill 875 home with me — bent on paying the final interest on my guilt by destroying myself and those around me. It was in that frame of mind that I lay awake one long night and talked to God. I wanted to commit suicide, but I was afraid I would go to hell. I cried, "God, why did you spare me from death on Hill 875? Why did I make it back? Where are You today, God?" How can any of us second-guess God? Yet, if it hadn't been for Hill 875, I may never had been driven to God in such absolute desperation.

The doctors told me I had black spots on my lungs from smoking three packs of Camels a day. My psychiatrist told me to join Alcoholics Anonymous. I just laughed it off, but now I know I was hooked on drugs and alcohol — anything to kill the pain. The next morning, I flushed all my booze down the toilet and threw my cigarettes in the trash. However, I clung to my dope. I rationalized that it was medicine. I hadn't stepped in a church for years, but I started going. I was looking for God. I was looking for a way off that hill.

About two months later in a friend's living room, for the first time in my entire life, I saw myself through God's eyes. The shield of self-sufficiency and hardness which I had thrown up around my life suddenly buckled. I was no longer better than the guy down the block nor was I worse. It was no longer a broken body which needed care, but a broken heart and soul. Somehow, at that moment of vulnerability, I knew that He understood the pain I was suffering. He knew what it was to be rejected, spit upon, cursed, and misunderstood by those He loved and sacrificed Himself for. That night some fourteen years ago, I accepted that peace which Christ, alone, can offer and realized at that moment that all the former guilt, hate, and fear had been buried forever.

When we came back, there were no bands playing, no drum rolls, no festive parades, no fireworks, no flag-waving, no "Welcome Home" banners. There was little pride or patriotism — only protests and profanity. It was a contemptuous homecoming for those quiet heroes who fought a thankless war for an ungrateful nation. Instead of appreciation, we faced scorn and galling humiliation.

Fifteen years ago, I stood to speak in a high school auditorium amidst a torrent of heckling and obscenities. Ten years ago, the crowds sat in silence. Today, some stand and cheer and, in their own awkward way, extend their hands and say, "Welcome back, John!"

It is a witness to the changing mood in our country. It is a reflection of our nation's painful reappraisal of that traumatic period. It is an attempt to understand something beyond the tired moralizing and political platitudes. Yes, war is hell. I know this better than most; but, even out of the rubble of Vietnam, something glorious and noble has been redeemed.

John Steer has been happily married to Donna for over eighteen eyars. He has two boys and two girls.

John is actively involved with veterans groups across this nation. He has served as Chaplain of the Vietnam Veterans Motorcycle Club of Missouri, the Veterans of America Chapter 70, and the Incarcerated Veterans of Missouri. He is the author of a book entitled, *Vietnam: Curse or Blessing?*, which is in its third printing and has completed a record album dedicated to Vietnam veterans called "Circuit Rider." John and his wife recently purchased a farm outside of Charlotte, Arkansas, which they are renovating for a comprehensive veterans outreach center.

Martin J. Glennon
E-4, U.S. Army
Combat Infantry Medic
2nd - 506th Infantry
101st Airborne
Jan. '70 - Dec. '70

11

The Decisive Battle

Fire Base O'Reilly had just received word that our company was moving to a new area of operation. We would soon be operating around the reactivated Fire Base Ripcord which was dug in near the A Shau Valley.

A Shau Valley was a North Vietnamese stronghold honeycombed with an underground labyrinth of weapons depots, supply dumps, field hospitals, classrooms, and sleeping quarters capable of sustaining several thousand well-armed and well-trained soldiers. The Communist forces had spent years reinforcing this area near the Laotian border and their primary supply arteries which snaked southward from their stockpiles in the north. Any operation which we mounted in or around this strategic area was guaranteed to trigger a fierce battle. Charlie wasn't about to be threatened, without a fight, just because we periodically airlifted patrols into his turf.

New moves were always met with a curious blend of excitement and anxious anticipation. Breaking well-worn patterns and hard-won adjustments to one area of operation and relocating to unfamiliar territory was always laced with the fear of the unknown, whether real or imagined.

We spent the next couple of days waiting, something you never seemed to get used to in the army. Finally, word was passed down that the choppers were scheduled to come in early the next morning to pick us up. As we packed up our gear and boarded the choppers, another company was coming on line to replace us on the fire base.

Even though O'Reilly couldn't be characterized as a

rest and relaxation center, it did provide a measure of relief from beating the boonies. The guys coming in after days of endless tension and the constant fear of death out in the jungle were always ready for the partial refuge which O'Reilly had afforded thus far. As the chopper motor revved up, churning up a cloud of dust, we lifted out of O'Reilly for the last time.

The choppers ferried us to a landing zone about five kilometers away from Fire Base Ripcord to an area bordering the A shau Valley. Our initial orders were to patrol a particular ridge and try to make contact with the enemy. We plodded through the jungle for what seemed like miles without spotting any sign of the enemy. In spite of the discomforts of humping many pounds of gear through the relentless heat and humidity of Vietnam, I was relieved we hadn't run into Charlie thus far. However, the knowledge persisted that we would soon be entering the heart of NVA territory.

That night, our company set up camp. As the men were settling into their nighttime positions, a single shot punctuated the sounds of the jungle. It wasn't the familiar crack of an enemy weapon but the sound of one of our own M16's. The call for "Medic!" soon followed, but since the wounded soldier was in one of the other platoons, another medic responded. We waited anxiously, not knowing whether the shot was a signal that Charlie was near or not. In short order, word filtered among the men as to what happened. One of our own men had supposedly shot himself in the foot by accident, but most of us knew that it wasn't really an accident but a deliberate act to buy a quick pass out of the field. The strain of jungle warfare could drive men to such acts of desperation. Some guys couldn't take the strain and figured it was better to suffer a self-inflicted wound in the foot than get blown away by one of Charlie's booby traps or ambushes. His med-evac chopper was in and out in a few minutes. The rest of the company then settled in for the long night.

Just as fast as the night curtain fell upon the jungle, the early morning sun spread its golden rays across the jungle canopy. It was July 20, 1970. I had weathered a restless night and spent my turn at perimeter guard filled with nervous apprehension. However, nothing had happened and I was still alive. No matter how depressing the previous day had been, there always seemed to be something refreshing about the sunrise. As the company gradually stirred to life, I made my morning rounds dispersing pink salt tablets with the usual yellow malaria pills which gave your skin a jaundiced hue.

We broke camp at 0700, split up into three platoons, and moved out briskly. First and third platoons headed out with the company commander, while our second platoon forked off in another direction. Our plans were to rendezvous later in the day with the other two platoons.

We had traveled about a klick along a ridge when our point spotted two NVA soldiers guarding a possible encampment. The point immediately opened up on the two. One of the guards bought it and dropped into the bush; the other was hit but managed to crawl into the jungle, leaving a trail of blood. Our lead elements pursued the wounded soldier but somehow he got away. Whether his body was lying in the undergrowth or he was able to warn his comrades that we were closing in was a question none of us could answer; however, knowing he couldn't be found left a nagging sense of insecurity.

While we waited for the order to saddle up and move out, I heard what seemed like an audible voice behind me whisper, "Your company is going to be wiped out." I quickly whirled around thinking that it was one of the guys with a sick sense of humor, but no one was there. While I tried to figure out whether I really heard something or was simply entertaining some stray thought, I couldn't shake the feeling that the message carried an ominous forboding of what really lay ahead. In a few moments, the point element returned. The word was passed down the line to move out again and link up with the other two platoons. As the shadows began to lengthen, we set up our position for another restless night waiting for the unexpected.

I had been in Vietnam for six months. Medics were only supposed to be in field combat for six months because their casualty rate was so high; but, because of the policy of gradual de-escalation, there were not enough replacements to go around so my field duty was extended. It was a bad break but, like most other things in the army, I didn't have much say in the matter. As the familiar lines in the "Charge of the Light Brigade" read, "It was not for me to reason why, but for me to do or die!" On the bottom line, that was precisely what I was afraid of.

Our platoon sergeant pulled the night watch before me. His tap on the shoulder awakened me from my sleep about three in the morning. As I came to, I was surprised to smell the pungent odor of fish in the air. My first impression was that the gooks were so close that I could actually smell them. After six months in the country, my senses were quite developed. I knew they were only a few feet away. I whispered my concerns to the sergeant, but he thought I was just imagining things and brushed my comments aside. Other than the smell, the jungle was quiet, but I knew they were out there waiting. I kept my finger on the trigger of my M16, strained my eyes and ears for the slightest sound of movement, and also waited.

Meanwhile, back at Fire Base Ripcord, our boys had come under heavy fire and were taking a tremendous pounding. Charlie had put the fire base on notice that he wouldn't tolerate us in his backyard. The NVA launched a coordinated attack to crush our resistance and overrun the base. The firestorm at Ripcord had actually started about three weeks earlier. On the morning of July 1, Ripcord received its first whoosh of incoming rounds. One of my buddies back at the base, James Kilgore, provided the following account:

> *I was on watch when the first round impacted. The first four or five rounds were bracketing rounds, which showed the enemy if his aim was too high or too low. The enemy had us in his sights and was adjusting his fire for maximum effect. The NVA gunners were sizing us up like a skilled boxer waiting to deliver the decisive knockout to his opponent.*
>
> *The incoming fire upset the base as if someone had just kicked over an ant hill. As the men swarmed for action or cover, the stream of enemy firepower intensified. During the next twenty-two days, Ripcord received a steady barrage of RPG's, 82mm mortars, 51 caliber machine gun and AK 47 fire. The casualty toll*

piled up. Many, like myself, suffered multiple wounds; others were not so lucky. The death toll also climbed. Both the battalion commander and artillery and field captains were killed.

The constant bombardment forced us into our bunkers. Charlie had us so effectively pinned down that we had become virtual prisoners in our underground shelters. A trip outside could be fatal. We were even forced to urinate in cans and dump them outside of the bunkers because the fire was too heavy to risk going out. When we ran low on water we sent a detail out, but they were quickly wounded and forced to scramble back like scared rats.

I was an 81mm mortarman with radio linkup with the fire control center and headquarters. We monitored all the radio traffic and had a pretty good idea of what was coming down. The news wasn't very comforting. Charlie was also listening to our communications and, by his repeated thrusts, seemed to know where to hit us. Company C had been all but wiped out. The defensive perimeter they had established was overrun in one night assault. At one point, the battle got so hot that we were forced to fire on their position to repulse the NVA attack.

The toll in killed and wounded was so high in the line companies protecting our perimeters that they could no longer adequately protect the fire base. It was only a matter of time before the combination of around-the-clock shelling and human wave assaults would completely overwhelm our defenses. An entire company was chewed up over a five day period. Each night the platoon was overrun. Like clockwork, the seesaw slaugher was repeated the next night until we were gradually whittled away.

After nearly three weeks of uninterrupted hell, our situation had deteriorated to a point of desperation. A breakout was impossible. Fresh reinforcements or supplies were unable to make it into Ripcord. We seemed trapped in a V.C. stranglehold which they were methodically tightening. Each day the number of dead increased. We had no recourse but to stack their plastic body bags near the chopper pads to bake in the sun. The choppers couldn't get in so they just kept piling up. I'm sure an unspoken question among many of us was whether we would be the next one on the stack. At this point in the siege, we were so completely encircled by incoming fire that the enemy was walking rounds all around our fire base at will. With our line support crumbling, escalating enemy pressure, and an inability to resupply, our commanding officers found themselves caught between the difficult decision of calling for outside help or evacuating.

When a supply chinook tried to run the NVA gauntlet and resupply us with a load of much needed equipment, it received a direct RPG hit and crashed into our ammunition site. The dump exploded and burned for six hours, pro-

viding a spectacular fireworks display. At this point, it was no longer a question of whether to hold out and take our chances. We were inevitable statistics if we stayed any longer. It was now simply a matter of how to get out. The only glory left was not in sacrificially staying but surviving.

Our officers hatched a plan to call in CH47 choppers which would land at alternating positions on the three chopper pads on the base so the enemy would not know where we were going to land next. Hopefully, we'd outguess the NVA gunners with our hopscotch plan of evacuation. Our plan worked, but before we left, we blew up everything we had to leave behind so Charlie would be deprived of any aid and comfort.

While the events back at Fire Base Ripcord were reaching their disastrous climax, my unit was continuing to probe deeper into enemy territory. It was the morning of July the 22nd. As we assembled our gear and once again prepared to move out, I couldn't shake the nagging feeling that we were being watched. The jungle seemed to have eyes even though there was no evidence of the NVA. I felt like we were entering a trap which would soon be sprung.

At about the same time, the Battalion Command Post back at Camp Evans was intercepting an NVA radio transmission concerning our company. The Battalion Command radioed us to immediately regroup and move out in the opposite direction. They knew something that we didn't.

The company C.O., lieutenants, and sergeants gathered in a huddle to compare notes. The rest of the company, which now numbered only about seventy-five men, were wondering what they were planning for our lives. We were now positioned about one mile due east of what was left of Fire Base Ripcord. I had a gnawing, gut feeling that things were going to heat up very soon. The tension in the air was a token of the gathering storm which would soon break with a lethal fury. However, before the day was out, I would discover that proverbial silver lining.

During this lull, I pulled out my Gideon pocket New Testament which I had repeatedly been drawn to over the previous two months. Our platoon radio man by the name of Bill had been instrumental in encouraging me to open the pages of that little book. He was already a seasoned Christian when he arrived in Vietnam and had proven to be a vital source of inspiration to the rest of us. As I picked my way through the scriptures, the words took on a fresh relevance. The scriptures were alive — they were speaking to me. On the last couple of pages were written several key passages which cut to the heart:

> *For God so loved the world, that he gave his only begotten Son, that whosoever believeth in him should not perish, but have everlasting life (John 3:16).*

> *That if thou shalt confess with thy mouth the Lord Jesus, and shalt believe in thine heart that God hath raised him from the dead, thou shalt be saved (Rom. 10:9).*

> *These things have I written unto you that believe on the name of the Son of God; that*

ye may know that ye have eternal life, and that
ye may believe on the name of the Son of God
(I John 5:13)

As I pondered the meaning of these verses, I found myself praying to receive Christ as my personal Savior. As I muttered a prayer under my breath, a tremendous sense of release welled up in my spirit and, in spite of the pressure of battle, an unseen burden suddenly lifted from my life. As I knelt on the life and death threshhold of one decisive battle that I didn't want to face, I found myself voluntarily settling another silent battle warring in my heart which would have a decisive, life-changing effect upon my eternal destiny. At that pivotal moment of truth, I accepted God's terms for salvation and unconditionally surrendered my life to Christ. This was not just another shallow, foxhole conversion uttered insincerely under the stress of battle. It was a genuine decision to serve Christ. When I finished my prayer, I quickly scribbled my name and date of salvation in the back of my New Testament and tucked it back into my fatigues. Little did I realize how far-reaching that decision would be at the time.

The break soon ended. The lieutenant returned and clued us in to the new change of plans. We were going in a different direction. My platoon was ordered to move out first. As we headed out, we all sensed that the lieutenant was not telling us everything. The tension was so thick you could cut it with a knife. Droplets of sweat broke out on my forehead. It was 11:30 in the morning and getting hot.

As our point started out, we could hear the faint thunder of explosions far off in the distance. Something big was happening back at Fire Base Ripcord. Our point element had advanced no farther than 150 feet when an explosion shredded a tree in front of them. The V.C. had fired a rocket-propelled grenade to stop us from going any further. As if on cue, we all hit the jungle floor in unison. The popping of AK 47 small arms fire erupted on all sides. The rear two platoons were also taking heavy fire. As I hugged the ground I heard the cry, "Medic! Medic!" Someone was calling for me to move forward to the front, but I couldn't move. I found myself frozen in fear, on the razor edge of panic. I just started calling upon Jesus. All I could say, over and over, was "Jesus, Jesus, Jesus!"

One of my buddies, who was a Christian named Tom, crawled over to me and said, "Doc, I think it's going to be all right." He knew what was happening. Even though he appeared tough as leather on the outside, he had a sensitive heart of gold. He knew I had to get it together because the lives of the others depended upon it. "I think we're going to make it." Within an hour after speaking these words, a lethal round slammed into him. Those words of comfort were the last ones he spoke, but they gave me hope that my prayer of desperation would be answered.

I pulled myself together and decided to respond to the cries for help. I couldn't afford to lose it now. I was scared to death, but this was no time to be a coward. Anyway, I had long since lost that false illusion of invincibility and immortality so peculiar to youth. To keep my sanity in the constant face of death, I had repeatedly reconciled myself to the fatalistic conclusion, as so many others in war, that when your number's up, it's up. When God decides to check you out, nothing is going to change His mind. Anyway, my life was in His hands now, and if He decided to call me in, at least I was ready to go.

Some of the men in the point had suffered shrapnel wounds. As I started crawling forward, Bill said, "Doc, wait! Don't go up now!" I wondered why he said that, but I now know he was speaking with the voice of experience. Charlie knew that the medic provided the pivotal moral support for the platoon. If the medic was put out of commission, the rest of the men would be forced to treat their own wounds plus fight the battle. Often, he was the fine line between life and death. His absence would undermine the unique sense of security which he, alone, provided.

As quickly as the firefight erupted, it died down. We were wondering whether this was simply another hit and run ambush of Charlie where he had now quietly faded back into the jungle. After a few anxious moments, the platoon sergeant decided to stand up and check out our position. But no sooner had he raised his head when the crack of a sniper round ripped through one side of his face and out the other, taking teeth and tissue with it. The pop-pop-pop of AK 47 fire ignited. I rushed over to the sergeant. There was a gaping hole torn in his cheek, and he was bleeding profusely. "Doc," he tried to get the word out, but he was having difficulty speaking with his mouth filled with blood. I pulled off my medic's pack and gave him emergency treatment: a blood filler and a transfusion of dextrose. He was bordering on shock. He looked at me and said, "Things are getting dark. I think I'm going to die." I told him, "No you're not! You're going to make it!" I spoke as confidently as I could, but

I really wasn't sure whether he'd make it or not. Still,
I tried to calm his fears the best I knew how.

About 500 feet behind us, the 3rd platoon, under Captain Hankins, was also pinned down and taking heavy
fire. A friend by the name of Buster Harrison described
what was happening:

> *When the lead elements in 2nd platoon got
> hit, all hell broke loose. The NVA started drop-
> ping mortars in on us. Luckily, they overshot
> us with the first salvo. By the time they zeroed
> in, we had safely shifted our position.*

> *After several mortar rounds exploded
> harmlessly a few yards away, the NVA rushed
> our position. I remember looking through the
> thick brush and seeing the khaki-clad soldiers
> with their telltale pith helmets and AK's
> blasting away as they charged us. One was run-
> ning right towards me, and I had my machine
> gun pointed right at him. Just as I began to
> squeeze the trigger and send a burst into him,
> another one of our guys dropped him. I opened
> up with a raking stream of automatic fire which
> chopped up the jungle like a weed eater. I pull-
> ed the pin on a grenade, lobbed it into the
> jungle, then hurriedly scrambled over to Har-
> rington's position. We moved cautiously along
> the hillside until we ran into a few more guys
> from our platoon, including Doc Draper and
> a guy named Alabama.*

> *In the confusion of the firefight, our platoon
> had been hopelessly splintered in the dense
> jungle. We formed a protective circle and*

waited for Charlie's next move. We could hear rustling in the thick undergrowth on our right flank but didn't know if it was some of our guys crawling towards us or the enemy, so we shouted out our secret platoon password "CURRAHEE!" The counter call shot back, "CURRAHEE!" We sighed an air of relief and relaxed our trigger fingers. Another call rang out. "Medic!" Doc Draper and Alabama started towards them, crouching as they went. Even in the midst of the most vicious firefight, the medic was duty bound to a sacred, unspoken covenant of mercy with the men which he had to respond to, even if it cost him his own life. The guys we thought were ours were gooks. They had suckered us into a trap. I remember as a kid watching those old World War II movies when the Japanese would use the same cries for help to lure our guys out of their positions and pick them off. Doc and Alabama had gotten only a few feet when the NVA opened up and cut both of them down. Doc was killed instantly, and Alabama was hit so bad that he died later that night. We, too, opened up and drained a few clips into the NVA position until their firing stopped.

A million thoughts raced through my head. None of us knew what was going to happen next. I didn't have much hope we'd get out of this one, but I forced myself to stay calm. If I panicked, I would only seal my death warrant. During those desperate moments, I prayed and asked God to spare our lives. Suddenly, the roar of jets filled the air. They thundered over our position, just above the tree tops. They released their payload right on top of Charlie. The concussion was unbelievable. I thought, "If Charlie doesn't get us, our own bombs are going to wipe us out." The heat from the blast hit us in the face like a hot gust of desert wind. Those pilots were good. They placed their bombs with precision just a few yards in front of us and right on top of Charlie. I'm absolutely convinced that if they hadn't arrived when they did, the only way our unit would have gotten out of that firefight was in body bags. Those bombs were an answer to prayer.

Somehow through the confusion, word got to us to move up the hill and secure the high ground. We were still taking sporadic sniper fire. Rick, our squad leader, made his way to the crest of the ridge before he was seriously wounded. The rest of what was left of 3rd platoon had managed to regroup on the slope of the hill, but none of us wanted to move to the top, even though we could hear Rick yelling for help. I looked around and asked if anyone would go with me, but no one wanted to volunteer. Finally, a black trooper said he'd go. We started cautiously up the hill, watching each other's flanks. Every few moments, a round whizzed overhead or thudded into the ground near us. After what seemed like hours, we spotted Rick lying in the bushes. While I crawled

*over to him, I whispered in a low voice, "Rick,
can you hear me?" I could hear the weakness
in his voice. "I don't know." "Can you
move?" I asked. "No." I rolled him onto his
side, grabbed him under his arms, and dragged
him back to the black guy who had been covering me. There wasn't much we could do
because our medic, Doc Draper, was already
dead. As dusk settled, we did the best we could
to dig in and hoped we'd make it till morning.*

Meanwhile, those of us back in 2nd platoon were also
trying to regroup. Our lieutenant gave the word to pull
back and try to join up with 1st and 3rd platoons. I guess
he felt we'd have a better chance by concentrating the
remnants of the entire company tnan waiting out the night
alone with our small platoon. As we started edging back,
a torrent of small arms fire suddenly opened up and again
pinned us down. We were cut off. Charlie had surgically
isolated us and was moving in for the kill. We all crawled together into a tight protective circle just in case the
NVA charged us. I felt like I was in an old western when
the settlers formed their wagon train into a tight circle
to fight off an attacking war party of Sioux. We each
held our M16, watching for any movement immediately
in front of our position. We had only one M60 machine
gun, which was capable of laying down enough concentrated fire to cut a tree in half, so we set it up to cover
a fire zone with about a 45 degree sweep of our circle.

The NVA usually had special units called "sappers."
They were gooks stripped down to a loin cloth, covered
with camouflage paint, and loaded down with grenade
belts filled with special charges which gave off tremen-

dous flash explosions to produce confusion and fear. These guys were nothing more than suicide teams. They were often doped up and had their arms and legs tied off with tourniquets so that they could take several rounds and still keep coming before we could drop them. Little did we know that a sapper unit was slowly crawling towards us through the thick undergrowth.

The small arms fire had subsided, bringing a deceptive calm in the battle. Bill and the lieutenant were on the radio with the fire control center back at Camp Evans. They were directing artillery fire around our position. The rounds were roaring overhead like an oncoming locomotive. It was comforting knowing that their destination was Charlie's position. The wounded platoon sergeant who had taken a round through his face was in stable condition. It was the first time in three hours that things had quieted down. It was 2:00 in the afternoon, and things were not over yet.

While we waited, I took my New Testament out of my pocket and started reading from the Psalms. My eyes fell upon Psalms 91: "He that dwelleth in the secret place of the most High shall abide under the shadow of the Almighty. I will say of the Lord, He is my refuge and my fortress, my God; in him will I trust." As I read on, the words of that soldier's Psalm written by David, the warrior king, flooded my heart with comfort. David had long ago discovered the refuge of peace in God that I, too, was finding in the heat of battle.

While we were laying in that protective circle watching for movement in the jungle in front of us, we were periodically lobbing fragmentation grenades into the bush to keep Charlie off guard. Suddenly, the enemy sapper squad which had been quietly closing in heaved about ten satchel flash charges into our position. We immediately opened up and sprayed the jungle with fire. The smell of burnt powder hung in the air. Fortunately, the satchel charges were not as powerful as our grenades so only a few of the guys suffered minor shrapnel wounds from the dirt and debris kicked up by the explosions.

The muffled "thooomp! thooomp!" of mortar rounds exiting their tubes signaled incoming fire. The NVA had opened up with 61mm mortars and were trying to drop them right on top of us. However, because the terrain was very irregular, it made it difficult for them to locate our exact position. Things died down again. I felt a slight pain in my head and instinctively reached for the area and felt the telltale moisture of blood. I had taken a tiny sliver of schrapnel in the temple, but it was only a superficial wound.

Cobra gunships finally arrived on the scene and were circling protectively overhead, but the enemy was lying low. They feared those lethal gunships like a field mouse caught out in the open fears the predatory eye of the hawk. The Cobras were crisscrossing our position, firing their rocket pods into the jungle around us. The undergrowth was so thick that they couldn't see if their rockets were hitting the mark. One round exploded near a cluster of our own men. I heard their screams and crawled over to them to give medical aid. I found one of the guys had taken a jagged piece of rocket shrapnel which ripped his cheek wide open so that it just hung down his face like a flap on a tent door. I tried to stop the bleeding but had difficulty trying to put a compress on his jaw for fear it would restrict his breathing. After about 45 minutes, the Cobras had exhausted their ammunition and flew off. We hoped that the enemy had also packed up and left, but when one of our men stood up for a look, a sniper round cracked by just missing him. The NVA hadn't gone anywhere, they had only dug in deeper.

Meanwhile, back at Camp Evans, headquarters had again intercepted enemy radio communications all around us. The picture painted was not good. If they didn't send in help soon, we were going to get wiped out. As we waited for the NVA to charge, we could hear the roar of jets screaming in low from the east. Our air support was back, and this time they intended to finish the job before the day was out. It was already dusk, and the darkness was closing in rapidly. The pilots radioed us to pop off a smoke canister to locate our position. They soon spotted the dye-colored smoke filtering upwards through the jungle canopy, pinpointing our position. At the same moment, Camp Evans picked up an order to the NVA battalion surrounding our position to move in and annihilate us. Charlie intended to deliver the decisive "coup de grace" in a matter of moments. We were hopelessly outnumbered and outgunned, and he knew it.

At that crucial moment, our F4's and F100's knifed in along the jungle edge of our position releasing their 750 lb. bombs. The explosions gouged huge craters into the jungle floor and heaved tons of dirt and jungle growth into the air which rained down all around us. The concussions were so enormous that they made my ears ring. A few of our guys had their eardrums ruptured by the blasts. The jets streaked in again on another pass and dropped the rest of their payload. The jungle was being chopped up like it had been placed in a huge blender. Every time a bomb went off, the ground lurched in one immense upheaval before settling back upon itself.

The jets had accomplished their mission and veered off for the safety of their bases. Camp Evans was still monitoring the radio frequencies, but the NVA radios had gone silent. It was 6:00 p.m.; we had been in battle for seven hours, but we had survived. We had one more night to spend in the jungle. If we made it, we would be airlifted out in the morning.

The next morning, Delta Company tried to link up with us. Knowing that reinforcements were on the way was a tremendous morale booster. They couldn't locate our precise position on the map, so we used sporadic rifle shots to direct them to us. When they found what was left of our decimated unit, it wasn't a pretty sight. The head count was fifty-one wounded and twelve killed. The other two platoon medics were dead. The C.O. was wounded in the neck, and one of the lieutenants was killed. However, by the grace of God I was spared.

I had spent most of the night tending to the wounded. The wounds varied from minor shrapnel wounds to bullet wounds in the chest, arms, and legs. The worst were the abdominal wounds. I had difficulty stopping the bleeding in these. One of the men who had taken a hit in the gut died the next day.

When Delta Company arrived, they started blasting out a clearing for the med-evac choppers to come in. By afternoon, we had loaded up the last of the living plus a pile of green body bags. The blades spun faster and faster as the engine torque mounted, whipping the scrub brush and small trees back and forth in its wake. With a final surge of power, the chopper tilted slightly forward, then lunged upwards in a slow, spiraling ascent through the hole in the jungle canopy, slapping the surrounding trees with the departing downdraft. As my chopper lifted off, we were cramped for space and a few of us were forced to sit on the body bags containing the remains of our fellow soldiers who had died in the battle. As we climbed above the jungle, tears started rolling down my face. My mind was replaying the vivid scenes of yesterday's battle. The torrent of emotions was overwhelming as I considered the mercy of God on my behalf. The only thing which separated me from those young men in the plastic bags was God. Though grateful, I knew I couldn't take any more without cracking up. I had seen enough of the horrors of war in six months to last forever. As we passed over the deceptive tranquility below, the door gunner turned and looked into my eyes but said nothing. The expression on his face was a study in emotions — all of which showed that he understood.

That was my last flight out of combat. In a few months, I boarded a plane for home. I was not the same man that had touched down in the Republic of Vietnam a year before. The innocence of youth had been lost somewhere in the jungles of 'Nam. I was returning now a different man: not just a man who had been forced to grow up before his time or a man changed by the sobering realities of war, but a man who had been profoundly changed by what I had experienced on that July morning.

Though, at the time, I didn't fully understand the full impact of what had happened when I surrendered my life to Christ, in the years which followed my tour in Vietnam, I gradually came to realize just how decisive that battle really was. It had been a conflict not just of flesh and blood but a battle which involved my very soul. It was a battle of immense proportions which had encompassed the very scope of my eternal being. The decision I made that day on the jungle floor permanently altered the course of my life. Though difficult months of adjustment followed, the decision that had been made during the heat of combat was honored by Christ. He spared my life and has faithfully preserved my footsteps to this day.

Martin Glennon, his wife Lea, and four children live in Valporaiso, Indiana. He is an independent insurance agent in his area and an active spokesman in the Gideons. Martin and his family attend the Hegewich Baptist Church.

Robert L. Peragallo
S/SGT, U.S.M.C.
M-60 Gunner
1st Battalion, 9th Marines
July '65 - May '66

12

Tail-end Charlie

It was July, 1965, when my replacement company of green grunts came ashore in Da Nang. Unlike hundreds of thousands of servicemen who would follow as the war escalated, we didn't have the luxury of arriving by commercial jet but arrived by a cramped troop ship. I was soon assigned to 1st Platoon, Bravo Company, 1st Battalion, 9th Marines. We'd been brought over to replace the whole battalion which was rotating back to the States. Da Nang was supposed to be a relatively safe rear area. It was our platoon's duty to run security patrols around the air base about six miles south of Da Nang. We occupied a piece of high ground on the last hill between the ocean and the jungle. Looking east, you saw the sparkling bluegreens of the South China Sea. Looking westward, you saw the lush beauty of the jungle which stretched in a chain of moss green mountains towards Cambodia. In many ways, Vietnam offered a visual paradise of land and skyscapes. But the breathtaking beauty of summer sunsets splashing iridescent pastels above an emerald horizon veiled many a subtle danger.

Each night, our platoon ran two ambush patrols, one squad from 6 to midnight, the other from midnight to dawn. That night, we pulled ambush duty on the first shift. Our squad leader, Corporal Bradly, informed me that I would be walking "tail-end Charlie," a term for the last man in the column whose responsibility was to cover rear guard, something I would psychologically be doing through the rest of my tour, even after I graduated to other positions in the platoon. Though I was always guarding my rear, whether consciously or unconsciously, it would slowly dawn upon me that someone else, far more perceptive than myself, was walking tail-end Charlie for me, even though I didn't recognize it at the time.

Though it was my first patrol assignment, it was not without significance. It was my responsibility as rear guard to protect those in front of me in case Charlie popped up out of some spider hole or hit us from behind.

I was still so green that I couldn't understand what I was doing walking tail-end Charlie. I had been trained as an M-60 machine gunner — a dangerous if not prestigious position. But I knew I'd better not ask any stupid questions. I figured it was for my orientation. Still, I had only the vaguest idea of what was happening, and I wasn't sure I really wanted to know, for that matter.

As I prepared for my initiation patrol, I wondered what I was doing here. When I had enlisted in the Corps, I had visions of being handsomely decked out in dress blues on romantic sea duty. There was no Vietnam in June of '64. I kept telling myself that I was too young for this. I soon found out that the oldest man in the squad was only 24 — he was affectionately referred to as "gramps."

As the evening shadows deepened, I moved out awkwardly on my first patrol in the bush. I was a bit self-conscious but tried to act as if I had been walking tail-end Charlie all my life. I did draw some comfort from the knowledge that being the last man in the column lessened the odds that I'd step on any booby traps. If one of our guys tripped one, it would be in front of me. However, I soon discovered that this position also had its drawbacks. I kept getting dizzy in the darkness,

twisting and turning around, and was having difficulty
keeping up with the column because of jungle density.
Unless you kept your attention on the guy in front of you
as you zig-zagged through the jungle, you might zig when
you should have zagged and get swallowed up in the bush.
I later heard stories about guys wandering out of the column, never to be heard from again. However, the grunt
in front of me didn't seem too concerned. Why should
he? He was secure in the knowledge that I was covering
his rear. But as I struggled on, I reminded myself to keep
cool. This was no t.v. war but the real thing, and if I
didn't want to get one of those proverbial rounds in the
neck that everyone in the squad was always joking about,
I better watch myself.

After plodding nervously through the bush for several
hours, we backtracked to our base. When we reached the
top of the hill overlooking our air base below, the night
suddenly lit up with a spectacular fireworks display. The
yell went out, "Dig in, dig in!" Sapper squads had infiltrated our perimeter and were running helter skelter
through the base lobbing their satchel charges. From our
perch, we could see choppers burning and the elongated
shadows of men silhouetted against the flames running
in frantic patterns.

The guy I was digging in with half jokingly said, "Your
first night, huh? Well, welcome to Vietnam," cynically
drawing out the word V-i-e-t-n-a-m. I felt stupid but asked
him what was going on. He said the air wing was getting
its butt kicked. He told me to relax because the heat
wasn't coming our way. We wouldn't do anything until
the show was over; then we'd move out in the morning
to sweep the area.

In a bizzare sort of way, it did seem like we had box seats for a lethal light show. A violent cacophony of machine gun bursts and flash explosions filled the night. Every few moments, a satchel blast would light up the sky like an enormous flashbulb. Staccato streams of tracers traversed the base, scratching red streaks through the blackness. With so much fire power being released, I was sure that hundreds of V.C. were getting hit. The fireworks lasted about an hour and a half before dying down.

About an hour before first light, we moved out cautiously to sweep the base perimeter. We were all jumpy. Each of us carried a green flare to signal our own guys if they accidentally opened up on us in the darkness. We were extremely nervous, knowing that the perimeter bunkers were manned by equally nervous, trigger-happy office pogues which we sarcastically referred to as "Remington Raiders." My body was clammy with sweat as we moved cautiously across the sandy perimeter. The acrid scent of burnt cordite still lingered faintly in the air. We were all praying for the light of dawn.

Our squad leader relieved the pressure by popping a flare to announce our intentions. A languid sun revealed scores of V.C. strewn across the perimeter. Many were grotesquely tangled in the twisted strands of razor wire. Some still had undetonated satchel charges the size of backpacks strapped to their bodies. Others lay nearly naked, stripped of their satchel charges by their comrades. Those that had made it past the gauntlet of our outer perimeter ran indiscriminately through the base heaving their explosives at helicopters and cargo planes. The battlescape was a scene of chaos. It looked more like the V.C.

sappers had ravaged a wrecking yard than an air base. Twisted metal and the gutted remains of aircraft littered the tarmac. The charred hulls of choppers and disembowled transports were still smoldering from Charlie's devastating free-for-all.

A thorough search of the area uncovered only a few satchel charges and the stripped bodies of slain V.C. They hadn't carried any guns. All the frenzied firing had been from our side, yet they had still devastated the base.

The whole experience was sobering. Marines prided themselves in the art of camouflage, but what we encountered revealed that the V.C. could teach us a lesson. They had floated in along the coast in little wicker baskets. They had coated their bodies with oil and then rolled in the fine white sand. Except for the jet black hair and crimson splotches, the bodies almost blended into the sand. The saying that "experience is a hard teacher because it gives the test first and the lesson afterwards" suddenly took on a new sense of reality. Somehow, my green uniform and big steel helmet seemed clumsy and ill-suited for my new line of work.

The events of the previous 24 hours had stunned me into a new respect for the enemy and a deep forboding of things to come. I had survived my first patrol, but I was not sure that I would be so lucky in the days ahead. What tightened the knot in my stomach was the passing comment of another grunt who said that our company had earned the name "Bloody Bravo." They acquired the nickname the old-fashioned way; they earned it through the highest K.I.A. and W.I.A. ratio in the batallion. I couldn't shake the fear that I would one day contribute to that score card. I didn't know then, nor would I fully appreciate the fact until after Vietnam, that my fearful premonitions were premature.

Looking back, I've had years to refine my reflections of Vietnam. From the experiences and afterthoughts, one supreme conclusion has been distilled: I survived to write this account because of the all-pervasive grace of God on my behalf. Even back in 'Nam, separated from home, alienated from God, and scared spitless, His providential hand was protecting me.

In a few days, we moved from the rear area to a hill called "55." These hills usually got their designation from some undulation on a grid map. Our new home got its name because it was 55 feet above sea level. There were many godforsaken hills in Vietnam with impersonal numbers for names. However, they weren't impersonal to the loved ones back home who received telegrams from the Dept. of Defense that their husband or son or lover had died there. Those hills were consecrated ground in the memories of those who were left behind. By war's end, these barren outcroppings stood all over Vietnam as silent memorials, marking some of the fiercest battles in the war.

Hill 55 was a maze of barbed wire, sandbag bunkers, and trenches. Our command post occupied one of the larger bunkers. We would be running patrols from our new home into two gook strongholds known as the "Iron Triangle" and "Happy Valley." We called it Happy Valley because you were always happy if you made it out.

As the weeks passed, we made many patrols into the bush. I saw numerous W.I.A.'s, but had yet to experience a K.I.A. firsthand. The Iron Triangle was notorious for its booby traps, and almost every patrol returned with a foot blown off or a shredded leg. Some booby traps were so powerful that after some poor guy tripped it, there was barely enough of him left over to put in a poncho liner. We all knew this was happening daily, but so far, it had maintained its distance. Things would soon change. Intelligence had received reports that a large unit of V.C. had penetrated the area. Our orders were to try and make contact.

We were huddled in our bunker one night trying to keep dry from a downpour when Sergeant Al came in and told us we were moving out in the morning for a long patrol. He was noticeably aggitated by the assignment. We started out early the next morning in the predawn darkness. We took two gun teams. I manned the first team. We also took along a 60mm mortar team, an indication that things would probably get hot. After an uneventful morning passing through the serenity of several villages, we got orders to set up an ambush at a designated site along the China Sea. Corporal Wilson, our point man, said we'd hole up until sunset then dig in on a bluff overlooking a road near the beach. Intelligence expected the V.C. to come in by sampans under the cover of darkness and move down the road. Our job was to intercept them.

As night fell, we hurried to our new position. As we left the beach and started up the hill through the jungle edge, Wilson snagged a trip wire. Wilson had been in 'Nam for nine months and was a seasoned "salt." He had developed an uncanny sense for smelling trouble. Fortunately, he had been cautiously feeling his way forward, looking for possible booby traps in the undergrowth, when his hand touched the telltale wire. It didn't go off. We all froze. For a few anxious moments, Wilson didn't move either. He just held the wire in his hand.

While we waited, Wilson gently followed the wire to its source. We could hear him whisper, "It's not a booby trap; it's a noise-maker." We all sighed an air of relief. I could remember playing "kick the can" as a kid. If you got to kick the can, it sounded the alarm to the whole neighborhood that you had made it to home base. The Viet Cong had their own version of the game, but with deadly results.

The noisemaker was a large can containing a wound-up spring attached to a string tied to several smashed cartridges which would spin and beat against the can if released. It was crude but effective.

Wilson yanked it free, wrapped it up, and tucked it in his fatigues for a souvenir. We then set up on top of the hill in a straight line perimeter. One foxhole faced the road and sea; the alternating hole faced a small village set back in the jungle. We were keyed up as we waited for Charlie to make his move, but as the hours passed, nothing happened. Except for the normal noises of the jungle and the faint sounds of waves breaking on the beach below, the night was uneventful.

At dawn, Wilson had a little surprise for us. He called me over to his hole and showed me what we'd thought was the harmless noisemaker. It had a homemade grenade attached — one of Ho Chi Minh's special. It was a 3 inch piece of bamboo with a lead ball and filled with gun powder, wax, and a little reservoir of acid. When you pulled out the string, the acid dripped down the hole, ignited the powder, and we were calling for a med-evac. Wilson treated it like a toy, but we were just glad it hadn't gone off.

Our orders were to stay put until noon then head back. We dug in deeper and waited. After an hour or so, I was told to give my position to a buddy named Dutchnowsky and set my gun up closer to the road. As I was moving into place, the lone crack of a rifle shot, followed by a hail of sporadic small arms fire, suddenly opened up all around us. We, too, opened up. We couldn't see anyone — just the muzzle flashes.

Then it stopped. I heard Sergeant Al call out for Dutch. There was no response. The next thing I saw was a couple of our guys dragging Dutch's body up the hill. Sergeant Al was crying. Dutch had taken that first sniper round just above his left ear. I almost vomited. The impact of a high velocity round in the head had the same effect as splattering a watermelon with a shotgun. Suddenly death became very personal. As I looked at what was left of Dutch, the lethal seriousness of being an M-60 gunner hit home. It was not a very enviable position after all, seeing that the average life expectancy of a gunner in a firefight was only seven seconds. Along with corpsmen and F.O.'s, we had the highest mortality rate. Charlie wanted the machine gun knocked out of action as soon as possible and concentrated all his firepower to accomplish that task.

Only five minutes earlier, I had been in Dutch's hole. It could have been me getting wrapped in a poncho liner instead of Dutch. My heart was pounding so hard I felt like my chest would explode. The adrenaline rush was overwhelming my system. I could hardly speak. Burned in my mind was the visual horror of Dutch's head. We were all badly shaken.

Sergeant Al radioed in and received word to search the

V.C. village a few hundred meters to our east. None of us liked the idea. We knew Charlie was waiting for us to make his day. Common sense, emotions, and physical instincts protested, but when the familiar "saddle up" echoed across the hilltop, we all seemed to respond mechanically. As we clambered out of our holes, the tree line opened up again and pinned us back down. It was a free fire zone, and everything was fair game.

Just then, a gook in white pajamas darted out of a hooch and sprinted across a clearing on the edge of the village. It was like trying to tag a fleeing jackrabbit. Like idiots, we all opened up. He didn't have a weapon and had obviously been forced by the V.C. to run out to draw our fire so they could locate where our automatic weapons were positioned. It worked.

Rounds started whining by my head and kicking up dirt all around us. Boyhood fantasies of being a John Wayne soldier suddenly faded. I just buried my head in the dirt and prayed the firing would end. They kept it up for about a minute then stopped. Then it was our turn. We opened up on the village with our M-60 fire and started chewing up every hooch in the village. If we weren't going to search the village, we were at least going to destroy it. The red tongues of tracer fire we were pouring into the hooches set the village ablaze. Even at a distance, we could hear the crackling and popping of dry thatch and brittle bamboo going up in flames.

As soon as our command post on Hill 55 heard about our firefight, they sent a reinforcement platoon to help. They were coming up the beach on tanks. We were in trouble and Charlie knew it. If our guys didn't get here soon, there wouldn't be anyone left to rescue. I felt like

a beleaguered cavalry detachment waiting for Rin Tin Tin
and the 7th Cavalry to show up.

Finally, we heard the distinctive clanking of treads and
the throaty diesel roar of three tanks as they rumbled up
the hill. What followed was an awesome demonstration
of American firepower. M-60's, 50 calibers, and 105
rounds from the tanks cut loose on the burning village
and leveled the smoking remains.

We then loaded our dead and wounded on the back
of the tanks and climbed aboard. There was something
comforting about sitting on the solid hulk of thirty tons
of warm steel. But we were all frustrated. We didn't know
if we had won or lost. We hadn't even pursued Charlie
or established a body count. We had simply made contact, shot up the countryside, and retreated with a load
of casualties. We hadn't destroyed the enemy. There was
a silent, seething rage building in each of us. We wanted
to fight instead of run. We felt like a boxer with one hand
tied behind his back. We wanted to do to Charlie what
he'd done to us. All that we wanted was our pound of
flesh. What made matters worse was that suddenly it
dawned on me that we'd been sent out here in the first
place just to serve as bait to lure the V.C. out. The plan
had worked, but the whole experience didn't sit well. We
were heading back with the hollow accomplishment of
confirming Intelligence's suspicions.

I never met a Christian in 'Nam, but God was a regular
topic of conversation. Often, our casual raps drifted into questions about why God allowed wars, why innocent
people suffered, or why God's dealings seemed so unjust. Back in the world, it was convenient to pass the buck
and blame natural disasters on "acts of God," but war

was another matter. After all, whether we were willing to admit it or not, even in the most vulnerable sessions of bar talk, we were the ones killing and being killed, and we didn't seem to need any help from above. Deep down inside, I think we all knew this.

The life and death sobrieties of combat inevitably led to other discussions about God and eternity. At some point, the blunt realities of war forced most men into considering their chances of making heaven. I believed God existed, but He seemed so distant and unable to be related to. At the time, I had serious doubts whether the Man above really cared enough to involve Himself in my private affairs. Riding back on that tank with some of our guys lying dead beside me only reinforced those doubts. Looking back, however, I now know how intimately God was involved in my life. The fact that I had walked away from my baptism of fire was God's way of laying the foundation for understanding His providential protection. I didn't appreciate it then, but this firefight was the first in a series of close calls which would eventually cause me to face the facts.

The first of these close calls involved a temporary assignment to chopper duty. Command had come up with a rapid deployment plan called "Sparrowhawk." Several squads were kept in reserve with two twin-bladed Chinooks to be airlifted in just in case other units in our battalion got caught in a heavy firefight or were in danger of getting overrun. Because we were only scrambled in critical situations, we spent most of our spare time hunkered down in our bunkers secretly praying that requests for our assistance would never come in. We were not so lucky.

We got an urgent distress call from Delta Company who was pinned down and getting wiped out. As we were descending into the hot LZ, the entire chopper shuddered violently as a recoilless rifle round slammed into the tail section blowing the door to pieces, freezing the rear rotor, and rupturing the hydraulic fluid lines. Hydraulic fluid was spraying everywhere, the chopper motor was smoking badly, and we were spinning nearly out of control with only the use of the front rotor. It was near panic in that claustrophobic cabin as we rapidly rotored down. Charlie saw we were hit and started pouring all his firepower into the disabled chopper as we descended. We were all terrified that the fuel tanks would go up and cremate all of us trapped inside. Just then, the bulky chopper dug into the ground with a bone-jarring crash. Like frantic rats on a sinking ship, we clawed our way to safety before the chopper went up in a fireball.

Another flirt with death happened on Christmas day. We were into a three-day truce pulling a local security patrol through a rice paddy about three klicks from our base when we stepped into an ambush. Charlie was not very good at honoring cease-fires. In the panic of the first few seconds, we took several casualties. As I was dragging one of the wounded back, a bullet hit my magazine pouch on my right hip, spun through the casing, exploded out the other side, and jerked me around before lodging in my belt buckle. It felt like someone had punched me in the stomach. At first, I feared the worst and looked down expecting to see my guts hanging out, only to discover a hot piece of lead stuck in my buckle.

There was an added bonus with that miracle. As the rest of the squad was spraying the tree line, I pulled out

a collapsible "LAW" rocket, jerked it open to firing position, and, in the process, somehow dislodged the rocket
from the tube assembly thereby arming it. There I was,
standing out in the middle of a rice paddy, holding a live
round in my hand which could disable a tank, waiting
for it to go off and turn me into history. The firefight
suddenly stopped with me standing there waiting to explode. All I could do was lay it down gently and walk
away as fast as possible.

The last confirmation that God had cast Himself in the
role of "tail-end Charlie" on my behalf came towards
the end of my tour. We were on a big operation just
outside of Hoa Thay, eighteen miles south of Da Nang.
It was my eleventh month. I was a "short timer" with
only 45 days left before I would be rotated back to the
world.

I was now walking point and leading the first squad.
I was still a gunner, but anybody that survived more than
six months was usually given a squad regardless of your
M.O.S. On this large search and destroy operation, our
squad was assigned the point position. Because of my
bush experience, the skipper asked me to walk point. We
had two M-60 gun teams. My expertise with the gun gave
my squad an extra edge in knowing where to place it. We
would need it because we would be crossing the most
hazardous field of fire in 'Nam: a wide open rice paddy.

Wading out in the open through the muck of a rice paddy towards a possible ambush lying in a tree line fifty
yards in front of you wondering if some V.C. sniper had
silhouetted your neck in his sights was a horrible feeling.
Being completely exposed with your life a potential split
second away from a bullet's sudden impact heightened

every physical sensation. Time seemed to slow; the visual images of jungle green, the sounds of sloshing through 2½ feet of gunk, the sucking sensation of mud and water oozing in and out of your combat boots, the position of your platoon members, the calculated distance to the safety of the nearest dike, the stench of the rice paddy, even the distant contrail of a jet passing safely miles overhead electrified every nerve.

If the tree line opened up, your anchor of hope was in setting up those guns in the most strategic spot to lay down fire superiority as fast as possible. That's why I was selected to walk point. The rest of the squad felt secure in my experience of directing the gun teams in a firefight.

Early into our sweep, we entered the village of Hoa Thay. It bore the signs of being recently evacuated. The cooked food in the hooches gave every indication that the villagers knew we were coming and had fled in a hurry. Even the stray dogs looked like they sensed danger.

I halted the platoon and radioed our lieutenant that something was coming down. I sensed a possible ambush. The lieutenant heard me out but ordered us forward. He was green and gung-ho. That's why we lost so many overly zealous lieutenants.

We moved forward cautiously until I spotted three V.C. running up ahead carring Russian carbines. I opened fire and apparently wounded one. The rest of the squad came on line and laid down a base of fire. This sighting confirmed my suspicions. Charlie was ahead of us, shifting men into positions. The lieutenant came running up to get a handle on what was happening. After explaining the situation, he told us to check out a body count. We found none, but located some fresh blood and signs they had dragged the wounded man away.

I recommended to the lieutenant that we set up our night perimeter and he agreed. But the lieutenant spread us out too far: two men in a hole with one sleeping for an hour, the other watching. We liked to have visual and voice contact in our perimeter, especially when you knew you were in Charlie's backyard. The lieutenant didn't see it that way and had us dig in a good 50 yards apart. He'd also positioned my squad at the point of contact. We didn't like it — his inexperience was going to get us killed.

To make matters worse, we got a replacement sergeant dropped off on that night's resupply run. He had been a desk jockey lifer with no combat experience. He was also full of Marine Corps zeal, the kind that had little practical experience. Between the lieutenant and sarge, we were in a world of trouble.

However, us old-timers had a special little game we would play on those occasions when we wanted to regain control from the greenhorns. It was called a phony firefight. There's a distinct sound to a carbine. Our corpsman carried one, and our radio operator carried a 45. About a hour after sundown, we'd have them fire their weapons like crazy to simulate a V.C. attack. Then, the rest of us would open up, empty a few clips, throw a few grenades, scream "incoming!", run around, make a lot of noise, call in mortars, and make an urgent request to the lieutenant to tighten our perimeter before Charlie overran us. It always worked. The way we were running around in our combat version of a "Chinese fire drill," we should have all been awarded the Bronze Star — if not for valor, at least for acting! The V.C. probably thought those crazy Marines were wasting ammo again.

Morning brought a new day and new problems: the rookie sergeant took over my squad. I was given second squad. I thought it was a bad call at the time, but the tragic events which soon unfolded showed me that the switch saved my life. First squad was told to move out first and run a security patrol. About an hour out, we lost radio contact with them. They had run into an ambush of two fully-equipped V.C. companies of 200 men. They had inadvertently wandered beyond their zone and had sprung a trap. Only two of the fourteen squad members lived, and they were severely wounded. When the V.C. searched their bodies, they were so shot up and unconscious that they thought they were dead.

As we rushed to their assistance, we could hear the tail end of the firefight. The silence was not a good omen — we all suspected the worst. As we broke into a clearing of two large rice paddies bordered by clumps of six foot elephant grass, Charlie opened up. It was the most intense field of fire I had yet experienced. The bodies of first squad were strewn ahead of us in the clearing. We were skirting the edge of the elephant grass when they opened up. The fire was so thick that it literally scythed down the squad. At least every other man was cut down. We managed to make it to a shallow trench, then returned fire with our automatic weapons and M-60's.

The rest of the platoon and portions of 2nd platoon came up and started firing. Just then, the lieutenant led 3rd squad on a frontal assault on the tree line directly in front of us, but half of them dropped in the paddy before they reached a narrow dike about 100 yards from their goal. The lieutenant was killed along with several others.

While the remnants of my squad set down a strong base of fire, we moved forward through the elephant grass trying to flank Charlie. The V.C. saw what we were doing and shifted their fire towards our movement. Though the V.C. were hidden in the tree line, we could still make out their muzzle flashes and see where their rounds were hitting around us. At least I hadn't got it in the neck yet. They say you never hear the one that has your name on it. If you hear it, it was history and they were on target. We were hearing a lot of rounds around us at that moment.

We linked up with 3rd squad and, with our combined firepower, we seemed to be gaining fire superiority as we moved forward. This was the impression Charlie wanted us to have. They were allowing us to funnel in so the rest of our company would also be sucked into the trap. With so much sustained fire, we were starting to run low on ammunition. The rest of the company had not yet reached us and we were wondering where they were. In about five minutes, the lead elements of the other platoons came in sight in their efforts to link up. The tree line erupted again. Suddenly our situation grew desperate; we were running out of ammo and were sandwiched in a crossfire between our guys and over 200 V.C. The rest of the company had to fire over our heads to hit Charlie. We were pinned down and getting picked off like flies.

We had dead and wounded Marines lying all around our position. Some were crying for a corpsman, but the pressure was so intense that we didn't have time to treat the wounded. We were locked in a deadly impasse; we couldn't pull back, and we couldn't move forward. The only bright side was that our radio man was still alive.

He had only a bullet wound in the leg. We still had a radio lifeline to the rest of the company. They, in turn, were calling in artillery and air strikes.

Waiting in that no-man's-land for artillery support seemed like it took forever. Finally, the familiar locomotive sound of shells rushing overhead signaled relief. The wood line exploded with huge geysers of smoke and debris. Charlie stopped firing.

We all sighed a premature air of relief and called for an urgent med-evac to take out our wounded. It seemed like the battle was over. In a few minutes, a lumbering twin-bladed Chinook settled down. When the dust cleared, we rushed to load our dead and dying into the bowels of the waiting med-evac. But the deceptive calm was abruptly broken. The V.C. again opened up, peppering the chopper with a fusillade of disabling fire. Those poor guys in the chopper were getting it again, but it made no difference to Charlie. The only thing he wanted to get out of the battle was dead Marines.

Just then, two Phantoms showed up overhead. They were circling like hungry vulture sizing up their prey. They dove fast and came in at treetop level along the jungle's edge firing Zuni rockets and dropping 500 and 1,000 lb. bombs. The sky was soon swarming with Skyhawks and F-8 Crusaders which screamed in, dropping napalm and strafing the tree line with the buzz saw sound of 20mm cannons. With each pass, the napalm pods would detach from the jet's underbelly and tumble end over end until they rolled through the canopy, engulfing the tree line with boiling orange balls of liquid hell. We were so close that we could actually see the pilots as they made their passes. The distinctive smell of burning napalm floated across the paddies. With each blast, we felt the invisible shock wave of heat rush over our position like a hot gust. We were all praying that, in the attempts to take the heat off, one of those napalm pods wouldn't fall short and incinerate us in the process.

While our jets were pounding Charlie's position, Alpha and Delta companies were being airlifted in, in an end-run maneuver to cut off their retreat. It was now our turn to give the V.C. some of their own medicine. The plan worked perfectly. The enemy withdrew right into our trap. It was a Vietnam turkey shoot. The body count the next morning stood at over 175 confirmed V.C. dead.

Even though there was little left of our original platoon, Stars and Stripes listed our casualties as light! First squad had been wiped out, my second squad sustained 50% killed or wounded, and our platoon had only twenty men fit for combat duty after the battle. I helped load the bodies of twelve close friends on the choppers beside a number of other dead marines heading back to the morgue unit at Da Nang.

Flying out of the scene of the battle, I couldn't shake the knowledge that it could have been me leading first squad into that fatal ambush instead of someone else. I had a gut feeling that that last minute switch was more than coincidence. Too many near fatal misses had occurred thus far to conveniently write off as mere luck. Something else was responsible for protecting my neck. Still, the full confidence that a sovereign someone was pulling tail-end Charlie for me had not sunk in.

When our tattered unit returned, our C.O. took pity on what was left of Bloody Bravo. We were sent back to Hill 55 to stand perimeter duty and lick our wounds.

During the first week, I passed a kidney stone and was med-evaced to the Hospital Ship Repose. My health was shot. I had intestinal parasites and kidney stones. Besides my physical condition, I was psychologically shattered. I was teetering a hairbreadth away from a complete physical and emotional breakdown. I told myself I couldn't take any more.

I spent a month urinating in a bottle. I still had a month of combat duty remaining, so the Corps wanted to send me back to 'Nam to finish my tour. Fortunately, I had a compassionate doctor who gave me a thorough physical, checking for any excuse to keep me out of the field. He found a good one; I had a thyroid nodule the size of a golf ball. The surgery to remove it guaranteed a ticket home. After recuperating in a hospital in Okinawa for two months, I was eventually sent home.

My first exposure to the world was one of profound shock. At a stopover at L.A.X., I was confronted by the people I was supposedly fighting for. I was spit upon, ridiculed, and cursed as a baby killer. It was not the warm welcome home you might expect for a young man who had risked his life for the sake of freedom. That experience produced an intense frustration and disillusionment. However, in some ways God would redeem the injustice and misunderstanding for my eventual good. For one thing, it prevented me from fully putting my experience in 'Nam behind me. It forced me to reappraise my reasons for going and the reasons for my coming back. Over the next couple of roller coaster years, those nagging questions finally drove me to the recognition that my duty in Vietnam was not in vain. Whether it had been politically right or wrong is a matter which may never be settled. But whether God had a purpose, as far as my life was concerned, was personally resolved in 1971. The recognition that a merciful God had preserved me was slow in coming, but when the truth finally came to light, it caused me to break before Him. He had covered my tail through the valley of the shadow of death, and the assurance that He would continue to preserve my paths in the future has proven itself a reality until this day.

Bob Peragallo, his wife Linda, and three daughters live in Bonners Ferry, Idaho. Bob is the Senior Pastor of Praise Church — a thriving fellowship which he pioneered nine years ago.

Ronald E. Mason
Sgt. E-5, U.S. Army
Forward Observer
1st Battalion, 2nd Brigade
5th Mechanized Inf. - 25th Div.
July '66 - July '67

13

Forward Observer

I felt trapped. I had graduated from high school and had a job — that was all. There seemed to be no way out of the black ghettos of New York City. Because of the dead end look to my life, I volunteered for the draft. Besides, the handwriting was already on the wall. By that point in the war, the draft boards were already mailing induction notices to blacks in disproportionate numbers. The way I figured it, it would only be a matter of time before I was sucked into the "green machine" anyway. On December 12, 1965, at the age of nineteen, I received my draft notice to report for active duty in the United States Army. Six months later, our chartered 707 touched down at Tan Son Nhut Air Base and disgorged another load of adolescent soldiers.

My first impression of the country was offensive. Stepping from the air conditioned crispness of cabin air into the stifling humidity of Vietnam was like stepping into a steam room. In seconds, rivulets of perspiration were running down my face and neck, soaking my khakis with sweat. I soon learned that in Vietnam, you were always sweating — everything sweated in 'Nam. Not only was the heat unbearable, but the stagnant air had a stench of burnt gunpowder and human waste.

After a week of processing, I was herded onto a convoy of deuce-and-a-halfs heading south to Cu Chi, the base camp of the 25th Infantry Division. I didn't particularly like my destination since I was a proud paratrooper, fresh from jump school, heading for a "straight leg" outfit. I wanted to wear the "Screaming

Eagle" patch of the 101st Airborne, but was sent, instead, to the 25th. I'm now glad that I was.

The 25th Division from 1966-67, was a well-coordinated unit whose leaders were not ambitious glory-hounds or promotion-addicts. They were conscious that the men who filled the infantry squads and platoons were human beings just like themselves, with the same desires to return to the dreams and loved ones they'd left back in the world. Therefore, they operated in a manner which would insure the best results and give the soldier in the field the maximum chance of making it through the whole thing without being sent home in one of those reuseable metal coffins.

After a day-long truck ride, I was standing in formation at brigade headquarters waiting for orders that would send me to my unit. I had been in the country almost three weeks, having traveled on a convoy down the famed "Highway One," but the closest thing to action that I had noticed was the distant thunder of artillery and F-4's taking off for some air strike. "This is not such a terrible war," I thought. Then I was given my orders to report to the 1st Battalion, 5th Mechanized Infantry. As the Spec-4 handed me my orders, he commented, "The 5th Mech, brother — you're going to the butt-kickingest unit in the 25th!" At that moment, an uncomfortable mixture of pride and fear came over me. "Was this what you wanted Airborne Tuffy?" I asked myself, thinking I was heading for a little more than I thought I wanted.

Later, I arrived at Company A and was assigned to the heavy weapons platoon. Mortars were my M.O.S. I rather liked that job because it carried an extra edge of safety. In weapons platoon, I wouldn't have to go on any of those small killer team patrols and would always be safely surrounded by plenty of friendlies in case Charlie turned up. The sergeant led me to my "hooch," a large tent with a wooden floor, and showed me where I should stash my gear.

A week later, we were saddling up to go on my first operation. I was actually excited. I didn't really know what to expect but consoled myself thinking, "How bad could it be?" I had been trained pretty well back at Fort Gordon, Georgia, and I felt ready. I walked through the company area to the motor pool where we were boarding armored personnel carriers or "tracks." The 5th Mech went everywhere in tracks and, once in the area of operation, we dismounted and patrolled on foot. The tracks we loaded onto were modified and looked a little different from any of the ones I had seen back in the world. Each one had a powerful 50-caliber machine gun mounted on it with a half-inch thick steel shield welded around where the gunner would stand. The opening behind the "50" where the other squad members would stand was ringed with sand bags two layers high which gave great cover in a firefight.

My first two months in the field were spent in comparative safety. Not only was I in the weapons platoon, but I was also in the Fire Direction Center. This is where the data was computed for the mortars' firing direction during a fire mission. We always stayed with the company command post which was secured by 30 to 50 men, in addition to the tracks, while the line platoons were patrolling the bush. I felt we would always have a good chance if Charlie should hit us. Being with just a few guys or cut off in the face of a firefight was my greatest fear.

In October, my secret nightmare became reality. The forward observer in the second platoon was hit and I was chosen to take his place. "My God," I thought, "patrols, ambushes, and twelve man killer teams!" My greatest fears were coming to pass, and the heat under me would now be turned up some five hundred degrees. The statistics on F.O.'s were shocking. In the field, their life expectancy was about three days — three seconds in a firefight. Carrying that radio made you a primary target when the shooting started. It was like wearing a bull's eye on your body. Charlie worked at knocking them out, along with the machine gunner, during the first few seconds of a firefight. I didn't like being picked, but there was nothing I could do. My vacation was over, and, with the casualty stats on F.O.'s, I considered my future prognosis to be grim.

The new role I was suddenly cast in placed me in a critical life-and-death position directing the fire power that could save our men from getting wasted. The accuracy of my coordinates was often the thin line between life and death. It was an awesome responsibility which carried extreme risks. With my new assignment, I was sure that I had received a one way ticket to oblivion. But I wasn't the only one cast in that role. The only difference was that I had been volunteered against my will — He was doing it willingly. At the time, I had no way of knowing that, but God was guarding the fields of fire around me against the day when I would find Him.

I put my gear together and reported to the lieutenant. He welcomed me to the platoon and told me what he expected of me. I should stick with the leader of the patrols and know where I was at all times in relationship to a

map and our location on it. In the event we took fire,
I should get a fire mission started and mortar rounds falling on the target A.S.A.P. When I was back in the F.D.C.
and a "fire mission" came over the radio, there was a
sense of urgency, but that was nothing compared to the
anxiety of those in the bush who were waiting for friendly
fire to take the heat off.

The time came for me to go on my first ambush patrol.
First of all, it started at night. In fact, all of the activity
in the field started at night. During that day, our battalion had run smack into a dug-in, brigade-sized North
Vietnamese force of Regulars. Up until that point, I'd
been involved in minor firefights but never right in the
middle of one. Our battalion was traveling in a column
en route to an area of operation somewhere near Tay
Ninh. We were rushed there because Charlie had overrun the base camp of the 196th Light Infantry Brigade
stationed there.

An observation chopper had spotted some movement
and had pointed us in that direction. Company A led the
battalion, and the second platoon led Company A. The
first squad led the column through the bush in the first
track; and the second squad, Lieutenant Cuthbertson, and
myself were in the second track with the third and fourth
squads behind us, followed by the rest of the column.
All of a sudden, the familiar, methodic sound of Russian AK's opened up. The first squad had come under
heavy fire. With the first burst of automatic weapons,
we all hit the floor. The lieutenant shouted the order for
the platoon to come on line fast. As our rifle squad swept
to the left of first squad, firing as we went, we also began
to come under heavy fire. As rounds ripped by us, I could

hear the metal shield around the 50 begin to ring as AK and 30-caliber fire zeroed in on our gunner.

I fed four magazines through my M-14 in a matter of seconds. All along the line, our guys were firing in a frenzy like madmen. The air was saturated with the chatter of automatic and machine gun fire. Every two or three seconds, an exploding grenade would accent the battle. Sweat rolled from me as though I were in a shower, and my tongue felt like someone was trying to jump start it from a battery. Even though I was functioning with the precision of a military manual, I was on the razor edge of panic. Nothing I had been through in training could have prepared me for this. "I have to hold it together," I thought. To lose it would mean certain death.

At that critical moment, we had to gain fire superiority from Charlie. We had to pin them down so we could rush their position. Then I saw it, a trench only twenty-five meters to our front with a large bunker to the right about ten meters. There were AK flashes coming from all along the trench, with a steady stream of tracers coming from the bunker. As I dropped down to change magazines, our 50 gunner also dropped — he was hit. I looked at him, then scanned the faces of the other members of the squad. The common, unspoken question was "Who would man the 50?" I then found myself moving toward the gun. At that moment, it was the only weapon that could give us an edge. Its rate of fire is slower than that of an M-60, and even Charlie's 30-caliber firing from the bunker, but none of them had the slugging power of a 50.

After a couple of desperate moments, I reached the 50. I still couldn't see the first track to my right, and I knew the third and fourth squads hadn't made it through the thick bush to get on line yet. Their silence explained why Charlie was concentrating his fire power on us. Staying as low as possible with my face directly behind the shield, I grabbed the twin handles which brought the gun to life with its steady "boom, boom, boom!" I swung the 50 in the direction of the V.C. bunker and started pouring tracers into it. The shield around me began to ring and vibrate from Charlie's hits. The shower of rounds zipping by sounded like the cracking of a hundred bullwhips, but none found their mark.

The firing slits of the bunker were too small for me to consistently get the tracers into, but it didn't matter. The 50 was knocking fist-size chunks of sand bag away each time a round impacted. Moments later, the tracers stopped coming out. Then, to my left, I could hear the sweet sound of an M-60 open up along with a couple of 50's. It was the third and fourth squads. A guy by the name of Catalina was manning the M-60. He was trimming the forward edge of the trench and anything that moved in it. Our platoon was now on line and moving forward. Captain Pelphry, the company commander, was on the radio trying to find out what was happening. We were now some ten meters from the trench and could see Charlie falling back. The tracks were on line and laying down a withering base of fire. With at least three 50's, two M-60's, and automatic fire going at once, the jungle began to churn as though in a blender. Lt. Cuthbertson then gave the order for the platoon to stop and dismount — we were going in on foot. Selector switches were placed on "rock-and-roll," the rear doors came down, and the squads swarmed out screaming.

The rest of the column was moving past the protective perimeter we had established around the wounded for a med-evac. In a matter of moments, we picked up the familiar "whop, whop, whop" of an approaching Huey. We loaded the wounded on board for the flight back, then moved forward to consolidate a battalion-sized perimeter from which we would operate during the next two weeks in the field.

We soon received orders to move out on a night patrol. With only the stars to light our way, our 12-man team started out under the cover of darkness. Our purpose was to make and keep contact with Charlie until reinforcements arrived. Each man carried as much ammo as he could. Since we were to be picked up in the morning, we didn't need anything else. In the past I was never afraid of the dark, but the night was Charlie's element and knowing he was lurking out there gave me cause for concern. Walking around in the jungle in the dark looking for trouble just didn't appeal to me. I had heard about other patrols walking into Charlie's night ambushes and suffering heavy casualties. What heightened the suspense was the fact that we'd already made contact. We knew the V.C. were operating in the area and would also be moving around that night. Because they had left behind over six hundred bodies, we were sure there must have been quite a large force still concealed in the jungle. Charlie liked to discourage us by dragging as many of their dead and wounded away from the battle site to leave as little evidence as possible of what we had really done to them.

However, the patrol was uneventful. We walked all night and didn't make any contact, which didn't upset me a bit. We spent the next day cleaning up and fortifying our positions along the perimeter. While the rest of the platoon was digging in and setting up claymores, I called into Fire Control to check our coordinates. It was my job as F.O. to call in and register reference points or check points to our front which we would use in the event our position came under attack.

I called in for a spotting round of Willie-peter. "Four-zero, four-zero, this is four-seven-two," I called over the radio. "Fire mission — over." "This is four-zero — send your fire mission," the weapons platoon answered. I gave a compass heading and a map reference and asked for "one round W.P. — will adjust — over." As the seconds ticked by, I noticed the rest of the platoon waiting to see what kind of F.O. they had with them and whether or not they could count on my work in a squeeze. Just then, a mortar went off and a voice over the radio said, "Round on the way — over." The white phosphorous round came down fifty meters to the left and front of our positon. "Not bad," I thought.

"Where's this one going?" a voice from a foxhole to my right asked. "See that dead tree?" I asked, pointing to the front and middle of the area of our responsibility. Now, if I came within 25 meters of that tree, I would have been very happy. Hitting that tree would be like getting a ringer in horseshoes at a hundred yards. "Round on the way — over." "Round on the way — wait." I held my breath. Then "pop!" — the round exploded with a shower of white phosphorous in the branches of the very tree I had pointed out. I then adjusted my next shot 75 meters to the right.

I tried to act cool, but I really couldn't believe my accuracy. I was on a roll. "See that tree over there?" I asked with a slight air of cockiness, pointing to the right front of our position. "Let me see it!" a challenging voice replied. "From checkpoint two...," and I gave the numbers that would bring the round somewhere in the general vicinity of the tree I was pointing toward. I felt if I came close, and that was the most I could expect, I could at least say one out of two isn't too bad. "Round on the way — over." "Round on the way — wait." Again, the round exploded in the branches of the same tree I had pointed out. I knew it wasn't me governing the fire control — it was just too uncanny. I had an inexplicable sense that someone else was calling the shots. "But who is it?" I thought. For the first time, a strange feeling of Someone very much in charge watching out for me registered in my mind. I paused for an instant, then dismissed what had just happened.

A few weeks later we were on operation "Junction City," a multi-division operation near the Cambodian border. Large forces of North Vietnamese Regulars were sighted traveling south through Cambodia, then filtering into South Vietnam. As we drew near the area, we passed elements of the "First Cavalry" and the "Big Red One," two other divisions in Vietnam at that time. It brought a measure of relief knowing we had such a large force in the area. For us to have so many men involved meant that the area was crawling with gooks.

Two days later, we were on a platoon-sized patrol in the tracks; the area had small forests with large clearings. Spotting movement ahead, Lt. Cuthbertson gave the order to come on line. As we swept on line through a forest, the second squad reached the edge of the wood line a little ahead of the other squads to our left when the sudden "pop-pop-pop" of mingled M-16 and AK fire rang out. Seconds later, a squad of seven khaki-clothed North Vietnamese darted from their cover and sprinted across a clearing in front of us. Most of the platoon opened up with a volley which tumbled all but two of the NVA. I didn't have a clear line of fire so I couldn't take part in the turkey shoot. We then moved in a direction that would intercept the fleeing soldiers. Just as they reached a small patch of woods, one of them looked around to see where we were and was cut down. The other dropped into the tree line.

In all the firefights I had experienced, I had never looked down my sights and watched what my rounds were doing to the flesh as I squeezed the trigger. The density of the jungle concealed most of the dead and the dying in a firefight. Usually, you were just firing at some muzzle flash or Vietnamese phantom hiding in the darkness.

A moment later, twenty meters in front of me, the guy was coming out of the wood line, right toward me with his hands raised; he was giving up, but I didn't care. I placed his head on top of my sights and squeezed the trigger. My M-14, which always fired, did nothing — it had malfunctioned. I quickly pulled the bolt back, ejecting what must have been a dud round. As I did that, the magazine fell out. The months of fighting had left its effect on me. I had grown cold and hard-hearted, and even lost the worry of getting killed. I didn't care. The flood of letters I had received when I first arrived had dwindled to a trickle, and the hate I felt because of the waste of lives due to a political war raged within me. I was seething with hate and had an insatiable urge to wreak revenge on those that had blown so many of my friends away. As far as I was concerned, that little dink was dead meat.

Again, I took aim and squeezed the trigger. Again, nothing happened. In the haste of my bloodlust, I hadn't fully seated the magazine when I replaced it — a procedure I had done flawlessly in the past. "Why is all this happening now?" I asked myself. For the third time, I pulled the bolt back to see that there was no round in the chamber. I fully seated the clip, sent the bolt forward chambering a round, and finally I was ready to fire. As I looked up to find my target, someone from the third squad had grabbed the guy by the ear, and with his weapon pointed at his temple, was leading him back to our lines.

In hindsight, I now know that God was not only protecting my body from the lethal impact of war, but He was also covering my mind. He foreknew that the future slow-motion replays of that cold-blooded murder — the sensation of squeezing the trigger, the crack of the rifle, the split second before impact, the sudden jerk of the victim, and the lifeless results — would have been burned into my consciousness for the rest of my life making it hard for me to forgive myself, even though He would have.

That night, we got orders to saddle up and take a patrol out on tracks. They would drop us off in the bush, then we would backtrack to the perimeter hunting for V.C. Charlie wasn't dumb and would cause problems if we did things the same way each time, so we shuffled our method of operating from time to time. After waiting for the tracks to move fully out of the area, we then moved the patrol by foot to an ambush site. As we snaked through the shadows of the night, we came across a clearing. When we reached the wood line to our front, we then turned right along the edge of the wood line, keeping it to our left. I was hoping no one saw us, when suddenly we picked up movement in the bush. Instantly, everyone dropped to a kneeling position and held his breath. We could hear the faint voices of Vietnamese coming from within the wood line — they were very close. By the sound of things, it appeared to be too large a force for us to fire on, especially being in our vulnerable position out in the open. They didn't know we were there, and it would only be a matter of moments until someone spotted or smelled us. We couldn't open up or withdraw without being seen. "This is it," I thought. "You can kiss yourself good-bye." We found ourselves in a precarious situation where the chances looked slim to none that any of us would make it out in one piece.

The lieutenant passed a message down the line. "Don't fire," we whispered ever so softly. Just then, something jerked a bush which was right next to my position. "We've been spotted," I thought, as I sprang up turning to fire. I was extremely nervous, being left-handed with my weapon facing away from the wood line. As I straightened up beginning to squeeze a burst of automatic fire, something stopped me. In that critical instant, it seemed like some hand had stopped me from firing. I dropped back to my knees without a sound and waited. Sweat poured from my face, and my heart was pounding so loudly that I was sure everyone, including the gooks, could hear it. In the midst of reacting, God had grabbed me and controlled me so I wouldn't set off something that would have gotten myself and the others killed.

Then word was passed that on "three" we were to lay down a three-second burst of fire, then turn and sprint the two hundred meters across the clearing and take cover on the other side. Eternity seemed to pass during the counting from one to three. Finally, Lt. Cuthbertson opened up, with all of us right with him, spraying into the tree line. I could hear some screams blurt from the wood line and could not help feeling we had awakened a sleeping giant. As the short burst ended, we all turned for our mad dash across the clearing. As we sprinted across the open field, the visual images of rounds tearing into my body from behind flashed through my head.

In no time, we had crossed the great gulf. I was sure it was covered in record time. When we reached the other side, every man dove into the woods, scrambling for cover from the imaginary bullets chasing us. As I hit the ground, I was already on the radio screaming, "Fire mission, fire mission!" I didn't wait for a reply and began giving the coordinates of the target as the rest of the patrol fired into the clearing. I was so out of breath and overwhelmed with adrenaline that I could barely get the coordinates out fast enough. My words were tripping over each other as I called for fire support. The W.P. marking round was a direct hit, and I hollered "Fire for effect! Fire for effect!" The three mortar teams were pumping out rounds as though they had ten tubes. Orange flashes from the exploding rounds pulverized the target area.

After ten minutes, I called for a cease fire and we waited. As the sun began to appear through the trees, we knew we had made it again. Shortly after, the rest of the company linked up with us to search the area that had given us such great concern the night before. There was fresh blood splattered everywhere but no body count. Once again, Charlie had succeeded in dragging away the results of our impact. We knew, though, that we had tagged a number of them.

The calendar drifted into April. I was a "short timer" with less than ninety days left before I would be going home — something I doubted I would get to do. We were on a large "search and destroy" operation in the "Ho Bo" woods. This was an area just outside of Cu Chi filled with tunnels and underground caverns large enough to hide a battalion of North Vietnamese. Charlie had saturated the area with spider traps, camouflaged rifle pits, and booby traps. When we operated there, we suffered more casualties than any other place during my tour.

Every time we penetrated a V.C. stronghold on one of our so-called "search and destroy" operations, I couldn't help feeling somewhat uncomfortable with that characterization. In those hunt and kill sweeps, we were always gook-hunting. We were stalking human beings, the most elusive and cunning of all prey. We were playing the role of the hunter, while Charlie was the hunted. But out in the jungle, this distinction was often blurred — Charlie was jungle-wise. The jungle was his territory, his ally, and he was more skillful at this deadly cat-and-mouse game than we. After all, he'd spent years mastering the art of stealth and mobility in guerrilla warfare fighting the Japanese and French. We soon realized that, with very few exceptions, we did most of our hunting on his terms. In reality, we were his prey. He had set the traps and was waiting for us to search and destroy our way right into his snare.

It was late in the afternoon and the sky was turning a greyish-orange as we headed back to our perimeter. We had spent an exhausting day rooting out V.C. tunnels and blowing them up. Before we reached our perimeter, an uneasy darkness settled over the jungle. Another day in the nine-to-five war was coming to a close, and we all knew that in spite of all our propaganda boasts about pacifying the countryside, we only owned it by day — Charlie controlled it by night.

Suddenly, my head was jerked violently forward, causing my chin to bounce off my chest. The tell-tale sound of a 50 cal. followed immediately. I quickly dropped, grabbing my head, as sounds of automatic fire filled the air. Large beads of moisture were running down the side of my face, but, in the darkness, I couldn't tell whether it was blood or sweat. As I held my head in my hands, the fingers of my left hand dropped into a jagged gash ripped into the top left side of my helmet, like a part, about six inches long. It felt like a huge can opener had made a clumsy attempt to open my helmet. Quickly, I snatched my helmet off and strained to see. I turned the helmet to catch the reflection of moonlight until I could see a long gash cut into my pot and helmet liner revealing the suspension straps of the interior. Just a fraction of an inch and that slug would have literally taken my head off.

Again, as in the past, I wanted to chalk it off as mere luck, but I had a nagging uneasiness in my mind that luck had nothing to do with it. As quickly as the firing started, it ceased. Charlie slipped away. Our only casualty was my helmet.

The next night, we went out to set up an ambush. It wasn't quite dark enough to walk to the ambush site without being observed so we stopped some three hundred meters away and waited for the darkness to come on before we moved forward to set up. Minutes after we had stopped, the ground around us began to explode with the defeaning "Karumph, KaRUMph, KaRUMPH!" of incoming mortar rounds. Each man hugged the earth, trying to get flatter than a piece of paper on a wet street. The shrapnel ripped through the bush above us with each exploding impact. Charlie was walking mortar rounds all around us. It sounded like some huge monster was staggering through the jungle with explosive footsteps, trying to smash anyone who got in his way. "These are too close," I thought, and I prayed to God to get us out of there alive, promising to be good for the rest of my life. Just as I completed the prayer, I heard an ominous "tick," like something snapping a small branch high in the jungle canopy overhead. An instant later, I heard two more ticks, but much closer. The sounds were moving in our direction. I knew that in the next split-second, a falling mortar round was going to hit very close. Calculating that thought took almost all of that half second, leaving little or no time to react. In the midst of my flinch, the "thud" of a mortar round dug into the ground halfway between myself and Espo who lay only seven feet away. Gritting my teeth, I tensed for the shell burst that would send a thousand pieces of searing metal raking through my side. I waited for the explosion that would blow me unprepared into the next life. At that moment, I seemed suspended between life and death. Time crawled to a stop. I was frozen in space with the past im-

ages of my entire life rushing past my mind's eye. I was
a prisoner strapped to an electric chair, waiting for the
executioner to throw the switch.

After what seemed like the longest seconds of my life,
I opened my eyes and turned my head to see the fin of
a mortar round sticking up out of the dirt only three feet
away. I could not believe my eyes and neither could Espo
as we stared at each other in utter disbelief.

Three weeks later, my field duty in Vietnam abruptly
ended when the track I was riding in struck an anti-tank
mine. One moment we were riding through the forest,
the next instant there was a flash that heaved eleven tons
into the air. As the track came to rest, my head and ears
were filled with pain. In the midst of even this explosion,
He covered me. I only suffered a slight concussion and
a blown ear drum, enough to keep me out of the field
until my turn came to rotate back to "the world" and
my eventual reconciliation with the One who had preserved me in a place where, every day, more than a few
were being lost.

Only 48 hours after leaving the bush, I was beating the
pavement back home. Nothing much had changed, except me. I was no longer the frightened street kid when
I returned. That former self was left somewhere overseas.
Back in 'Nam, I looked death squarely in the face and
survived. You either mastered your fears under the constant strain of combat or you cracked up. The conditioning instilled in me a certain sense of self-reliance which
one seldom acquires outside the boundaries of war. On
the surface, I felt like I was ready to take on the world.
Even the hazards of an asphalt jungle looked tame in comparison to the murderous violence of Vietnam. It was with

that initial air of self-confidence that I came home to start over.

I made it back, but leaving the war behind me was another matter. I soon discovered that it was easy taking the soldier out of the conflict but not so easy taking the conflict out of the soldier. The "freedom bird" had carried me home, but it couldn't deliver me from the bondage of bitterness and anger which I carried with me. It was a pathos shared by many Vietnam vets. A thousand unanswered questions followed me home. "Why weren't we allowed to win? Why couldn't we talk about it? Why was our society so embarrassed about us? Why the mindless slaughter of 58,000 Americans? What purpose did it all serve?" These questions didn't die easily.

No matter how hard I tried to put Vietnam behind me — to put those questions to rest — I couldn't. I struggled to make something meaningful out of my life, but my private war raged out of control. As the years ticked by, I found it increasingly difficult to cope with the pent-up frustration. I may have appeared "together" to those around me, but I was emotionally scarred. In spite of a college degree and a fine management position with AT&T, I was demoralized and disillusioned with life. On the surface, I had achieved a relatively enviable position in life, but all was not well with Ron. The cosmetic trappings of my success were not cutting it. I was gradually awakening to the reality that the many things I once had thought were so necessary for life didn't really matter after all. There had to be answers somewhere.

Finally, in sheer desperaton, I quit my job, forsook responsibilities, and hit the road in one last search for a resolution to my inner conflict. That search inevitably led me back to my experiences in 'Nam. It was through those reflections that things began to come into focus.

I had known of Christ in Vietnam, had even thought about Him on occasion, but was unable to make the crucial connection between what had happened there and the fact that I had made it home. Yet, years before, back in the jungles and rice paddies, the all-knowing God foresaw that I would one day cry out for His help. He needed only to get my attention — something He had repeatedly tried to get by sparing my life. Finally, after years of fruitless groping, my quest led me to the answer I so desperately sought. In July 1980, I found Jesus Christ, and the peace which had seemed as elusive as quicksilver brought an end to the private war which raged in my soul.

Before I met Christ, I had found it extremely uncomfortable to talk about my experiences in Vietnam. I had so subconsciously suppressed my past that it often seemed like a distant blur. I suppose the memories were just too painful to deal with. The scorn and shame which an ungrateful nation dumped on us only intensified the silent cover-up. But as God began to heal the inner pain, I experienced a personal release which helped me make sense out of the confused impressions I had bottled up for so long. I had tried to forget those memories, but God wanted me to remember. I've had a lot of time to see things clearly, to savor what He did for me in 'Nam, to appreciate the depth of His grace in my behalf.

Since my tour in Southeast Asia, I have come to recognize that the killing fields of 'Nam were the fertile soil God used to plant the questions within me which would eventually lead to the answers my soul thirsted after. Though that revelation was slow in coming, I thank

God that it was better late than never. Since that day, I've often wondered how many thousands of other men and women scattered across this country have still not recognized that God graciously preserved their lives in harm's way, as well.

Ron Mason and his wife Michelle reside in South Lake Tahoe, Ca. They recently had a new baby boy. Ron works as a cabinet maker and attends the Church of Glad Tidings where he serves in the music ministry.

Eugene "Red" McDaniel
Lieutenant Commander, U.S. Navy
Medium Attack Pilot
VA/35 Black Panther
Attack Squadron
USS Enterprise
Nov. '66 - May '67
P.O.W.
May '67 - Mar. '73

JERE FULLERTON
BEST WISHES
Red McDa

14

The Hanoi Hilton

I was awakened from sleep by a call from the duty officer notifying me of our upcoming mission. It would be a maximum effort "alpha strike" against the strategic truck repair center and marshalling yards at Van Dien, south of Hanoi, — what we referred to as "Little Detroit." The strike would take us through "white knuckle alley" and heavy concentrations of anti-aircraft flak and surface-to-air missiles. We all knew that Van Dien was surrounded by clusters of batteries capable of peppering the sky with flak bursts and radar-guided SAM missiles.

After reviewing weather reports and surveying photographs of the target area, we finished our briefing and headed topside for our standard litany of pre-flight instrument checks. Kelly Patterson would be my bombardier-navigator for the morning mission. Checkout complete, I felt the sudden shock of the catapult hurling our A-6 Intruder off the pitching flight deck of Enterprise, loaded with 13,000 pounds of ordinance. In a few minutes, we rendezvoused overhead with the rest of the squadron, then headed towards the North Vietnamese coast. Our formation penetrated North Vietnamese airspace at 15,000 feet through a broken layer of sky blue and patchy white clouds. We had flown about sixty miles inland when we started seeing SAM missiles rising up in front of us. They looked like a barrage of telephone poles which had been flung skywards. I was starting evasive maneuvers when the red light on my ECM (Electronic

Countermeasure) started flashing, and the ominous warbling "whoooo, whoooo, whoooo..." echoed through my headset, warning us that a ground radar and SAM battery had locked on and were tracking us. We were twenty-five seconds into evasive dodging when a violent explosion jarred the aircraft, sending us into a dive. Red lights on the console indicated a fire in the port engine, hydraulic systems were out, the control stick was frozen, and we were dropping fast. We had to get out before our bomb load blew.

My Visual Display Indicator, which showed my flight path in relation to the ground, indicated that we were sliding off and down to the right. The altimeter gauge was spinning backwards as we descended towards a jungle mountain range in the distance. We were riding down a burning jet whose speed had reached nearly 550 knots. You were not supposed to eject at over 500 knots because the canopy could jam. I asked Kelly, "How about it? Do you want to try for the mountain?" Kelly gave the affirmative. We both knew from navy survival training that riding our aircraft to an uninhabited area gave RESCAP the greatest chance of getting to us before the Vietnamese.

At about two thousand feet above the approaching range, I yelled at Kelly, "Let's get out!" The canopy blew amidst a blast of high velocity turbulence and cockpit debris as Kelly shot out first, then my seat was ejected into a confused somersault before the violent jerk of shroud lines and the billowing parachute slowed my descent. I felt like a puppet on strings dangling over enemy territory. As I floated down, I could see Kelly's chute far off to the right and the pall of black smoke where our A-6 had plowed into the mountain.

The parachute had slowed my free-fall, but due to jagged rips in the chute, I was descending dangerously fast. All I could do was hang on helplessly and watch the jungle rush up towards me. In moments, I crashed through layers of canopy until an abrupt halt left me dangling fifty feet above the jungle floor, snagged on one of the branches. There I was, ten thousand miles from home, stranded in the middle of North Vietnam, gently swaying from a jungle tree while the Vietnamese closed in.

I knew I couldn't just hang there and do nothing. I had a better chance commiting myself to a hostile jungle than waiting to be taken prisoner. The only obstacle was getting down. I started crawling up the risers of my chute when the sickening sound of ripping nylon sent me slamming into the jungle floor with such an impact that two of my vertebrae were crushed in the fall.

"Red, are you O.K.?" It was Nick Carpenter, my back-up man, calling me on the radio. I reached into my vest and pulled out my small survival radio. "I'm O.K., Nick. My back's pretty bad, but I'm O.K." I looked up through the holes in the canopy and saw Nick's A-6 circling protectively overhead, then he veered off toward the coast. Still, I was thankful to God that Nick had pinpointed my location. I wasn't stranded. I knew RESCAP, who had a reputation for its uncanny ability to pluck pilots from hostile territory, would soon be on the way with a Jolly Green Giant to rescue me. I found myself praying, "And thank you, God. Dorothy will know I'm on the ground O.K ."

While I waited, I unzipped my G suit, buried my chute, strapped on my survival kit, and started climbing up the lush jungle incline, pausing every so often to listen to the whistles of Vietnamese search parties combing the jungle in pursuit. I tried to make contact with Kelly over the radio, but there was no response. As the darkness squeezed the last rays out of a brooding jungle, I fell into an uncomfortable sleep — waiting for my deliverance.

Apprehensive hours passed amidst the night sounds of the jungle, but nothing. The claustrophobic darkness of the jungle was slowly choking out my hopes for a rescue. I began to pray from a position of urgency which I had never confronted before, "Please, God, get me out of this." I was asking for a miracle. "Please, God, lift me out of this jungle and back to the deck of Enterprise." But more hours passed, broken only by the infrequent screech of a jungle bird, the chattering of monkeys and the snapping of twigs high in the overhead canopy. I strained to hear the distant drone of planes, but nothing. I reminded God in the darkness that I was a good Baptist, a deacon in my church, a believer in Him. I thought about my family — Dorothy, Mike, David, and my little baby daughter, Leslie. How would they take the news of my shootdown? And I found myself asking, "Why me, God? Why me?"

Dawn came around 5:30, but still no planes. I moved back down the slope to where I had buried the parachute to unfurl it upon the ground as a marking signal, even though I knew it would expose my position to the V.C. search parties, as well. It was a calculated risk I had to take. Moments later, I heard an A-6 overhead, accompanied by an F-4 fighter escort. I radioed them and was told to hold tight. A Jolly Green Giant would be coming in forty-five minutes to pick me up. "Outstanding!" I shouted back. My emotions soared. But the minutes dragged by, then several hours, with no chopper in sight. About one o'clock, I heard the lone crack of a rifle, followed by a sudden surge of adrenalin. I turned around, and all my hopes came crashing down around me. In moments, fifteen jabbering Vietnamese peasants had surrounded me. There was no escape.

After trussing my arms behind my back, they led me through the jungle until we reached a small hamlet where I was strip searched and left bound in a small room, waiting for the next move. Besides the nagging pain in my back, my arms and legs were swollen and numb from the tightness of the ropes. After an hour, I was given back my flight suit and began an agonizing journey by foot and truck to Hanoi. It was a painful trip through a gauntlet of rifle butts, taunts, leg kicking, face slapping, and the galling humiliation of feeling like a captured animal. The closer we got to Hanoi, the rougher the treatment from my captors. Sadistic specters of Oriental torture pricked my mind as we neared our destination — specters that would assume a ruthless reality in the years ahead.

I finally arrived at the Hanoi Hilton, the main American prison camp, on a Sunday morning. My introduction to North Vietnamese interrogation commenced shortly after my arrival. They began torturing me to extract information by tying my wrists, then pulling my arms high behind me so that my shoulder bones were ready to pop. It was a procedure I would become intimately acquainted with during my six years of confinement. My body was contorted into a position it wasn't designed to adjust to. The pain was excruciating. My numbed brain struggled to compute what they wanted. Military information? A confession? Every man possesses a different threshhold of pain — a different breaking point beyond which there is no endurance. I didn't know where mine was, but I was determined not to give in to their interrogating and political hammering. I would die first. Name, rank, serial number — that's all. All I could do was pray, "Please, God, give me strength to resist, to go out with some kind of dignity." After three days of relentless interrogation, the brutality had not budged me so they gave up and threw me into an isolation cell clamped in leg irons.

In my musty, gray, solitary cell, reality finally hit. I was a prisoner of war, facing an indefinite sentence. Preparing for eighty-one combat missions over the North, I had considered the possibility that I might be killed. To die suddenly was one thing. It was easier reconciling yourself to that potential than to capture. I wasn't prepared for that.

I knew it would be a long war, and I knew I had to resist. I had to find a way to resist. I couldn't let myself rot in resignation. I had to keep fighting. It was going to demand everything within me and then some. I knew there were other American prisoners facing the same grim future and fearing the worst, and I could tell by their screams that more was in store for me. We were up against an enemy who found pleasure in inflicting pain. I knew I had to establish communication with the other Americans to bolster our morale, to rally our resolve, to give and take whatever moral support we could during the long haul that lay ahead. If we wanted to keep our sanity, we had to stick together.

Yet, I also knew that I had to lay hold of God more

than I had ever done so in the past. I knew that the arm of man could only sustain me so far. I had to lay hold of the Rock which is higher than I.

Just then, the jiggling sound of the jailer's key turning the lock brought me out of my reflections. The dreaded metallic rattling sound would become a familiar, hated noise in the days and years ahead. It was always a portent of impending pain.

The guard unshackled the leg irons and jerked me to my feet. I was pushed down the dingy corridor, dragging my half limp leg, before being shoved into another gray cell. In the dimness, I focused on eyes shining from hollow sockets. It was another flyer grinning at me. He was lying on the concrete floor, naked, with his arm ripped open with an ugly laceration running twelve inches from his wrist to his elbow. He had a gaping hole in his left leg, caked reddish brown with blood, where a two pound piece of shrapnel had hit him; the other leg was broken.

When I saw young Bill Metzger lying there grinning up at me, I changed the question of self-pity I had asked out in the jungle from "Why me, God?" to "Why not me?" I remembered the times I had sat in the comfort of my padded pew on Sunday mornings back home and agreed with the words of the Apostle Paul: "For we know that all things work together for good to those who love God; to them who are called according to his purpose" (Rom. 8:28). It was so easy, in the sanctuary of America, to nod a casual assent to that great assurance. But now, the austere confines of a military prison forced me to contemplate the force of that promise in a way which I had never been challenged previously.

"If that verse is true," I said to myself, "if any of what

I call my faith is true, then that verse applies here in Hanoi, right in this forlorn cell. If, in God's scheme of things, there's a purpose for my being here, I can make it — even as a wretched prisoner caged like an animal, starved and beaten and brutalized. God, if I can muster what little strength I have to help Bill Metzger and he can help me, then we'll both make it.''

God's assurance so underscored my confidence that we would make it that I rapidly became known as the "camp optimist.'' In fact, this attitude became my mainstay and eventually a contagion which infected others in that dreary camp. In my very limited contacts with other incarcerated Americans, they would ask me, "When do you think we'll be going home, Red?'' "In about two months,'' I would answer in the upbeat. I lost a lot of credibility as the years dragged on, but they gleaned hope out of my tireless role as the "Positive Rumormonger'' anyway. I was kind of a reverse version of the boy who cried wolf.

It was optimism not built on the sand or the platitudes of wishful thinking but on the bedrock of a solid faith in the assurances of God — a rock solid faith that didn't waver with the passing of time but grew steadily stronger and sharper under the relentless pressures of our confinement. Even in a place where tomorrows seemed so dismal, where life and death hung so precariously in the balance, where every effort was exerted to exploit your weaknesses and undermine faith in God and country, His grace sustained me and checked the dark clouds of despair which threatened to overshadow us. Through Him, I learned to survive and even triumph over the sordid realities of boredom, anxiety, and despair. It was a victory we had to grasp in our imprisonment or resign ourselves to the darkness.

The long days turned into months, and the months drifted into years. I shared with others my long-held belief in the "power of positive thinking," and they, in turn, as the torture sessions came more often and grew ever more severe, would bolster my spirits in any way they could. For three years, we clung together like that, Bill and I and the others.

But worse than the torture was the isolation, the solitary confinement. Our captors knew they could break our spirits if they kept us separated from one another. They knew that a man can only endure more pain if he is linked with others in his suffering; isolated, he became weak and vulnerable. To break us was their single-minded mission.

They wanted our minds to be empty and bored so we would be receptive to the brainwashing propaganda that they piped over the loudspeakers in our cells. Besides the wholesale torture, we were alloted ample doses of free lance harrassment to wear us down. Exaggerated statistics of American casualties were broadcast over the camp P.A. We were informed of American soldiers defecting to Sweden, we were forced to listen to the "Voice of Vietnam" playing the melancholy recordings of homesick prisoners to their loved ones, and we were fed all the depressing news from America they could dig up: the anti-war demonstrations, the assassinations, the airline disasters, even news of anti-war delegations from the States.

Still, we struggled to beat the system and outwit the guards. I knew we couldn't survive if we didn't communicate with one another. That was a vital lifeline to survival. Any risk was acceptable to me if it held the slightest chance of making contact with others. We went to great lengths to keep the lines of communication open, even though it cost us dearly in repeated trips to the "quiz" room for torture. We invented a "tapping code" which we used to stay in touch with other prisoners through the walls and down the corridors, in the washrooms, and under the doors. Besides the camp code, we had other subtle signals such as cough codes, finger signs, clothes swaps, and thumping signals in the dirt with our reed brooms when we swept the courtyard. We even attached scribbled messages on scraps of paper to the underside of our toilet bowls which were placed outside our cells for pick-up. We affectionately called it our "pony express."

With our crude camp code, we tapped out short messages through the thick concrete walls. We shared stories, Bible verses, poems — anything we could think of to help each other cope with the dark hours. We even shared jokes to cheer one another up. Rapid taps signified laughter, while slow, heavy thumps indicated it was a dud. When a man came back from torture, needing encouragement, sometimes needing forgiveness because he hadn't measured up to his own expectations, we tapped our meager moral support to him through those thick walls. It was our way of redeeming a bit of moral victory from the system.

Between the pressure and pain were monotonous grey gaps — tedious hours of boredom, endless hours of nothing to do but think and wonder and sometimes worry. To combat the mind-numbing dullness, we invented elaborate mental exercises to while away the time. We taxed our ingenuity and mental resourcefulness with playing mind games, doing calculations, remembering, planning construction projects, planning vacations, thinking through adventures and fantasies, reliving history, composing poems — anything to keep our minds alert and active.

On Sunday mornings, we worshipped the Lord together, tapping our clandestine worship through the walls. We found bits and pieces of scripture buried deep inside our minds and shared them with one another — missing words, missing lines, passages paraphrased. We prayed together, through the walls. Then we closed our primitive worship service facing the east, each man in his own cell, toward the Gulf of Tonkin where we knew U.S. Navy ships were waiting offshore, as we pledged our allegiance to our unseen flag.

We learned to pray for our guards, Spot and Rabbit, Jawbone and Sweetpea, Slug and the others who inflicted such ruthless torture on us. We learned to share our sparse food, to tend another man's wounds, to find and share the courage and strength we needed to meet each day.

We put together, as best we could, a makeshift copy of the Bible. It could never be called the Living Bible or the King James Bible. We called it the Revised Prison Version. We wrote down all the scripture we could recall on pieces of toilet paper stuck together with glutinous rice. Ink was a problem. We tried brick dust and water. We tried blood and water. Finally, we tried cigarette ashes and water, and that worked. The V.C. gave us three cigarettes a day in the good times when they were feeling generous, and we found all kinds of uses for the tobacco. The nicotine was used to clear up toothaches and intestinal parasites. It may not have been effective, but we liked to think it was.

I made a conscious effort not to think about the past and not to dream too much about the future. I knew I had to take one day at a time. I tried to put the good life behind me, to meet each new crisis, each new challenge, with all the strength I could muster.

Two things weighed heavily upon my mind. What had happened to Kelly the day we bailed out? At every interrogation session, I asked about Kelly. The V.C. always claimed to have no knowledge of him. We had what we thought was a pretty good system of information in the prison network, but I never was able to ferret out any word about Kelly.

And I wondered about Dorothy. Did she know I was alive? Was there any way I could let her know I was in a P.O.W. camp? Since I couldn't think of a way, I was thankful that she at least had the knowledge that I had gotten out of my plane after we had been hit.

Through all of this, I was acutely aware that my struggle for survival was a learning time for me. I would never again be the same man. I would benefit in many ways from my suffering. I would appreciate my country and my freedom when, and if, I ever experienced freedom again. I knew I would be a free man again, that it couldn't go on forever, that there would be an end, that our country would not forsake us. I always believed my country would come to get me some day. But I wondered when — and I wondered how.

In 1968, when the bomber missions stopped coming, our hopes soared with a new wave of optimism. The Paris peace talks had begun, unbeknownst to us. "We're going home," I thought. As the weeks and months ticked by and the bombers didn't return, it was hard to hang on to that slender thread of hope, but I knew if I let go, I would not make it through this. And so I did hang on. And I was making it, one day at a time. After every torture session, I would thank God that I was still alive. I would thank Him that I had resisted once again. And I would cling to my belief that my country would never abandon me. I was making it. I would make it. Some day I would go home.

And then came the summer of 1969. I had taken my place as the main communications liaison between two camps. The V.C. had shuttled us from camp to camp to disrupt our organization and communications system. Early in 1969, they moved me from the Hanoi Hilton to the Zoo Annex, and then over to the compound directly behind the Annex we called the "Zoo." From my cell, I could see my old cell in the Zoo Annex and was familiar with the layout of both camps. From my new vantage point, I could link the men in both camps to our communications system.

All of this meant that I knew the inner workings of what was secretly going on in both camps. It also meant that the Vietnamese knew that I knew. Consequently, on the night of May 10, 1969, when John Dramesi and Ed Atterbury got caught in a desperate attempt to escape and were returned to the camp for punishment, the authorities came down hard. They retaliated with an unprecedented vengeance. Some of the men were tortured to death in the enemy's attempt to finger the escape committee.

After they'd beaten their way through about twenty-four men, I was taken to an interrogation room called the "chicken coop" to confirm the information which had been extracted from the others under vicious torture.

Some of what they wanted, I had — some, I didn't. Our captors were in a brutal dispositon and determined to get me to say what they wanted me to say. But I was equally determined to resist, even if it cost me my life. As they prodded me to the torture room at the point of a bayonet, I kept telling myself, "I've made it this far. I can still make it." I gritted my teeth and prepared for the worst.

I was placed in loop-shaped U-bolt leg irons intertwining both ankles. My arms were locked behind my back with wrist irons. For the next seven days and nights, I was ruthlessly beaten in that torture room with no sleep and almost no food. I was forced to strip, then sprawl spread-eagle on the floor with my buttocks exposed to repeated blows from a 3½ foot rubber fan belt until my buttocks became a bloody pulp. I was subjected to relentness demands for information, karate chops, and tire sandal slappings across the face. I was beaten with bamboo sticks and suspended from an overhead beam in agonizing positions which dug the ropes into my flesh, cutting off circulation and paralyzing nerves. They twisted my body into grotesque positions with those dreaded ropes until the bone in my left arm snapped. My face, mouth, arms, shoulders, legs and open wounds were pulsing with pain. My body was wracked with fever, but I refused to give in to their demands. They then tied cords around my arms and chest, wrapped wet cloths around the cords, and hooked the wires up to a battery. Each time the wires were touched to the terminals, violent jabs of voltage jerked my body into spasms. After a week of unrelenting torment, I began to slip in and out of consciousness, occasionally drifting into hallucinations.

At some point during the seventh night, I became dimly

aware that I wasn't going to make it after all. All the positive thinking, optimism, and hope I had so carefully nurtured for long years was exhausted. I was going to die. And death would be welcomed.

As I knelt crumpled on the floor in my own blood and wastes, I found myself yielding control to God. I found myself surrendering my fate to Him unconditionally. There was no more human resolve or pride or tenacity of spirit — just surrender to Him: "Lord... it's all Yours.... whatever this means, whatever it is supposed to accomplish in me, whatever You have in mind now with all of this, it's all Yours..." God knew my breaking point. He knew exactly when the torture had to stop. And it did stop, at the threshhold of death. He had a larger purpose for me. He had spared me at my shootdown. He had graciously allowed me the privilege of serving beside men of great courage — to help them find strength, and to receive strength from them in turn. He had preserved me through two long years of torture and deprivation. He delivered me that seventh night, as well. Kneeling there, empty before God, I was overwhelmed by the sheer awesomeness of His presence and profound awareness that He was forging a deeper dimension of faith and commitment in my life to glorify Him in the years ahead.

He was not ready for me to die. He would bring me through four more years of imprisonment, back to my home and family, back from the brink of the grave. He would give me back my health, and I would testify of His power to heal. He would help me to see His divine purpose in allowing me to suffer, and He would use me as an example that others might know of His power and turn to Him for life.

To my amazement, I was put in a cell with Windy Rivers and Ron Bliss, two outstanding Christians. They didn't recognize me at first because I looked like a specter out of hell. My eyes were sunken, my skin turning jaundiced, legs pitifully swollen, body caked with scabs and sores, and my hands dangling limply at my sides. But they rallied on my behalf and lovingly nursed me back to health. They fed me, shaved me, washed my wounded body, and even helped me relieve myself. Jack Van Loan, another prisoner, massaged my hands for hours on end over several months, slowly bringing back circulation. During that time, my broken arm finally began to heal.

The V.C. left me alone for the next five or six months. And then one day, the dreaded turnkey came and escorted me back to the interrogation room. I was still very weak, and I knew I would not survive another torture session. "Write a letter confessing to your war crimes," Spot demanded, "and we'll let your family know you are still alive." I refused. "You know we can force you," he said. "You will have to force me," I answered. I knew "force you" meant "torture you," and I knew they were more than qualified to physically destroy me in methodic, maniacal stages. "But when we force you, it makes us look bad in the eyes of the world," Spot replied. That was a very strange statement, coming from him, I thought. And I decided that someone, somewhere, was talking about us. Somewhere, in the real world, someone was aware of our plight, and I thought, surely this is the beginning of the end.

It wasn't the end. I would spend three more years in captivity. But there was no more torture. The public outcry back home was putting pressure on Hanoi to improve their treatment towards us. The food was better. I got some mail from home, and I was allowed to write to my family to let them know I was alive. The North Vietnamese were trying to manipulate the world's press and reap the propaganda value of giving the illusion that they were giving the American P.O.W.'s "humane and lenient" treatment. However, our living conditions only marginally and seasonally improved during the next three years.

On December 18, 1972, the B-52's returned. For the next twelve days, they came around the clock, one wave after another, rocking Hanoi with earth-rending concussions. The massive bombing strikes were a sign that our government was fed up with the stalling and was turning up the heat to force the North Vietnamese to negotiate a peace settlement in Paris. Our hopes were rekindled. The punitive air strikes were a clear signal that we would soon be freed. For the first time, I dared to look ahead, to think about the future.

Would there be a place in my country for me? After six long years in a Communist prison, where would I fit? And what about my family? What kind of toll had this separation taken on them? Would I be a stranger in my own home? With babies now grown into teenagers, where would I fit? What about my shipmates? My squadron? My country? Would there be a place for me? Back home in America, would they still know me? Where would I fit? And would I be able to share, in some small way, the sure and certain knowledge, developed in the darkest hours of a prison cell, that the love of God follows us wherever we go and protects us in all circumstances?

In January, we knew we were really going home. Early on the morning of March 4, we were herded into a bus and driven to the Gia Lam airport in Hanoi to board our freedom bird for home. When I saw the waiting C-141 on the field, I choked with emotion as warm tears streaked down my face. The knowledge that our country had not abandoned us was moving, but even more so the awareness of the Lord's words, "I will never leave you nor forsake you," was so overwhelming. As I waited in line, I scanned the familiar faces of the guards. I saw Spot, his face unreadable as he watched me move along the line towards my moment of freedom. He had locked me in my cell at night. He had withheld my meager rations, beaten me in the torture room, watched me bleed and almost die. The guards had always seemed so heartless, so stoical. In those six years, we saw no compassion, no tenderness, no human decency. Out of the same mouth they would tell us, "I am here to give you your rations and bury you when you die." Now he stood, along with the others — the guards, the interrogators, the skilled purveyors of torture — and silently watched us go.

For six long years — two thousand one hundred and ten days — these little stoney-faced men had been my tormentors. What were they thinking as they watched the long-term inmates of the Hanoi Hilton file by, in such orderly fashion, to board the plane that would fly us to freedom? They had performed their tasks well. They had broken the wills and the spirits of a long list of proud men. They had broken the bodies of others. And they had snuffed out the last little breath of life in the bravest of us. Were they glad to see us go, to be relieved, finally, of their charges? Were they preparing, even now, to go on to their next assignment, as I was, to do their part in advancing their cause? Were they thinking, as I was, of returning home to their families and to some semblance of normal life outside prison walls?

I had tried before in the Hanoi Hilton, the Zoo, and the other P.O.W. camps scattered throughout North Vietnam, to fathom the thoughts of these little inscrutable men who were my daily enemy. I had lain on my board-bed on sleepless nights and said to myself, "If I can get a handle on how they think, I'll be able to anticipate, to prepare for the next interrogation." But they were always unpredictable and mercurial in their reactions towards us. We had given them names: Spot, Rabbit, Jawbone, Little Caesar, B.O. Plenty, Sweatpea, Slug, World's Tallest Gook, and Hanoi Fats. Now, as I waited for release, I wondered about their lives. I thought of them, for the first time, as men. I was going home to my family and freedom. But they would never know the joy of breathing free. They were prisoners, too, victims of a brutal, harsh system that controlled their actions just as they had tried to control mine for those two thousand one hundred and ten days. As I shuffled across the tarmac, I felt no gloating, only pity.

I was leaving with no bitterness. I knew that fate had not dealt me a cruel hand. God had allowed the non-crisis cadence of my life to be thrown off. For six years, my life had been subjected to a higher purpose. I had been broken in prison and brought to the end of myself under the hands of my captors, yet it was not man but God who shaped me through the sufferings so that I could minister to others in their hurts. Someone had once said that "before a man can become bread to feed the multitudes, he must first be ground under the millstones of life." I was returning to pick up the pieces of my life a better man — a man with a new depth of sensitivity which could empathize with the suffering of others. I was carrying back a knowledge birthed through affliction that "all things" do "work together for good to those who love God."

My turn came. "Welcome home, Commander McDaniel!" The Air Force Colonel smiled broadly as he shook my hand. I was free! As the C-141 lifted off, my thoughts turned once more to home and what would await me there. The jet ascended over the familiar green jungle, heading for the coast. When we reached the Gulf of Tonkin, all pandemonium broke loose aboard with choruses of "Feet Wet!" The roar was deafening. It was a roar of men now free. It came from deep in our souls. Pent-up emotions, years in the building, released the familiar cry, from long-ago days of combat missions, "Feet wet!" Over the water, out of North Vietnam, we were free!

On the long flight home, I thought of Kelly and others like him who were not among us — still missing — brave men who had died in the jungles, in the torture rooms, in the solitary cells, alone. Or so I believed. "Why me, God? Why not Kelly?"

We landed at Clark Air Force Base in the Philippines for medical tests and intelligence debriefings. My forty-five minutes on the telephone with Dorothy and our children left me with the question still unanswered, "Where do I fit?" But four days into freedom I gathered them into my arms — Dorothy, Mike, David, and Leslie — and I knew that I did fit. I knew that all the strains and uncertainties of my absence had not sullied or soiled our relationship. All the hell of six years couldn't destroy the love between us.

The Navy let me get back into my aircraft, the A-6, and I knew that I did fit. They gave me command of the aircraft carrier USS Lexington, and I knew that my country still had a place for me. I could continue to serve the land I loved. Just as I had always believed in America, I found that America still believed in me. When I thought of Kelly and the others who did not come home, I thought of them as having died in captivity or on some mountainside or lonely jungle. Our country told us that all the living came home in the Big Release of '73, and I had no reason to question that accounting. Holding her ideals close to my heart, I felt that America could do no wrong.

Then I was assigned to duty on Capitol Hill, to serve as the Navy and Marine Corps Liaison to the House of Representatives. I took members of Congress to the Pentagon for briefings on various defense issues. One of the issues that caught my attention was the unresolved issue of Americans still missing in Southeast Asia. They had died in the jungles, in their prison :lls, in the torture rooms — or did they? The question began to haunt me — almost torment me. Were men like Kelly still struggling to survive their captivity in bamboo cages and prison cells somewhere in Indochina?

In 1981, I started to ask questions. My questions are still unanswered. I'm not sure at what moment I learned the truth about America's handling of information concerning Americans still missing in Southeast Asia. At what point in freedom did I cross the line from questioning my country's integrity to the absolute certainty that America knowingly left some of us behind? I'm not sure.

I am sure that I could have been one of them.

When did the Hanoi goverment decide that I would be one of the 591 Americans included in the Big Release? How did I escape the fate of an unknown number of men still held by the Communists in Southeast Asia?

For me, the Vietnam War is not over. It won't end until we bring home those men who were left behind in 1973. The ordeal won't end until my questions about my country's honor are answered. America has forsaken some of her bravest men. Worse than that, America has forsaken some of her highest ideals: liberty, justice, loyalty, righteousness. It was these ideals that kept me going from day to day in my captivity. They are the ideals that keep me going from day to day now in my search for answers to some deeply disturbing questions about my country.

I know that God will give unmeasured grace and mercy to those men still held in bondage, just as He ministered to me in the Hanoi Hilton. He has not forsaken those forgotten heroes in their quiet suffering. He shares in their suffering as He shared in mine. God is in Hanoi, in the jungle camps of Laos, and in the boxcars of the trains that move our men from one location to another so they can never be found. Nothing can separate them from the love of God. He will hold them in the hollow of His hand.

God continues to sustain me as I try to unravel the mystery of our missing men and determine the motives of the political powers in Washington who have failed to bring them home. I have not lost hope for those who long for freedom's light. Their burden is my burden, their suffering is my suffering, and I cannot forget them.

And, because He is God, He will teach me, once again, to forgive, just as He did in the Hanoi Hilton. To forgive free men who could act, and don't, is definitely more difficult than to forgive those whose brutality and injustice is orchestrated from within a totalitarian state.

As the American people become aware of the tragedy of the men still held prisoner by the Communists in Southeast Asia, I believe there will be a national outcry to bring them home. I pray that it will not be too late.

Eugene "Red" McDaniel is still happily married to his wife Dorothy and currently resides in the Washington D.C. area. Their three children are now grown. After returning home, Captain McDaniel authored a book about his P.O.W. experiences entitled *Before Honor*. He also resumed active duty and served as Commanding Officer of USS Niagara Falls and as Commanding Officer of the aircraft carrier USS Lexington. He served as Director of Navy/Marine Corps Liaison to the U.S. House of Representatives from 1979 to 1981, providing legislators with information vital to the strategic deployment of naval forces throughout the world. He retired from active duty in 1982. Today, Captain McDaniel is the founder and President of the American Defense Institute and the American Defense Foundation, headquartered in Washington, D.C. — non-profit organizations founded to increase public awareness of the need for a strong national defense.

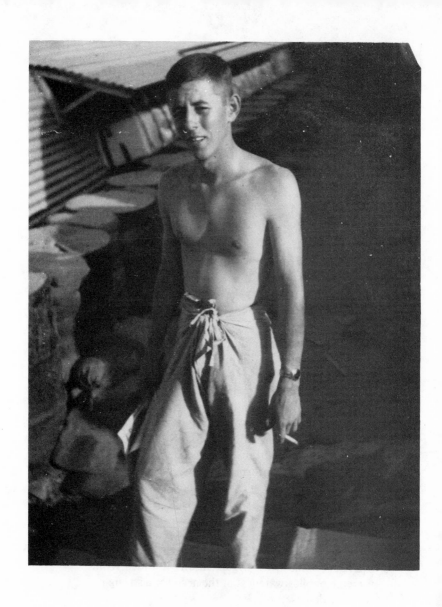

William R. Kimball
Mortarman,
1st Air Cav.
March '68 - May '68

Epilogue

Looking back, the most vivid reflections of my tour in Vietnam involves the day I was med-evaced out of country. It was early May 1968, on the backside of the Tet Offensive.

Somehow, I'd picked up a massive chest infection in the tropical filth of 'Nam which required specialized medical treatment in Japan. 'Nam was a breeding ground for all forms of death and dying. The dirt-soldier days of constant humidity, heat, bacteria, and stench had taken their toll. Though I hadn't been wounded in combat like so many others, I was a casualty nonetheless. The only difference was my chest wound wasn't bleeding externally. But it was my million dollar wound and potential one-way ticket home.

I remember the sense of guarded elation as we were unloaded from the hospital bus into the C-130 parked on the rain-drenched tarmac at Qui Nhon. It was a joy which carried an undercurrent of apprehension that I might be returned after the doctors healed the infection. Still, I savored the prospects of breathing free again. That flight was the culmination of countless prayers from an eighteen-year-old soldier who, less than a year before, had been cruising the strip on Friday nights, chasing girls or worrying about senior finals.

Those last few moments are still with me. I remember the awkward feeling of shuffling up the boarding ramp into the cargo bay of the waiting transport wearing my blue hospital pajamas and jungle boots. I remember my last glance westwards toward the mist-shrouded hills and the brooding slate gray clouds pregnant with rain. I remember the shudder of the fuselage as the props roared to life and the excitement as we slowly taxied into take-off position. And I remember the parting prayer which would forever alter the course of my life. Staring out of the rain-splattered window at the receding runway as we lifted off over the South China Sea, I promised God that I would serve Him if He would keep me from returning.

It was nearly twenty years ago when He honored the cry of my heart. As with so many anonymous men and women who sacrificed a season of their life in 'Nam, an awareness has grown over the ensuing years that it all was not in vain. It seems as each passing year places more distance between myself and that last day I, too, have grown more conscious of the significance of that pivotal, turning point in my life.

If there remains an unwritten chapter or a fitting epilogue to our involvement in Vietnam, it is a tribute to how the Lord redeemed something glorious out of the suffering.

A Final Note . . .

Ray Lockman's lead-in story concerning the tragic death of the young medic left the reader with an uncertain resolution. Ray served two consecutive tours as a combat rifleman with the 173rd Airborne Division. After his discharge, he returned to his home in West Virginia where he went to work with his father in the coal mines while performing as a part-time musician in local bars. He married and began to ride with the Devil's Disciples motorcycle gang before drifting to the Pacific Northwest. In short order, Ray began to manifest the classic symptoms of post-traumatic stress syndrome. His life and his marriage began to unravel as he sunk deeper into drugs and alcohol abuse. The restlessness and pent-up hostility eventually led to a barroom brawl which resulted in a second degree assault conviction and a ten year sentence in the Washington State Penitentiary. After several years as a leader in the biker gang within the prison, Ray's life reached rock bottom. In desperation, he turned to the pages of the Bible his mother had given him and finally found the resolution to his inner conflict through Jesus Christ. After seven years, he was parolled from prison and, shortly after, remarried. Ray is now a successful high-tech machinist and resides with his wife, Vicki, and four children in Monroe, Washington.

Glossary of Military Terms

A.I.T. - Advanced Individual Training

AK 47 - A Russian assault rifle

A.P.C. - A tracked Armored Personnel Carrier

Artie - Artillery Support

A.R.V.N. - Army of the Republic of Vietnam

A.W.O.L. - Absent Without Leave

A-6 Intruder - A jet fighter

Bennies - Benefits

Body bags - Plastic zipper bags for corpses

Boonies - The jungle or areas where infantry units operated on patrols

Bouncing Betty - A mine designed to pop about three feet into the air and explode at waist level after being tripped

Bush - The outer field areas where infantry units operated

B-52 - A long-range heavy bomber

Charlie - Slang for "the enemy"

Chinook - A large, twin-bladed helicopter used for transporting men and materials

Choppers - Helicopters

Claymores - Mines packed with plastique and rigged to spray hundreds of steel pellets

Cobras - Helicopter gunships heavily armed with rocket launchers and machine guns

Concertina wire - Barbed wire that is rolled out along the ground to hinder the progress of enemy troops

C.P. - Command Post

C-rats - C-rations or pre-packaged military meals eaten in the field

C-4 - Plastique explosive

C-7 - A transport plane

C-130 - A cargo plane used to transport men and supplies

Det-cord - Detonation cord for explosive charges

Deuce-and-a-half - A heavy transport truck used for carrying men and supplies

Dinky-dau - Vietnamese for "crazy" or "off the wall"

DMZ - Demilitarized Zone

Dragon ship - Helicopter gunship

Dust-off - A medical evacuation flight by chopper

E.C.M. - Electronic Countermeasure

E.O.D. - "Explosive Ordinance Disposal" units

F.D.C. - "Fire Direction Center" where artillery and mortar fire is coordinated

Fields of fire - Designated free fire zones where our units were permitted to shoot

Fire base - Reinforced bases established to provide artillery fire support for ground units operating in the bush

Fire mission - Artillery support which has been requested

Flak jacket - A protective vest worn to protect the chest area from shrapnel and bullets

F.O. - Forward Observer

Frags - Slang for fragmentation grenades

Freedom bird - Slang for the flight which carried you home after your tour was up

Friendlies - Friendly Vietnamese

F-4's and F-100's - Jet fighter aircraft

Gooks - Slang for an Oriental person, especially in reference to the enemy

Grunt - Slang for any combat soldier fighting in 'Nam

Harbor site - A camp

H.E. rounds - High explosives

Hueys - Helicopters used extensively in Vietnam

H & I - Harrassment and Interdiction fire

Ho Chi Minh Trail - The main supply route running south from North Vietnam through Laos and Cambodia

Hooches - Slang for any form of a dwelling place

Humping - Slang for marching with a heavy load through the bush

H-34 - A helicopter

I Corp - The northernmost military region in South Vietnam

"Indian country" - Slang for enemy territory

I.V. - Intravenous injection

Jolly Green Giant - A term for helicopters used in rescuing downed pilots

K.I.A. - Killed in action

Klick - One kilometer

Kit Carson scout - A former enemy soldier who defected and actively cooperated with American forces

Lai dai - Vietnamese for "Come here!"

L.A.W. - Light Anti-tank Weapon

LZ - Landing Zone

MAG-13 - Marine Airgroup 13

Med-evac - A term for medically evacuating the wounded by chopper or plane

M.I.A. - Missing in action

M.O.S. - Military Occupational Specialty

M-16 - Standard automatic weapon used by American ground forces

M-60 - A machine gun used by American combat units

M-79 - A grenade launcher

N.D.P. - Night Defensive Position

Nouc-maum - A strong smelling Vietnamese fish sauce

Number ten - The very worst

NVA - North Vietnamese Army

NVR - North Vietnamese Regulars

Papa san - A term for an elderly Vietnamese man

Phantom - A jet fighter

Pogue - A Marine assigned to rear area duties

Point man - The lead man on an American patrol through the bush

Punji pit - A camouflaged hole containing sharpened stakes in the bottom or sides

Recon - Reconnaissance

"Rock and roll" - Slang for "fully automatic"

RESCAP - The rescue units whose job was to retrieve downed pilots

R.O.N. site - Remain Overnight Site

R.P.G. - Rocket Propelled Grenade

R & R - Rest and Relaxation

R.T.O. - Radio Telephone Operator

"Saddle up!" - An order for soldiers to put on their packs and move out

S.A.M. - Surface-to-air Missile

Sappers - Viet Cong infiltrators whose job was to detonate explosive charges within our positions

Satchel charges - Explosive packs carried by V.C. sappers

Search and destroy - American ground sweeps to locate and destroy the enemy

Short-timer - Someone whose tour in Vietnam is almost completed

S.K. - A Russian carbine

Smoke grenade - A grenade that releases colored smoke used for signaling

S.O.G. - Special Operations Group

Sortie - A bomber mission

Spider hole - A camouflaged one man foxhole and firing pit

Stand down - A period of rest and reorganization after an infantry unit is pulled in from the field

Supreme Six - Army call sign for God

Swift boats - Armed search boats used on the waterways

S-2 - An abbreviation for "intelligence"

Tail-end Charlie - The last man who covers the rear of a column

Tracer - A bullet with a phosphorus coating designed to burn and provide a visual indication of the bullet's trajectory

Tracks - Any vehicle with treads

Triage - A term for the process of sorting out the patients according to the seriousness of their wounds

V.C. - Viet Cong

Viet Cong - The local militias fighting Americans in South Vietnam

Web gear - Canvas suspenders and belt used to carry the infantryman's gear

W.I.A. - Wounded in Action

"Willie-peter" - White phosphorus round

"Yards" - Montagnard tribal groups living in the highlands of Vietnam

XO - Executive officer